Measurement
of Intergenerational
Relations

SOME OTHER VOLUMES IN THE
SAGE FOCUS EDITIONS

Measurement of Intergenerational Relations

Edited by
David J. Mangen
Vern L. Bengtson
Pierre H. Landry, Jr.

SAGE PUBLICATIONS
The Publishers of Professional Social Science
Newbury Park   Beverly Hills   London   New Delhi

To Our Parents
Lucille Zschetzsche Mangen
and
Victor Eugene Mangen
(1914-1958)
and
Julia Falk Bengtson
and
Bethel Nils Bengtson
(1910-1965)

For information address:

SAGE Publications, Inc.
2111 West Hillcrest Drive
Newbury Park, California 91320

SAGE Publications Inc.   SAGE Publications Ltd.
275 South Beverly Drive   28 Banner Street
Beverly Hills   London EC1Y 8QE
California 90212   England

SAGE PUBLICATIONS India Pvt. Ltd.
M-32 Market
Greater Kailash I
New Delhi 110 048 India

Printed in the United States of America

Library of Congress Cataloging-in-Publication Data

Measurement of intergenerational relations / edited by David J.
   Mangen, Vern L. Bengtson, and Pierre H. Landry, Jr.
      p. cm.—(Sage focus editions ; 92)
   Bibliography: p.
   ISBN 0-8039-2989-7—ISBN 0-8039-2990-0 (pbk.)
   1. Family.   2. Intergenerational relations.   I. Mangen, David J.
II. Bengtson, Vern L.   III. Landry, Pierre H.
HQ518.M42 1987
306.8′5—dc19   87-28466
                  CIP

Contents

Acknowledgments

This volume, whose gestation has a history of its own, represents the efforts, influence, and patience of many collaborators and well-wishers.

Collection of the data on which this report is based began in 1970, when Vern Bengtson received funding from NIMH to investigate patterns of similarity and contrast among grandparents, parents, and youth following the "generation gap" decade of the 1960s. It was during this time that the original formulation of "intergenerational solidarity" was developed. A full analysis of the measurement had to be delayed, however, because of the death of the Principal Investigator's wife. In 1980, Bengtson secured funding from NIMH and NIA to continue these analyses, many of which are reported in this volume.

David J. Mangen, who joined the faculty of the University of Southern California in 1980, served as Co-Principal Investigator of the project. He developed the overall measurement strategy reflected in this volume, in addition to drafting many of the chapters, and was instrumental in applying structural equation (LISREL) modeling as well as hierarchical cluster analysis to the family solidarity data.

Pierre H. Landry, Jr., was the project coordinator from 1981-1984. In addition to his coauthorship (Chapter 7), he provided the initial programming and data analysis for many of these chapters. He helped hold the project together during some difficult times in this volume's development, and a special acknowledgment is due to him for his efforts.

The remaining authors of chapters in this volume were graduate students on the project between 1980 and 1985. While identified with particular chapters, they were in every sense collaborators on the overall research program.

Acknowledgment should be made to many other individuals who have been instrumental in this project's design and conceptualization. In 1969, when the original proposal was submitted, the Principal Investigator (Bengtson) was just out of the University of Chicago's Committee on Human Development, where the first-year research project involved the collection of data from three-generation black families recruited from Chicago's South Side new high-rise ghettos. That experience, as well as the research project by Neugarten and Richard Flacks on the socialization influences of student activists, helped lay the foundation for the original three-generation design to examine intergenerational contrasts and similarities. To these Chicago faculty, especially Bernice Neugarten, go special acknowledgment for what they taught concerning the necessity for explicit conceptualization and adequate measurement of life-course phenomena. Most of all, we thank them for the focus on *ideas* that they emphasized.

To the late Reuben Hill is due another special acknowledgement. A faculty adviser and colleague to Mangen, and a consultant and friend to the original project, Hill's emphasis on conceptual precision and theory development shaped the course of American family sociology for several decades. Throughout this project he gave advice, encouragement, and criticism; many of our concerns for measurement rigor grew out of what he suggested he should have done in his monumental study of Minneapolis three-generation families (Hill and associates, 1970).

The focus on conceptual and measurement rigor is, indeed, the central theme of this volume; a preoccupation that is perhaps unusual in the social sciences today, and that might be considered old-fashioned. Our project consultants should be acknowledged for their encouragement of this quest. Paul Baltes, Glen Elder, Gunhild Hagestad, John Nesselroade, and Victor Marshall provided assistance at crucial stages in the project's development.

Acknowledgment is due to the funding agencies that have provided support during this project's 16 years: the National Institutes of Mental Health (grants #MH-36290, and MH-38244) and the National Institutes of Aging (grants #AG-02823 and AG-04092).

Linda Hall and her staff, particularly Deborah Wallace and Adriene Mixon, have done much to ensure this volume's accuracy in text and tables during production. Sheila Miyazaki, Miriam Kmet, Grace Greer, and Citas Vanderpool assisted in this role during earlier stages. Jan Ragsdale and Myrna Del Mundo provided fiscal management.

Finally, we wish to thank James E. Birren, Dean of the Andrus Gerontology Center, for his intellectual leadership and personal support, which were instrumental at many points in this project's history. He had a vision of what adult development research should be; he had the patience to encourage what it might become.

—*David J. Mangen*
Vern L. Bengtson
Pierre H. Landry, Jr.

PART I

Conceptual and Theoretical Overview

1

Generations, Families, and Interactions

An Overview of the Research Program

VERN L. BENGTSON
DAVID J. MANGEN

The most fundamental questions in sociology, suggests Nisbet (1970), pertain to the nature of the social bond: ties that link individuals to groups and one group to another. Inquiry into substantive concerns as diverse as mate selection and interorganizational linkages have often used the concept of the social bond as an important construct guiding research and theory.

Social theorists have focused on two general dimensions of the social bond. The *status* dimension emphasizes the vertical ordering or ranking of relationships in terms of power, prestige, and privilege. The focus on vertical structure allows examination of influence patterns, relative importance, and differential access to the valued goods of society. Thus the status dimension emphasizes the issue of *differentiation* in society and social groups.

In contrast, the second dimension of social relationships emphasizes the grouping together or bonding of individuals into groups, and groups into organizations or societies. The dimension of *solidarity* opens examination of issues of warmth, affection, attraction to and interaction with one another, and providing assistance when needed. Thus the solidarity dimension focuses on issues of *cohesion* in social groups.

Families, as special instances of small groups, manifest both solidarity and status. Both are represented in several ways, none of which is necessarily internally consistent with the others. Deference and respect may be given to the oldest family member, but the ability of a financially successful midlife offspring to influence family decisions may be greater. The interaction between parents and their children may be quite frequent, but this does not necessarily imply that they like one another or assist one another. These examples illustrate that solidarity and status are higher order constructs, each of which is composed of several dimensions that are most certainly *not* perfectly correlated.

How these two constructs are manifested in the *intergenerational* family system constituted the central question of the original research. This research was launched in the decade of the 1970s, immediately following a lengthy era of protest. The era of 1960-1972 included five social movements (civil rights, student rights, anti-Vietnam, women's rights, and the counterculture), and the disruption of Watergate was on the immediate horizon. In large part, these movements seemed to pit the young against the old. "Don't trust anyone over 30" became a rallying cry that directly emphasized the counterculture's mistrust of the older generation. "Those damn hippie radicals" were lamented by many a parent upon learning that a heretofore "good kid" had decided to attend protest-racked State University. The point here is that the divisions between age groups in society were creating strains in the social order. Highly visible confrontations over values, opinions, and political behavior (Bengtson, 1975; Bengtson, Furlong, and Lauffer, 1974) illustrated on an almost daily basis the age-related differences within society.

Contemporary theorists of that era frequently tied the macro-social implications of these age-group differences to divisions within the family (Bettelheim, 1965; Friedenberg, 1969; Mead, 1970). Was it true that these social movements were tied to generational rebellion in the family, in which youth were carrying out their own version of Mannheim's "fresh contact" with the establishment (Braungart, 1974)? Alternatively, were protesting youth acting out a socialization agenda in keeping with their parents' own values concerning commitment, responsibility, and honesty (Flacks, 1967)?

The data used in this book were collected between 1971 and 1972. The original aims of the research were (1) to assess the extent of differences between youth, their parents, and their grandparents, and (2) to examine the correlates and consequences of those contrasts in terms of the psychological well-being of family members. The original question-naire was designed to explore the *aggregate* or group-level contrasts between the generations involved in the study, and to address *intra-familial* issues concerning family relations and involvements during this era of age-based conflict. In this conceptualization, the construct of status was represented foremost by age and/or generational position, with controls for economic facets, while the construct of solidarity was represented by several sets of multi-item scales.

Initial analysis of the data in the mid-1970s revealed that the conceptualization of family bondedness was incomplete, and that the issues of intergenerational cohesion were far more complex than envisioned. During this same period, contemporary theory and research methodology in sociology began to address some of the issues raised by the original analysis. Much more concern with conceptualization and measurement (Mangen and Peterson, 1982a, 1982b, 1984) as well as theory development (Burr et al., 1979a, 1979b) characterizes current social research on family and gerontological subjects. Statistical procedures enabling analysis of more complex theoretical models have been developed (Jöreskog and Sörbom, 1979). In light of these several developments, we decided that these data warranted further exami-nation.

In 1980, we began a secondary analysis of the original data.[1] Our focus was on the family relations between the oldest (grandparent: G1) and middle (parents: G2) generations. This study examined some of the dimensions of solidarity or cohesion in families, with a special emphasis on the overall measurement properties of the instruments used in the original instrument. Detailed assessments of reliability and validity were one part of our overall goal of constructing adequate measures of the dimensions of solidarity. Adequacy of measurement was seen as a necessary precondition to examination of issues of continuity or change within the family, and as the critical first step in carefully exploring the causes and consequences of differential solidarity. Later, we extended this analysis to include consideration of the youngest (grandchild: G3) generation.[2] This book reports the detailed results of our analysis of the measurement properties of the instruments used to measure solidarity in the original Southern California Three Generations Data.

This book is laid out in three major sections. Part I, including Chapters 1 to 3, focuses on the conceptual and methodological underpinnings of the research that we report. Chapter 2 includes an overview of the conceptual development of the family solidarity construct, and traces the development of this construct from Durkheim to the present. Chapter 3 presents a detailed examination of methodological issues involved in measurement of solidarity, with special attention to constraints and opportunities that emerge when using three generations of respondents within the same family.

Part II includes Chapters 4 to 9. Each chapter focuses on the measurement of one of the six dimensions of solidarity (Bengtson and Schrader, 1982; Bengtson et al., 1985). The conceptual background and operationalization of each dimension are presented, and the measurement properties of the data gathered in the original study are analyzed. Basic data on central tendencies and dispersions of the items, as well as an analysis of the reliability, validity, and factor structure, is presented for each of the dimensions. Because of complexities introduced by the three-generation design, we test a number of alternative measurement models at the lineage level of analysis using LISREL. In some cases, the data for these measures are quite good, and adoption by others is recommended; in other cases, modifications are suggested that will improve the quality of the original measures.

Part III attempts to consolidate some of the findings of our work. An empirical consolidation is attempted in Chapter 10 by developing a typology of families based upon four of the six dimensions of solidarity. This typology clearly illustrates that simple linear models do not adequately explain the complex relationships among the dimensions of solidarity in these data. Chapter 11 attempts to synthesize the results of these analyses. The goal of this final chapter is to pull together the wide-ranging findings of the substantive chapters and to present recommendations for future work in the measurement of solidarity as an aspect of intergenerational relationships.

In sum, this book represents an extensive series of tests regarding the theoretical and empirical structure of the family solidarity construct. The data that are brought to bear in testing these issues are quite broad. Nonetheless, the analyses reported here constitute only one test in the validation of these measures. We hope that others who use these measures will contribute to their validation by examining substantive measurement issues.

NOTES

1. The contribution of the National Institute of Aging grant number AG02823 to the University of Southern California is gratefully acknowledged. This grant enabled us to begin the secondary analysis.

2. The National Institute of Mental Health (grant number MH36290) enabled us to extend our reanalysis to include all three generations. We gratefully acknowledge the assistance provided to this research.

2

Solidarity, Integration, and Cohesion in Families

Concepts and Theories

KAY YOUNG McCHESNEY
VERN L. BENGTSON

Why is it that members of one family seek each other out and seem to enjoy each others' company, while members of another family act more like individuals "doing their own thing" who happen to be related to each other? This is a version of Hobbes's (1651/1950) "problem of order," framed at the level of the family group. Restated at the societal level, the question becomes, "Given the ability of people to act for themselves, how does order in society come about?" This question has been asked since antiquity (see Aristotle, c. 340 B.C. [1961]; Hobbes [1651/1950]; Kaldoun [1348/1958]; Locke [1690/1960]; Plato, c. 368 B.C. [1962]; Rousseau [1762/1962]). Social theorists have attempted to answer it by positing the existence of a force or property that renders a collection of individuals an ordered group. This force or property has been termed *solidarity*, *bonding*, *cohesion*, or *integration* by various social theorists (Durkheim, 1893/1933; Kaldoun, 1348/1958; Parsons, 1951). Early in American family sociology, the term *solidarity* was used to assess the variable manifestations of cohesiveness within the family group (Jansen, 1952; Nye and Rushing, 1969, p. 134). In keeping with this tradition, within our research group we have chosen to use the term *solidarity* to describe this property.

This chapter presents the intellectual antecedents of our current conceptualization of intergenerational solidarity. We trace the conceptual development of this construct in terms of macro- and micro-social assessments of solidarity, from Durkheim through the current work of the Olson group (Olson et al., 1979, 1983). Our approach is selective, not exhaustive, and, in keeping with the remainder of the chapters, presents alternatives to be considered in future empirical treatments of family intergenerational relations.

Societal Solidarity

The first tradition informing the conceptualization of inter-generational family solidarity comes from structural-functionalism. The term *solidarity* became widely used in American sociology with Simpson's (1933) translation of Durkheim's (1893) *Division of Labor in Society*. Durkheim distinguished two types of solidarity, mechanical and organic, based on a biologic analogy. In mechanical solidarity, members of society are "undifferentiated" or interchangeable in function within the social structure, much like the atoms of a rock. Durkheim (1893/1933, p. 109) attributed this interchangeability of members as being due to a "common conscience," which may be interpreted as the norms and values shared by group members. In organic solidarity, members of society are "differentiated," which is to say that members of the social group are complementary and interdependent. This comple-mentarity of members is due to the division of labor present in an "organically solidary" society but not present in a "mechanically solidary" society (Durkheim, 1893/1933, p. 63).[1]

Durkheim (1893/1933) pointed out that most societies and groups are not pure types characterized solely by mechanical or organic solidarity. Thus Durkheim's nominal definition of societal cohesion might be stated as the combined product of both mechanical and organic mechanisms of solidarity within a society.

Durkheim's (1893/1933) concept of organic solidarity as a function of the division of labor was the basis for the concept of functional integration, which in turn became one of Parsons's (1951) four functional requisites necessary for the continuation of any social system. Parsons (1955a) later developed the idea of functional integration as a structural requisite in the family. He posited two complementary roles as being necessary to the family: the instrumental role of supporting the family's physical needs, and the expressive role of supporting the family's social and emotional needs (Parsons, 1955a).

Cohesiveness in Small Groups

The study of group dynamics in the 1950s provided a second point of departure in the conceptualization of intergenerational family solidarity. The group dynamics movement emerged from three independent traditions: applications of Durkheim and Comte, the field theory of Lewin and his students, and the cognitive perspectives of Heider, who built upon the work of Homans. These three traditions generated considerable research. We felt that the empirical findings resulting from this research might be applicable to the family as a special type of small group.

Three conceptual links tie Durkheim to the social psychological literature on small groups. First, Durkheim's concept of mechanical solidarity emphasizes similarity, or shared norms, among members of the society. At the level of the small group, Brown's (1965) concept of symmetry or similarity as the basis of his solidarity dimension within interpersonal relationships is very similar.

Second, Durkheim's concept of organic social solidarity is based on a pattern of relationships where group members have different but complementary and interdependent functions within the society. This ties directly to Lewin's conceptualization of the group: "The essence of a group is not the similarity or dissimilarity of its members, but their interdependence" (1948, p. 54).

The third link from Durkheim to the social psychological literature is at the level of the relationship of the individual to society. Durkheim's (1893/1933, p. 148) definition of cohesion was "the variable intensity of the forces which hold the individual more or less strictly attached to his group." While social psychologists' usage of "cohesiveness" varies (Shaw, 1976, p. 197), most researchers in group dynamics tend to use a definition of group cohesion derived from Lewinian field theory. They define *group cohesion* either as "the complex of forces which bind members of a group to each other and to the group as a whole" (Shepherd, 1964, p. 26) or, alternatively, as the result of "forces acting on the members to remain in the group" (Festinger, 1950, p. 274; see also Collins and Raven, 1969; Shaw, 1976). Thus they subsume cohesion under the general heading of interpersonal attraction, treating cohesion as the attraction of the individual to other group members or to the group as a whole. Conceptually, these definitions of group cohesion are virtually identical to Durkheim's definition of cohesion.

The work of Homans (1950) and Heider (1958) on interpersonal relationships is less closely related to Durkheim's mechanical and organic solidarity than the work of the Lewinian group dynamists, but both contributed substantially to social psychological theories of small group cohesiveness. Homans (1950, p. 231) posited four basic elements of social behavior—activity, interaction, sentiment, and norms—that can be seen as dimensions of group cohesion. For Homans, *activity* was defined as what group members do together. *Interaction* referred to the relationship of the activity of one member to the activity of another, such as the functional complementarity and interdependence of work roles. *Sentiment* referred to the sum of the feeling that one member holds for another group member. *Norms*, while not behavior per se, were inferred from "what people say about the way they ought to behave" (Homans, 1950, p. 231).

Homans suggested that cohesion within a group could originate from both similarity among members, as in Durkheim's mechanical solidarity, and from functional interdependence of group members, as in Durkheim's organic solidarity. From his case studies of several different groups, he deduced a general rule, "the more frequently persons interact with one another, the greater in general is their affection for one another . . . other things being equal" (Homans, 1950, p. 242). Building upon Homans's general postulate and balance theory, Heider (1958) systematized the following two propositions of cohesiveness in social relationships:

P similar to O induces P likes O

P in contact with O induces P likes O

where P means person and O means other (Heider, 1958, pp. 184, 188). Thus, for Heider, there were three basic elements of cohesion: similarity, sentiment ("likes"), and contact.

The theories of Lewin (1948), Homans (1950), Heider (1958), and many others interested in group dynamics generated considerable empirical work, much of it experimental (Festinger, 1980). The empirical findings resulting from this research are important because they may be applicable to the family as a type of small group. In summary, findings from empirical group dynamics research suggest that feelings of attraction toward the group are associated with (1) taking responsibility for group organization (Larson, 1953), (2) attending meetings (Sagi et al., 1955), (3) participation within a group meeting (Back, 1951), (4) choice of group activities over competing alternatives (Collins and Raven, 1969), (5) satisfaction and morale (Collins and Guetzkow, 1964; Collins and Raven, 1969), (6) readiness to be influenced by other group members (Back, 1951; Berkowitz, 1954; Festinger et al., 1952; Schachter et al., 1951), (7) perception of other group members as similar to self (Collins and Raven, 1969), (8) accurate estimation of other group members' feelings (Suchman, 1956), (9) favorable attitude toward other group members' behavior (Collins and

Raven, 1969), and (10) association with group members outside of group activities (see, e.g., Collins and Raven, 1969, pp. 122-123; Deutsch, 1968, p. 469).

Researchers in group dynamics also found that group cohesion is associated with (1) amount and quality of communication among group members (Bovard, 1956; Deutsch, 1968; Lott and Lott, 1961; Turner, 1957), (2) consensus among group members on attitudes and beliefs that relate to group functioning (Deutsch, 1968), (3) satisfaction and morale (Collins and Guetzkow, 1964; Deutsch, 1968), (4) mutual influence (Deutsch, 1968), (5) rejection of deviants (Festinger, 1950), (6) spatial distance among group members during interaction (Kipnis, 1957), (7) both task effectiveness and productivity when the group values the task being performed (Collins and Raven, 1969; Deutsch, 1968), and (8) "functional closeness" or meshing of task-oriented behaviors during task performance (Collins and Raven, 1969; Kipnis, 1957; see, e.g., Collins and Raven, 1969, pp. 122-123; Deutsch, 1968, p. 469).

Because the family is a type of small group, it seems intuitively logical that many of the characteristics of cohesiveness observed by researchers in group dynamics may be applicable in some way to family cohesion or solidarity. Groups studied by social psychologists, however, differ significantly from the typical family group in a number of ways (Bales and Slater, 1955, pp. 299-300). Two differences, membership and duration, seem especially important. In most types of small groups, membership and termination of membership is voluntary. Membership in a family is involuntary, however, terminated only by death. Thus membership in a family group is ascribed and definitional, rather than achieved and voluntary, and duration of membership is permanent, rather than temporary.

Solidarity in the Family

A third tradition informing the conceptualization of solidarity arises directly from family studies. There is a long tradition of research specifically delimited to the family, most of which includes concepts of solidarity, cohesion, and integration as central to the analysis of the family. The contributions of four groups of researchers to the conceptualization of family solidarity will be reviewed: (1) family sociologists working in the first half of the century, (2) clinicians studying the schizophrenic family in the 1950s, (3) family sociologists working from the 1970s to the present, and (4) recent clinical work on the Circumplex Model.

Early Family Sociologists

Three American family sociologists, Angell (1936/1965), Koos (1946), and Hill (1949), were among the first researchers to examine family relationships empirically. All three used concepts similar to Durkheim's as explanations of why some families appeared less affected by stressors than others.

In an attempt to describe types of families that responded well to significant decreases of income during the Depression, Angell (1936/ 1965) studied the retrospective reports of 50 University of Michigan sociology students on characteristics of their families before, during, and after the Depression. Drawing on symbolic interactionism, he was interested primarily in the integration of personal roles or functions within the family (Angell, 1936/1965, p. 13). His description of the integration of personal roles is similar to Durkheim's (1893/1933, p. 109) definition of organic solidarity as interdependence in pursuit of common goals.

One of the two analytic dimensions on which Angell (1936/1965) based his typology of families was integration (the other was adaptability). He referred to integration as the "bonds of coherence and unity running through family life, of which common interests, affections, and a sense of economic interdependence are perhaps the most prominent" (Angell, 1936/1965, p. 15). His idea of family integration as stemming from common interests and mutual affection seems to be similar to the idea of integration or solidarity due to similarities among family members. Thus, while Angell's conceptualization was limited to the life space as perceived by the family, his conceptualization of integration includes both the idea of similarities among family members and the idea of interdependence in pursuit of common goals.

A study of families in a New York City working-class neighborhood on the subject of family troubles employed as a major analytic criterion the adequacy of a family's organization (Koos, 1946, p. 10). While adequacy implies a value judgment, included in his concept of adequate organization was the idea that family members have complementary roles subordinated to "some common definition of the good of the family in preference to the good of the individual members" (Koos, 1946, p. 11). Thus, although Durkheim's concept of organic solidarity was not as central to Koos's analysis as it was to Angell's analysis, it was still implied within his conceptualization.

Hill's (1949) study of the war-induced stress of separation, adaptation, and reunion focused on the "roller-coaster" course of adjustment to family crisis. One of the three major factors that was important for successful adjustment to crises was family integration as measured by Cavan and Ranck's (1938) family integration scale (Hill, 1949, p. 128). Building on Angell's (1936/1965) usage, Hill (1949, p. 131) defined family integration as

> the unifying phenomena seen in the sense of economic and emotional interdependence: the strong affectional ties between husband and wife, father and children, mother and children, and among the children; a certain pride in family traditions, and high participation as a family in joint activities.

Thus Hill's usage of family integration again includes both the aspects of similarity among family members (joint activities, shared traditions) as in Durkheim's mechanical solidarity and interdependence in pursuit of common goals as in Durkheim's organic solidarity.

Clinicians of the 1950s

Several clinical researchers studying families with schizophrenic members developed labels for types of family interaction patterns that appeared to contribute to the development of pathology in one family member (Bowen, 1960; Hess and Handel, 1959; Lidz et al., 1957; Vogel and Bell, 1960; Wynne et al., 1958). Although the terminologies are unrelated, in each of these analytical schemes, there are linkages to family cohesion. Although some authors seem to describe families only at one or the other end of a continuum ranging from low to high cohesion (e.g., Lidz et al., 1957; Vogel and Bell, 1960), two researchers describe families at both extremes of the cohesion continuum. Their descriptions are in process terminology.

Hess and Handel (1959) hypothesized five processes that described the shape and coherence of the psychosocial interior of the normal family. These processes included the establishing of boundaries, developing congruent family images and patterns of dealing with biosocial constraints, and evolving family themes. They suggested, however, that the most essential family task was to create a satisfactory pattern of separateness and connectedness (Hess and Handel, 1959, pp. 12-13). In measuring connectedness, they asked, "In what way does this event or tendency or action bring the members together?" (Hess and Handel, 1959, p. 13). Note that this question is very close to the social psychologists' definition of group cohesion as "the complex of forces which bind members of a group to each other" (Shepherd, 1964, p. 26).

Bowen (1960) also described pathological families with an analytical scheme that fits into a cohesiveness continuum. He described families in which husband and wife interacted as though they had an ex officio emotional divorce. At the other extreme, he described families that seemed to have an undifferentiated family ego mass characterized by emotional fusion. In contrast, Bowen's nonpathological families had a balanced level of connectedness and separateness.

Contemporary Family Sociologists

In the late 1960s, researchers from the family sociology tradition began to work on family solidarity as an important component of family relations. Nye and Rushing (1969, p. 135), influenced by Landecker (1951), discussed family integration as a multidimensional phenomenon with six components:

(1) associational integration—the range and frequency of interaction in various types of activities;
(2) affectual integration—the degree of positive sentiments held about other family members;
(3) consensual integration—the degree of agreement on values, attitudes, and beliefs among family members;
(4) functional integration—the degree to which family members exchange services;
(5) normative integration—the degree to which members conform to family norms; and
(6) goal integration—the degree to which family members subordinate individual goals to those of the family.

Nye and Rushing divided the concept of family integration into these six components for purposes of operationalization and construction of indicators. They saw them, however, as aspects of three derived concepts of group life: associational integration (see Heider's [1958] contact), affectual integration (see Homans's [1950] and Heider's [1958] sentiment), and consensual integration (see Homans's [1950] and Heider's [1958] similarity) (Nye and Rushing, 1969, p. 136).

Nye and Rushing's (1969) three summary concepts—associational integration, affectual integration, and consensual integration—are also similar to those employed by Bowerman and Kinch (1959, p. 206) and Elder (1980, 1984), who suggested that association, affection and similarity of interests, norms and values were central to the analysis of parent-adolescent relations and their socialization consequences.

Note that Nye and Rushing's (1969) conceptualization of normative integration and consensual integration emphasizes shared norms, beliefs, attitudes, and values and thus fits Durkheim's (1893/1933) description of mechanical solidarity. Their definition of associational integration also suggests mechanical solidarity in that it is concerned with shared activities. On the other hand, the functional integration and goal integration dimensions, which are part of Durkheim's (1893/1933) definition of organic solidarity, were not included in their list of summary derived concepts. This suggests that mechanical solidarity was a primary aspect of family solidarity, while organic solidarity was a secondary aspect of family solidarity in the Nye and Rushing (1969) conceptualization.

Bengtson, Olander, and Haddad (1976) rejected the structural-functionalist connotations of Nye and Rushing's (1969) use of integration. However, they adopted Nye and Rushing's three derived concepts as significant and highly interrelated dimensions of family solidarity (Bengtson et al., 1976, p. 256). They conceptualized family solidarity as the interaction of associational solidarity, affectional solidarity, and consensual solidarity (Bengtson et al., 1976, p. 247). Their definitions of these three dimensions of family solidarity were similar to those of Nye and Rushing, and emphasized the degree of similarity among family members. This emphasis on shared behaviors, emotions, and cognitions suggests a conceptualization of family solidarity reflecting mechanical solidarity. The fact that their conceptualization of family solidarity did not explicitly include Durkheim's (1893/1933) organic solidarity is further suggested by their discussion of factors affecting solidarity. There, interdependence was implied but not discussed, and interdependence among family members in pursuit of common goals was never mentioned.

Bengtson and Schrader's (1982) discussion of parent-child relations included six "distinct but interrelated" (Bengtson and Schrader, 1982, p. 116) constructs related to family solidarity, reported here because they represent the nominal definitions for the remainder of this book:

(1) associational solidarity—the frequency and patterns of interaction in various types of activities;
(2) affectional solidarity—the type and degree of positive sentiments held about family members, and the degree of reciprocity of these sentiments;
(3) consensual solidarity—the degree of agreement on values, attitudes, and beliefs among family members;
(4) functional solidarity or exchange—the degree to which family members exchange services or assistance;
(5) normative solidarity—the perception and enactment of norms of family solidarity; and
(6) intergenerational family structure—the number, type, and geographic proximity of family members.

The most noticeable change in these components as compared to Nye and Rushing's (1969) set of dimensions is the substitution of an "Intergenerational Family Structure" dimension for Nye and Rushing's goal integration. In addition, there are changes in their specification of three other dimensions. First, associational solidarity includes frequency of interaction and patterns of interaction (Bengtson et al., 1976) as well as types of family activities (Nye and Rushing, 1969). Second, Bengtson and Schrader (1982) discuss the exchange of services as part of functional solidarity (as did Nye and Rushing), but omit the aspect of interdependence among family members that is central to the structural-functional perspective implied by the use of functional solidarity (Bengtson and Schrader, 1982, p. 117). Third, normative solidarity is limited to norms of family solidarity (e.g., shared expectations of how often we should get together as a family), whereas Nye and Rushing (1969) included all family norms within their conceptualization of normative solidarity.

The omission of the concepts of interdependence and goal integration from Bengtson and Schrader's (1982) dimensions of family solidarity suggests that their conceptualization of family solidarity has continued to evolve toward the notion of mechanical solidarity, or solidarity due to similarity among family members, and away from Durkheim's (1893/1933) organic solidarity.

The Circumplex Model

Recently, considerable work in the area of family solidarity has been done by clinicians interested in the differences between families with impaired as opposed to optimal functioning. Most notable of these has been the work of Olson, Russell, and Sprenkle (1979, 1983). Their two-dimensional Circumplex Model was an outgrowth of their frustration with growing lists of seemingly unrelated analytical schemes. In an attempt to integrate the field conceptually, Olson et al. (1979) studied terminologies relating to marital and family behavior developed by clinicians, family sociologists, small-group theorists, social psychologists, and anthropologists. Using these analytical schemes, they synthesized two dimensions that seemed conceptually to unify the diverse conceptualizations they reviewed. They presented these two dimensions—cohesion and adaptability—as a conceptual framework for the analysis of patterns of interaction within the family.

Olson et al. (1979, p. 5) defined *cohesion* as having two components: "the emotional bonding members have with one another and the degree of individual autonomy a person experiences in the family system."

Their discussion of cohesion suggests that they are in agreement with Festinger (1950, p. 274), who viewed emotional bonding as the result of cohesion, and in disagreement with some other social psychologists who equate bonding and cohesion (Shepherd, 1964). In addition, the Olson et al. (1979) definition includes the concept of cohesion as a continuum balancing forces of separateness and connectedness, and thus is similar to the conceptualization of Hess and Handel (1959).

Theoretically, the Olson et al. (1979) cohesion dimension is a continuum. For clinical application, however, they have divided their continuum into four discrete categories of families. Ranging from low to high cohesion, they have labeled the four categories as disengaged, separated, connected, and enmeshed, thus using Hess and Handel's (1959) terms, "separated" and "connected," for families in the center of the continuum and Minuchin's (1974) terms, "disengaged" and "enmeshed," for families on the extremes of the dimension. They suggest that a "balanced degree of family cohesion is the most conducive to effective family functioning and to optimum individual development" (Olson et al., 1979, p. 6). Thus they posited both separated and connected families as nonpathological, while the disengaged and enmeshed families were seen as pathological. The Olson et al. (1979) hypothesis of a curvilinear relationship between cohesion and a number of measures of family outcomes is not, however, substantiated by their data. As Broderick's (1984) review of the Olson et al. (1983) monograph points out, however, the relationships are clearly linear.

The Olson et al. (1979) definition of cohesion does not explicitly include either the aspect of similarity that characterizes mechanical solidarity or the aspect of interdependence in pursuit of common goals that characterizes organic solidarity (Durkheim, 1893/1933). Both concepts can be found in specific indicators developed to operationalize the dimensions of family cohesion. Their approach, however, seems to reflect more emphasis in assessing the similarities and differences among family members than on assessing the interdependence of family members.

Some of Olson et al.'s (1979) operational dimensions are conceptually similar to those of Bengtson and Schrader (1982). For example, Olson et al.'s (1979) emotional bonding dimension equates with affectional solidarity, their friends dimension and their decision-making dimension are types of familism norms, and their interests and recreation dimension is part of Bengtson and Schrader's (1982) nominal definition of the associational dimension. In addition, three of the Olson et al. (1979) dimensions (coalitions, time, and space) relate to specific patterns of interrelationships within the family, and thus are similar to Bengtson and Schrader's (1982) associational solidarity.

Olson et al.'s (1979) independence and family boundaries dimensions, however, have no counterparts within the Bengtson and Schrader schema. These two dimensions appear to be derived from Hess and Handel (1959), who included both the establishing of boundaries and the establishing of satisfactory patterns of separateness in their list of normal family processes. In addition, it should be noted that Olson et al. (1979) are strongly systems-oriented, and that the emphasis of their dimensions is on the evaluation of family process.

Summary

This chapter has reviewed the conceptual foundations for *solidarity* as a term to describe family intergenerational relations. Our purpose has been to outline the historical antecedents of the concept of solidarity as applied to the family, and to set the stage for discussion of the specific dimensions of solidarity and their measurement that will be presented in the remaining chapters of this book.

We began this chapter by asking what force, or unitary property, allows collective action and enables some groups to be more harmonious than others. We thus began with a single hypothetical construct, labeled "solidarity," and asked what could explain it.

Durkheim (1893/1933) posited two universal processes that produced order within the group: (1) mechanical solidarity, produced by similarities among members of the group, and (2) organic solidarity, produced by complementary differences that lead to interdependence among members of the group. While Durkheim's analysis was primarily macro-oriented, Parsons (1955a, 1955b) based his concept of "functional integration" on Durkheim's organic solidarity and specifically applied it to the family and the socialization of children. Thus Durkheim and Parsons hypothesize two concepts as explanations of the unitary property of the group called "solidarity." These two concepts can be viewed as being one level below the unitary construct of solidarity in terms of degree of abstraction.

We then selectively reviewed conceptualizations and empirical findings pertaining to solidarity within small groups and within the family, including research by social psychologists studying group dynamics, and research by clinicians and family sociologists. If Durkheim's concepts of mechanical and organic solidarity are viewed as a specification of grand theory, then the work of these groups of researchers represents additional elaboration. Their work may be viewed as a third level of abstraction below Durkheim's two types of social solidarity.

Two research perspectives can be observed within this large body of research on small groups and families. Some clinicians and family sociologists tend to be interested in family solidarity primarily as an explanation of other family phenomena. From within the positivist paradigm, they might be viewed as using family solidarity as an independent variable.

On the other hand, the work of the group dynamists, Homans (1950), Heider (1958), Nye and Rushing (1969), and Bengtson and colleagues (Bengtson et al., 1976; Bengtson and Schrader, 1982) seems explicitly designed to describe and explain the phenomena of family solidarity per se. To the positivist, they are using family solidarity as a dependent variable.

Conclusions

In conducting this review, we were impressed with the diversity of disciplines and approaches that have made significant contributions to the development of the concept of family solidarity. We value the diverse theoretical conceptualizations and empirical work of clinicians and basic researchers. In our view, this pluralism is healthy and we encourage further interdisciplinary collaboration on the topic of family solidarity.

For researchers interested in the cooperative advancement of a theory of solidarity, there are several additional conclusions that can be drawn from this review:

(1) Solidarity is best conceptualized as complex and multidimensional, rather than as a unitary construct.
(2) There is a trend toward explanations of family solidarity that emphasize mechanical solidarity and deemphasize organic solidarity.
(3) Current conceptualizations of family solidarity are frequently unclear and inexplicit.
(4) Measurement of concepts has not always been given adequate attention.

Each of these conclusions bears some elaboration.

Multidimensionality

There is a clear historical trend away from unitary constructs of solidarity at the level of grand theory toward a conceptualization of family solidarity as a multidimensional series of constructs within theories of the middle range. In spite of the diversity of paradigms, backgrounds, and purposes of the scholars whose work we have reviewed, and despite the fact that they sometimes appear to be working independently of one another, their work is congruent in that they seem to view family solidarity as multidimensional.

Emphasis on Mechanical Solidarity

There appears to be a trend toward an emphasis on similarities among family members (mechanical solidarity) as a basis for family solidarity and a corresponding deemphasis on complementary differentiation that leads to interdependence among family members (organic solidarity). This appears to be partially due to the decline of structural-functionalism in sociology. Given the renewed interest among clinicians in studying the family from the systems viewpoint, however, the deemphasis on organic solidarity is difficult to understand. After all, the definition of functional interdependence, which stresses interdependent members with complementary roles, could pass as the definition of a system. Indeed, Durkheim's thought is considered one of the bases for structural-functionalism, and as such represents an early systems viewpoint. Consequently, we would recommend that researchers rethink their conceptualizations of family solidarity. For those researchers whose conceptualizations emphasize mechanical solidarity, we recommend that they consider including both older functionalist ideas of organic solidarity such as complementarity of roles, interdependence of members, and commonality of goals, and new systems ideas regarding boundaries, coalitions, and so on within their conceptualizations of family solidarity.

Need for Conceptual Clarity

Several aspects of conceptualization seem particularly weak in the literature we reviewed. In this era of multiple paradigms, there is a need for a clarification of the basic assumptions or paradigms upon which a given study is based. A researcher proceeding within the framework of logical positivism may be looking at the antecedents and consequences of the construct of solidarity, while a researcher who is systems-oriented may describe a multifaceted phenomenon that cannot be temporally ordered. Either orientation is valid. We need to know the vantage point of the researcher, however,

In addition, researchers should strive for an explicit tie to a theoretical base. Even in the case where this theoretical tie serves only to inform the reader why the authors have rejected the received theories, such a tie will contribute to the building of a collective body of knowledge and, it is hoped, will cut down on the amount of time spent reinventing the wheel. This seems especially important if researchers from a variety of disciplines with disparate theoretical traditions are to build on each others' work.

Researchers should also explicitly formulate their conceptualizations. For example, it became apparent in the process of this review that by changing the nominal definition of "functional integration" as used by Durkheim (1893/1933) and Parsons (1955a, 1955b), and by deleting the dimension of "goal integration" as used by Nye and Rushing (1969), our own research group had eliminated the possibility of studying Durkheim's organic solidarity because none of our dimensions looks at differentiated and complementary roles within the intergenerational family system. Rather, we had emphasized the shared or similar aspects of the intergenerational relationship, an approach derived from the conceptualization of mechanical solidarity.

Need for Better Measurement

Once conceptualizations are clear, and a determination to contribute to a collaborative effort in theory building has been made, there is a need to focus explicitly on measurement issues in assessing family interaction. Where conceptualizations are vague, the inevitable measurement error is compounded. Clear concepts that are isomorphic to operational definitions that are in turn isomorphic to a series of multiple indicators will enable research to serve its intended purpose better.

We believe that good measurement is fundamental to both the testing of extant theories as well as the process of theory building. The study of family solidarity now has an extensive history, and the time for exploratory, atheoretical descriptive data gathering has passed. This book represents one contribution to the development of theories of intergenerational relationships, in that we explicitly analyze the conceptual and statistical foundations of our measures.

The chapters that follow are presented as an attempt to examine carefully both the conceptualization and the measurement of family solidarity. While we have not entirely succeeded in meeting these goals, it is our hope that this volume will contribute to the improvement of the theoretical and conceptual understanding of family solidarity.

NOTE

1. It should be noted that Durkheim (1893/1933, p. 63) credits Comte with being the first to recognize the consequences of the division of labor for social solidarity.

3

Measuring Intergenerational Family Relations

DAVID J. MANGEN

As Blalock (1979) notes, human behavior is so complex that failure to conceptualize adequately and measure carefully makes theoretical development and integration difficult if not impossible. In recent years, social scientists have increasingly recognized the importance of careful measurement, as evidenced by publications describing substantive measurement attempts (Schuessler, 1982), comparing question form and wording (Schuman and Presser, 1981; Bradburn and Sudman, 1979; Sudman and Bradburn, 1974), reviewing existing measures (Mangen and Peterson, 1982a, 1982b, 1984), and providing guidelines for effective measurement (Sudman and Bradburn, 1982).

All of these publications share one central theme: social science research will be advanced if greater attention is given to conceptual specification, measurement reliability, and validity. That theme is present here as well.

Intergenerational relationships within the family system constitute a challenge for accurate measurement. In addition to the necessity of clearly specifying theoretical constructs and assessing the reliability and validity of operational indicators (Straus, 1964; Mangen, 1982; Mangen, Peterson, and Sanders, 1982; Bengtson and Schrader, 1982), effective measurement of family relations requires particular attention to the complexities introduced by different levels of analysis, that is, aggregation to the *family* as the unit of analysis. This chapter will first review some of the issues involved in measuring intergenerational family relations, focusing on problems in defining the unit of analysis. Following this, mathematical and statistical procedures are briefly reviewed, with a special focus on the procedures we employ in analyzing the Southern California three-generation data (Bengtson, 1975). Finally, an overview of measurement goals for the dimensions of family solidarity outlined by Bengtson and Schrader (1982) and analyzed in this book are presented.

Measuring Families: Units of Analysis

As Hagestad (1981) and Bengtson et al. (1985) note, analyses of intergenerational relations are conducted on two levels: (1) the *generational* level, where the unit of analysis is the individual in the family who occupies a specific position within the intergenerational family structure, and (2) the *lineage* level. Generational analysis often begins with an age- or cohort-based model assumed to measure generational status accurately and completely. That is, by virtue of membership in some age or cohort group, a respondent individual is *assumed* to hold a certain generational status (e.g., child, parent, or grandparent) within his or her family. For example, the generational model typically assumes that a 40-year-old person has living parents and children, and the questions asked of that individual focus on those two role relationships.

The fact that very many 40-year-old persons actually have living parents as well as children legitimates the assumptions of the generational level of analysis as appropriate for many research issues. Note, however, that the status of a 40-year-old person is neither necessary nor sufficient for accurately measuring generational position. It is quite possible that any specific 40-year-old might be the oldest generation (G1), the grandchild (G3) generation, or even a great-grandchild (G4). He or she may even be both a grandparent and a grandchild in a five-generation family. The point here is that the assumption linking age or cohort status with generational status is often incomplete or inaccurate, and that these errors often stem from the fact that data are gathered from a specific *individual* in the family.

At the generational level of analysis, analysis of the efficacy of measurement usually presents few problems in that the standard psychometric procedures used in classical scaling models may be applied. The goal is one of maximizing reliability and validity while achieving cross-generation equivalence of measures. It should be noted, however, that these may well be conflicting goals in that achieving equivalence across generations may require elimination of some items that improve scale reliability within a specific generation.

A more important conceptual issue at the generational level of analysis involves the use of a key informant within the family to provide data about the total family system. Over 15 years ago, family sociologists debated the utility of employing the responses of only one family member (usually the wife) in studies of marital power (see, e.g., Safilios-Rothschild, 1969), because they recognized that the perceptual biases of a single observer have negative consequences for validity. Most survey studies of aging and the family rely upon the older person as the key informant for the family, although there are notable exceptions (Bengtson, 1975; Cicirelli, 1981; Hagestad, 1981; Hill and associates, 1970; Markides and Vernon, 1984; Marshall, Rosenthal and Synge, 1983). Using only one informant, regardless of generational position, to provide data on intergenerational relations presents problems of validity (Bengtson et al., 1985; Hagestad, 1981).

At the lineage level of analysis, the observations of several individual family members are linked into a single analytical unit. Generational position is determined by genealogical position within the vertical family system. Moving to the lineage level of analysis alleviates the problems of relying upon a single source of data. A number of additional issues become germane, however. The first is to define what constitutes a lineage. This concern is very similar to the problem in network analysis of defining the parameters of the network. Not all families are the same size, and thus the number of distinct role relationships present in any family differ widely. How then does research proceed in developing equivalence of measures when families are objectively unique?

Figure 3.1 presents two hypothetical family trees to attempt to explicate this issue. Family 1, a high fertility family, is characterized by eight bloodline relationships in the grandparent-adult child (G1-G2) dyad, and two in-law relationships in that same dyad. In the adult child-grandchild (G2-G3) dyad, 14 direct bloodline relationships are present, and 28 uncle/aunt-nephew/niece relationships. The grandparent-grandchild (G1-G3) dyad is also characterized by 14 unique relationships.

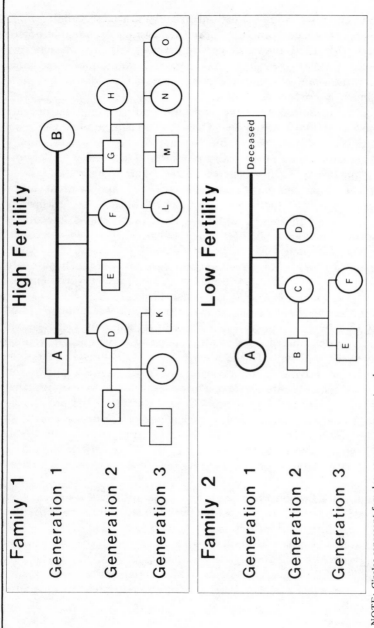

NOTE: Circles represent females; squares represent males.

Figure 3.1 Hypothetical Family Trees

34

Contrast this with Family 2, a low fertility family, where the G1 grandfather is deceased. This family has only two bloodline relationships in the G1-G2 dyad, and one in-law relationship. In the G2-G3 relationship, four bloodline relationships are observed, while the G1-G3 relationship is manifested by only two ties. In terms of the *family structure,* these families are objectively quite different. How then can research effectively proceed?

One strategy is to attempt to develop aggregate measures that characterize the entire family system. An aggregate measure of family affect could be defined as the arithmetic average of the responses of the diverse family members. The variance of age within the lineage may be defined as a measure of age homogeneity. The technique of averaging or computing the variance may be theoretically inappropriate for the substantive focus of a given piece of research, but the central issue is that some strategy for combining the different *number* of responses is required. As Blalock (1982) illustrates, however, aggregation requires an underlying theoretical structure, and even then is likely to introduce measurement error and amplify specification biases.

A second strategy is to focus on the *role relationships* within the family. That is, each of the families represented in Figure 3.1 are characterized by four intergenerational relationships: (1) grandparent-adult child, (2) grandparent-spouse of adult child, (3) adult child-child, and (4) grandparent-grandchild. An even greater number of relationships could be derived if sibling, extended family, and husband-wife relationships are included, or if the grandchildren are married. Further complexity is generated if gender specificity is incorporated into the research. This complexity is simplified through definitional reduction. The researcher elects to focus on a limited number of role relationships in order develop a manageable research problem. Observational procedures or questions can then be developed to evaluate the specific relationships from the perspective of each of the parties involved in that relationship, and measurement models appropriate to the data can be examined.

This strategy yields two measures for each role relationship, taking into account the perspective of both parties. If these measures are strongly correlated with a slope of 1.0 when using regression through the origin, then strong agreement regarding the nature of the relationship exists. Under such circumstances, development of a single measure to describe the role relationship presents no problem. Departures from this strict set of criteria result in problems in developing a summary measure of the relationship. If, for example, a G1 report of face-to-face contact with G2 correlates with the parallel G2 report at $r = 0.70$, then over one-half of the variance is unexplained, indicating a substantial difference in perceptions of a supposedly objective behavioral phenomenon. One solution is to analyze the individual level data linked within the lineage system. Using this strategy is valid, but quickly results in complex theoretical models as the number of concepts must be multiplied by twice the number of role relationships in the lineage to obtain the number of variables.[1] Another strategy emphasizes multiple indicator models that incorporate estimates of correlated measurement error. This strategy is discussed in greater depth later in this chapter.

A focus on the role relationship permits developing equivalent measures without introducing the biases of aggregation, and thus has some advantages when compared to the strategy of aggregation. In addition to the analytical complexity outlined above, other potential confounding factors emerge when using the role relationship approach.

One confounding factor stems from sampling relationships as opposed to people. Assume for the moment that data are gathered from all members of Family 1, represented in Figure 3.1. In a data file where the unit of analysis is the role relationship, some information will be excluded. Other responses, however, will be overrepresented and appear more that once. To illustrate, a data file of grandparent-adult child-grandchild triads in Family 1 yields fully *14* possible triad combinations.[2] The grandmother and grandfather are represented seven times, while the G2 daughter is included six times and the G2 son is included eight times. Thus a problem of *nonindependence of observations* would be introduced into the analysis, while some of the data concerning G1-G2 relationships would be ignored (i.e., for those G2s who have no children). Randomly selecting one person from each generation obviates the problem of nonindependence, but the resultant sample is likely to include a mix of role relationships. To illustrate, the A-E-N triad from Family 1 includes a grandfather-adult son relationship for the G1-G2, and an uncle-niece relationship for the G2-G3 portion of the triad. The A-C-J triad includes a father-in-law relationship at the G1-G2 level, and a father-daughter relationship for the G2-G3. While it is certainly desirable to explore these relationships, mixing them in one analysis causes conceptual and analytical problems. Finally, independence of observations may be obtained by theoretically defining the appropriate triads for the substantive analysis, and randomly selecting one triad if overlap exists. Note that this results in eliminating a substantial portion of the obtained data.

Assuming that an appropriate theoretical focus is developed for the lineage *and* that independent measures are obtained in data gathering, I suspect that the problems of overlapping observations are manageable without eliminating a large part of the data. From a theoretical perspective, the focus on role relationships implies exactly that constraint for independence: Are the *relationships* independent? The fact that a son has a relationship with both his father as well as his mother clearly implies two relationships, not one. To be sure, the shared environment of the family links these relationships. If the measures are independent, focused on the appropriate referent, and specifically do not mix or confuse the referents (e.g., "How often do you see your *mother*," as opposed to "How often do you see your *parents*?"), then the linkage of the relationship and hence the problem with nonindependence of observations can probably be addressed by using statistical models that allow correlated errors in equations and measurement.

In short, the tack of assessing role relationships requires specification of the specific roles to be tapped and hence the responses to be included within the analytical file. Almost certainly such specification stems from an underlying theory or conceptual focus. As a consequence, however, the definition of "lineage" will certainly vary depending on the substantive research problem. Note, for example, that a lineage file that incorporates intragenerational and intergenerational relations would exclude Family 2 from Figure 3.1 because the grandfather is deceased, and assessment of the intragenerational relationship in G1 is logically impossible.

What all of this illustrates is that drawing a three-generation sample and developing appropriate analytical files is notoriously complex (Bytheway, 1977; Hill, 1977). Not only is location of families characterized by a three-generation structure difficult, so too are the problems involved in constructing and defining a proper unit of analysis at the lineage level of analysis.

Generational-Level Measurement

Because most research on the aging family uses the generational level of analysis during some phases, discussion of some desired features of measurement at this level is warranted. Moreover, because lineage-level measurement is more complex than generational, the application of rigorous standards at the generational level serves to "pave the way" for the more difficult and often unwieldy task of validating lineage-level measures.

Measurement at the generational level of analysis is comparable to the assessment of any individual-level perceptual data, with the referent of measurement being some facet of the intergenerational relationship. As such, it parallels standard psychometric procedures of measurement, with the extending circumstance of requiring cross-generation equivalence of measures, if multiple generations are included in the study. Cross-generation equivalence is required to ensure that the derived scales are phenomenologically the same for the different generations.

In the present research, the first step in assessing the adequacy of the intergenerational solidarity measures is to determine the reliability, validity, and measurement properties at the generational level for the six solidarity constructs initially proposed by Nye and Rushing (1969) and discussed by Bengtson and Schrader (1982, pp. 119-122) in terms of their relevance for aging research. These dimensions are (1) structure, (2) association, (3) affect, (4) normative, (5) functional or exchange, and (6) consensual solidarity.

For each of the six solidarity constructs, items are delineated into two groups: (1) a multiple indicator group and (2) global single-item indicator(s). Note that respondents were asked a varying number of questions depending on generational position. For example, the measure of *associational solidarity* included nine items in the multiple indicator block and one global single-item indicator. The oldest generation was asked only this set of questions with reference to a specific G2 child, while the G2 were asked these questions with three referents: (1) their father (G1), (2) their mother (G1), and (3) a referent child (G3). In a similar fashion, the G3 respondents were asked these questions with two referents: their father and mother (G2).

The multiple indicator group serves as the basis of the scaling models, primarily principal factoring with iterations. A number of alternative scaling models, including multidimensional scaling (Borg, 1981; Davies and Coxon, 1982; Coxon, 1982; Schiffman, Reynolds, and Young, 1981) and cluster analysis of variables (Tryon and Bailey, 1970) were considered but rejected. The goal of scaling in this context is to define underlying dimensions that best explain the covariances among the multiple indicators. If dimensions that are congruent across generations emerges, then evidence of *construct validity* exists in that similar structures emerge in different contexts and with different groups. Procedures for determining factor congruence are discussed by Harman (1976, pp. 336-360) and Alwin and Jackson (1981).

Further evidence of validity is provided by the global single-item indicators. To the extent that these single items correlate with the multiple indicator scale score, evidence of *convergent validity* is available.

Evidence pertaining to the *discriminant validity* of these measures derives from two sources. First, measures of response bias such as acquiescent response patterns or the Crowne and Marlowe (1964) Social Desirability Scale may be used, although it is unclear as to the exact meaning of the brief form of the Crowne-Marlowe scale included in these data. It is hoped that measures of family solidarity are not contaminated by socially desired response bias, and thus negligible correlations are anticipated. Because the Crowne-Marlowe scale has poor reliability in these data, low correlations are somewhat expected due to attenuation. Thus the Crowne-Marlowe scale is a poor criterion of discriminant validity. Second, and more relevant from a substantive perspective, correlations across the role relationships that are negligible or moderate provide evidence of discriminant validity. To illustrate with the association dimension, the G2's report of interaction with his or her *mother* (G1) should correlate moderately with reports of interaction with a *child* (G3). This is in fact the case with these data ($r = 0.275$; see Chapter 6).

In sum, issues of validity are theoretical issues predicated on substantive concerns for the phenomena being studied (Mangen, Peterson, and Sanders, 1982), and what constitutes evidence of a valid measure is contingent upon those theoretical concerns. In some situations, extremely strong correlations are desired as evidence of a valid measure, whereas, in others, modest or even negligible correlations indicate validity.

Reliability is also of concern in assessing the quality of the measures, because it is a necessary but not sufficient condition for validity. Internal consistency reliability is favored over test-retest reliability for two reasons. First, the requisite data are always available for the multiple indicator models. Second, age-related theories generally predict longitudinal change in these data, and hence sorting out reliability from true change is problematic. Of course, if the elapsed interval between test and retest is short (e.g., two weeks), then test-retest reliability estimates are valuable. (See Heise, 1969, or Wheaton et al., 1977, for full discussions of this issue.)

Assessment of reliability at the generational level is grounded in the domain sampling model of reliability. The goal is finding replication across items (i.e., strong correlations) as opposed to replication across raters or time. As evidence of strong reliability for research purposes, α coefficients greater than 0.80 are desired. Coefficients as low as 0.50 are accepted within the research context but clearly suggest that findings are tentative, and that improvement in the scale is necessary.

Lineage-Level Measurement

When moving to the lineage level of analysis, new issues emerge. As noted above, the role relationship approach to solving the problem of what constitutes the analytical lineage group is one way to solve the problem of defining the family as the unit of analysis. Most of the analyses presented in this monograph use some form of a "triad file" that combines responses from one bloodline respondent from each generation in the family. For most of the concepts, scales are referent-specific in that items refer to a specific person in the family. For example, if two G3s are included in the data set, but the G2 bloodline respondent answered questions about only one of the children, then that *referent child* is the child included in the lineage triad file. Because the three family members are answering questions about the same facet of family relations, however, correlated measurement error is a potential problem as is specification error. When the triad file is overlapping (i.e., more than one triad is developed from each family) or when the data involve difference scores (i.e., the consensus dimension), concern for correlated errors increases because these factors will likely compound errors resulting from the shared role relationship.

In order to address the strong possibility of correlated error, analyses of measurement structure at the lineage level employs methods that permit testing for and controlling such errors. Most of the lineage analyses reported here use the LISREL (Jöreskog and Sörbom, 1981) program for maximum likelihood estimation of measurement and structural models. The LISREL procedure is a model fitting algorithm, where the analyst specifies a number of models—usually of increasing complexity and specificity—in order to test the fit of different theoretical structures to the observed covariances among the variables. The key advantage of this procedure is the opportunity to specify correlated errors of measurement while constraining the solution to test the hypothesized dimensional structure of the data.

The LISREL program provides as output unstandardized estimates of the measurement structure (analogous to "factor loadings"), and the variances and covariances of the dimensions and errors of measurement. If the specified model includes structural equations, these coefficients as well as the errors in equations are estimated. Standard errors and t-tests are provided for all estimated coefficients, as is a likelihood ratio statistic, distributed as χ^2, that tests the goodness of fit for the specified model.[3] In addition to these parameter estimates, several diagnostic statistics, including residuals, modification indices, and correlations of estimates, are provided to aid in modification of the model. In general, the goal is to find the model that is consistent with theory and parsimonious while at the same time adequately explains the sample variances and covariances. Campbell and Mutran (1982) provide an excellent review of the potential applications of the LISREL model in gerontological research, while Jöreskog and Sörbom (1979) document the mathematical and statistical theory of this estimation procedure. Because the LISREL procedures are extensively used in this book, however, a review of terminology and some of the basic models that are tested is included here to facilitate presentation in the following chapters.

The Lisrel Model

LISREL is a program for estimating linear structural relationships using maximum likelihood estimation procedures. It allows the researcher to estimate measurement models, structural equation models, and full information models that combine the characteristics of both measurement and structural equation models. Multiple groups can also be analyzed to determine if the same or variant structures are present in the different groups.

As a model fitting procedure, LISREL requires the researcher to specify the relationships among the variables. The algorithm then determines how well the hypothesized structure accounts for the observed covariances in the data. Relationships are specified as elements in matrices, each of which addresses one aspect of the measurement or structural equation model. Figure 3.2 presents a simple full information model to facilitate discussion of the matrices and their role in the LISREL system.

Figure 3.2 presents a two-wave longitudinal model with two concepts measured at each occasion. The six variables at Time 1 (X_1 through X_6) measure the two exogenous concepts, referenced in the LISREL

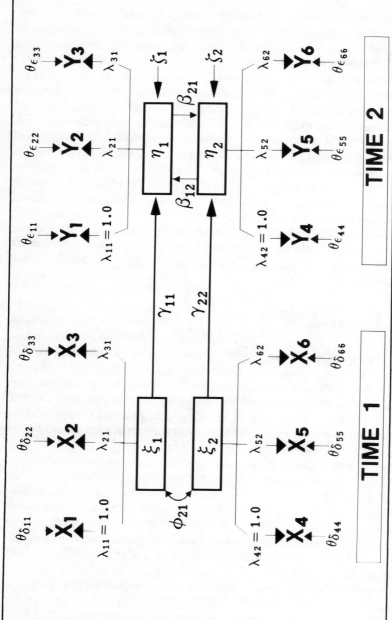

Figure 3.2   A Hypothetical Full Information LISREL Model

42

terminology as ξ_1 and ξ_2. The six variables at Time 2 (Y_1 through Y_6) are identical to the Time 1 items, and measure two endogenous concepts (η_1 and η_2).[4]

The *measurement model* relating the six observed items at Time 1 to ξ_1 and ξ_2 references elements in two matrices. The Λ_x matrix is a matrix of metric or unstandardized "factor loadings" that describe the relationships between the underlying dimensions (ξ) and the observed items (X_i). Specific elements in Λ_x are referenced by λ coefficients where the first subscript refers to the item (X_i) and the second subscript refers to the dimension (ξ). Errors in measurement are referenced in the symmetric Θ_δ matrix, with diagonal elements referencing error variances and off-diagonal elements referencing covariances (i.e., correlated measurement error). Measurement at Time 2 is analogous, except that these matrices are referenced as Λ_y and Θ_ϵ.

Elements in the Φ matrix refer to the variances and covariances of the ξ dimensions. Because these are exogenous measures, no causal relationships are assumed. Elements in the Γ matrix are metric regression coefficients that describe the causal effect relating the ξ dimensions to the η dimensions, while the β coefficients describe the causal relationships among the η dimensions. Note that reciprocal causation can be tested. The vector of errors in structural equations is represented by ζ, the variances and covariances of which are described in the Ψ matrix.

Coefficients in the various matrices can be freely estimated, constrained to equal any value, and constrained to equal other coefficients, given that the entire model is identified. Note that one λ coefficient is constrained to equal 1.0 for each ξ and η in the measurement model in Figure 3.2. This is done to establish a common scale for the underlying measures. The ability to specify constraints and values on the coefficients of the model enables examination of a wide range of theoretical models to determine the most appropriate explanation for the observed data. Because the focus of this book is on measurement, most of the analyses presented throughout this book use only the measurement models in LISREL (i.e., the Λ_x, Θ_δ and Φ matrices). Three measurement models that are examined in several of the chapters are now discussed using Figure 3.2 as a point of departure.

Assume for this discussion that X_1, X_2, X_3, Y_1, Y2, , and Y_3 are all measured on the same underlying interval scale of 0-50. Further assume that X_4, X_5, X_6, Y_4, Y_5, and Y_6 are measured on the same underlying interval scale of 0-100. Thus the items that are supposed to measure any

one dimension, regardless of period of measurement, have equal
theoretical ranges. Under these circumstances, three different measurement structures deserve in-depth examination.

The first of these models is the *parallel measures* model. This model
assumes that all variables within any dimension contribute equally to
that dimension, and that the error variances for each item are also equal.
In the context of Figure 3.2, this means that $\lambda_{11} = \lambda_{21} = \lambda_{31} = 1.0$ and $\lambda_{42} =
\lambda_{52} = \lambda_{62} = 1.0$ in the Λ_x matrix. It is not necessary in the parallel measures
model that all λ coefficients equal 1.0; this added constraint is a function
of establishing the common underlying scale. Furthermore, the error
variances are equal in the parallel measures model: $\theta_{\delta_{11}} = \theta_{\delta_{22}} = \theta_{\delta_{33}}$ and $\theta_{\delta_{44}}
= \theta_{\delta_{55}} = \theta_{\delta_{66}}$. A similar pattern is found in the Λ_y and Θ_ϵ matrices. These
criteria give the model its name—all items are assumed to operate in
parallel in defining the measurement structure of a given set of items.
This is a very restrictive model that uses few degrees of freedom. A
further restriction involves equating error variances across periods of
measurement as well, thus establishing an even more strict criterion of
parallelism.

The model of *tau equivalence* is very similar to the parallel measures
model, except that the equality constraints on elements in Θ_δ and Θ_ϵ are
relaxed and the error variance for each item freely estimated. The items
are *equal* in their contribution to the underlying measure, but some
uniqueness is permitted; hence the measures are equivalent.

The third model of special interest is the *congeneric measures* model.
This is the measurement model depicted in Figure 3.2 without any
additional constraints on Λ_x, Λ_y, Θ_δ and Θ_ϵ. Each item contributes to the
definition of only one dimension, and uniqueness is permitted in both
the loadings and the error variances.

Many of the chapters included in this book use these basic models, or
variations appropriate to the measures used in that concept area, as the
point of departure for the lineage analysis of measurement structure.
Broad alternative structures for the data are tested, and a general model
of choice is pursued. Usually, after a general model (e.g., congeneric
measures) is chosen, off-diagonal elements in Θ_δ are estimated to control for the significant correlated errors of measurement present in
the data. It is hoped that these correlated errors are substantively
interpretable.

Despite the ability of the LISREL methodology to estimate widely
divergent models with many constraints, the technique is not a panacea
for all research applications. A key assumption made in the model is that

the data are multivariate normal. While this assumption may be relaxed, little is known about the robustness of LISREL to violations of multivariate normality. Skewness in the distributions requires care in model estimation and testing (Campbell and Mutran, 1982). Models also assume linear, additive effects for both the measurement and causal structures. While transformations of the variables may be used to address issues of nonlinearity, and the multiple groups aspect of the model will address interaction effects *if* the interacting variables can be used to define nominal-level groups, many researchers will find LISREL incapable of addressing their substantive needs. Furthermore, incorrect specification of the model may result in incorrect parameter estimates, and it is often difficult to make substantive interpretations of correlated errors. Clearly there are limitations to the use of this methodology.

Constructs and Measures

In order to illustrate some specific issues that arise in measuring intergenerational relations, the six dimensions of solidarity (Bengtson and Schrader, 1982) analyzed in this book are reviewed with special attention to the different issues raised in measuring these concepts at a generational versus lineage levels of analysis. Table 3.1 presents a summary overview of these different issues, and briefly describes the research strategies used in the analysis of the three generation data.

Family Structure

The analysis of family structure on the generational level is primarily descriptive in nature, detailing the number, sex, and geographic proximity of the children and grandchildren of subjects in each of the three generations. This also is a goal of the lineage-level analysis, but the sample is redefined such that responses of family members are paired. This affords examination of additional questions, such as analyses of the transmission of tendencies for large families, or geographic distance between parents and children. Chapter 4 focuses on the description of this sample in terms of structural characteristics. Theoretically, the generation- and lineage-level analyses of family structure emphasize the *opportunity structure* that children and grandchildren provide within the intergenerational family system.

TABLE 3.1   Measurement Goals of Generation and Lineage Analysis

	Generation Analysis	Lineage Analysis
Family Structure:	Descriptive summary of the number and sex of children and grandchildren, and their geographic proximity.	Analytical analysis of the transmission of family size, child spacing, and proximity. Determination of the agreement between generations on objective structural characteristics.
Family Affect:	Descriptive summary of the degree of closeness present in each intergenerational role relationship as perceived by that individual. Assessment of the measurement structure of the affect items, with a focus on congruence across the different relationships and generations. Determination of the internal consistency reliability and construct, convergent, and discriminant validity.	Using a direct bloodline triad file, analysis of the degree to which paired responses of the affect perceived within each triad are correlated with the other. Attention given to error correlations due to overlapping triad membership and multiple raters of the same perceptual phenomenon.
Association:	Descriptive summary of the degree of contact as reported by each generation for each role relationship. Assessment of the measurement structure with a focus on congruence across relationships and generations. Determination of the internal consistency reliability and construct, convergent, and discriminant validity.	Reports of association by two generations are used as multiple indicators of same behavior. Measurement model of three constructs with correlated errors stemming from overlapping triad file and multiple raters of the same behaviors.
Norms:	Assessment of the degree of familism, by generation. Measurement structure of familism, with emphasis on congruence across generations, is assessed. Determination of reliability and validity of normative solidarity as perceived by the individual.	Two foci: (1) Assessment of the measurement structure in a nonoverlapping triad file with attention to correlated measurement error due to multiple reports of the same perceptual phenomenon. (2) Examination of the normative consensus within the same triad file; input variables are differences between the generations on normative content.
Exchange:	See the "Association" scale above, but with a focus on the giving and receiving of assistance or money. Attempt to infer perceived reciprocity from the perspective of each generation.	Same as "Association" above. Attempt to infer the objective and perceived reciprocity in a linked lineage file.
Consensus:	Descriptive summary of individual attitudes on social, political, and religious attitudes and religious behavior. Develop summary scales congruent across generations, with maximum internal consistency reliability.	Measure attitudinal and behavioral consensus within a nonoverlapping family triad file; input variables are absolute difference scores between adjacent generations.

An implicit analysis of "interrater reliability" can be obtained within the lineage analysis by examining the degree to which G1 or G2 reports of their proximity correlate with the G2 or G3 reports. While this is not truly a measure of reliability *per se,* it does provide data that are relevant to gerontological research in that strong correlations would imply considerable accuracy of these reports by members of adjacent generations, and hence justify use of only one informant to gather such data. In the reanalysis of the three-generation data, this is the case (see Chapter 4). Reliable and valid data regarding family structure can be gathered from almost any adult family member, with members of the middle generation being especially appropriate because of their generational position.

Family Affect

Regardless of the level of analysis, family affect represents an individually held cognitive evaluation of a shared relationship. That is, every individual has their own subjective perspective on intergenerational family relationships, as opposed to necessarily being linked to an objective reality. Conceptually, this implies that the measurement structure of a set of affect items should be specific to a role relationship and not merge dimensions across roles. To merge dimensions across roles would imply that the reports measure the *same cognitive property.* Rather, each report should measure a unique subjective evaluation specific to that respondent and that relationship. This has implications for both the generational and lineage levels of analysis.

At the generational level of analysis, it suggests that each role relationship will be uniquely evaluated and that a global family closeness scale is not present. Thus because the G1 report on the affect they feel toward the G2 and G3, two separate dimensions of affect are expected to emerge in the generational analysis. For the G2, however, a different pattern should result. Because G2 respondents evaluate the affect they feel toward their mother and father (G1) as well as the referent child (G3), three dimensions of affect are expected for the G2. Each dimension is specific to one of the three role relationships. Construct validity data are provided by the emergence of these hypothesized dimensions, especially if congruence across generations and referents is manifest. Discriminant validity data are provided by correlations between the scales within a generation. Again using the G2 as an example, the correlation of the mother affect scale with father affect should be moderate to strong, but the correlations of child affect with mother affect and father affect are expected to be negligible to modest.

At the lineage level, somewhat different models are of interest. Using a three-generation bloodline definition of lineage, the resultant file has reciprocated responses by all generations. Two models are important. The first model anticipates six dimensions: (1) G1s' evaluation of affect toward G2, (2) G1s' affect toward G3, (3) G2s' affect toward G1, (4) G2s' affect toward G3, (5) G3s' affect toward G1, and (6) G3s' affect toward G2.[5] This suggests that each relationship is uniquely evaluated by each generation, and that there is not a shared evaluation specific to each relationship that is consistent across the generational boundary. Certainly these dimensions are correlated, especially the scales paired by role relationship (e.g., 1 and 3, immediately above). The second model relaxes the assumption of generational specificity, and examines specificity to the relationship. In this model, three dimensions are anticipated: (1) affect in the G1-G2 relationship, which combines dimensions 1 and 3 above; (2) affect in the G1-G3 relationship, which combines 2 and 5 above; and (3) affect in the G2-G3 relationship, which combines 4 and 6 above. This model suggests that both parties define the relationship similarly.

Association

In contrast to affect, association represents supposedly objective behaviors (i.e., contact between the generations) that in three-generation data are described by both members of the relationship. Thus, while the goals of measuring association on the generational level are similar to the goals in measuring affect (i.e., congruence across generations, maximizing reliability, and assessing validity), a different goal emerges for lineage-level analysis. Given that these behaviors are objective, a substantial correlation is expected between the generations' reports of association in that role relationship. This substantial correlation represents a multiple indicator of the same behavior. As such, three dimensions are anticipated.

Therefore, at the generational level of analysis, we expect to find a total of eight dimensions of association: (1) G1 reporting on contact with G2; (2) G1 report of contact with G3; (3) G2 report of contact with mother, (4) father, and (5) child; and G3 report of contact with (6) mother, (7) father, and (8) grandparents.[6]

At the lineage level, respondents are grouped into an overlapping triad file. Consequently, the reports of association included in this file include only those that refer to the other actors *in that triad.* The objectivity hypothesized as stemming from the behavioristic features of this dimension suggests that only three dimensions will emerge: (1) G1-G2 association, (2) G1-G3 association, and (3) G2-G3 association. If six dimensions are required to explain the covariances at the lineage level, then the adequacy of the measures must be questioned. Alternatively, and congruent with a symbolic interactionist perspective, perhaps even objective behaviors are extensively filtered and result in distinct evaluations by each generation.[7]

Norms of Familism

At the generational level of analysis, assessment of the measurement structure of norms of familism is similar to both association and affect. The normative measures assess the beliefs held by respondents regarding expectations of other family members. The goal of scaling at the generational level is to determine that the items share a common meaning, and that the resultant measures are congruent across generations. Unlike association or affect, however, the normative concept is not conceptualized as specific to the role relationship. Rather, norms of familism are defined as a global concept perceived by each member of a family and assumed to operate throughout the entire family system. Thus only one dimension is expected for each generation.

As noted in Table 3.1, however, at the lineage level of analysis, yet another conceptual dimension emerges. While the *degree* of familism held by each respondent is assessed, the derived concept of *normative consensus* is also assessed. (See also the discussion of the consensus dimension below.) Here, the goal is one of determining whether members of the lineage share the definitions of appropriate behavior in the intergenerational relationship. Regardless of how familistic any member of the lineage is, this approach suggests that conflict between family members over the definitions of "right and proper behavior" is an important component of family solidarity. We generally expect to find substantial agreement or, barring that, relatively greater familism in the older respondents. The normative consensus approach suggests, however, that G2 or G3 family members *may* have a higher degree of familism than their parents. Indeed, because parents want their children to succeed in life, normative consensus may be absent if parents believe that "too much" familism is present to permit geographic and status mobility by their offspring.[8]

Exchange

As an objective behavior within the lineage, the concept of exchanges of assistance and support is very similar to the association concept on both the generation and lineage levels of analysis in its implications for measurement. In addition, inference of some perceived (generational) and objective (lineage) reciprocity of exchanges in the family network is possible. The concept of reciprocity appears to be underutilized in gerontological research. To illustrate with these data, items regarding the giving and receiving of *service assistance* and *financial assistance* are present. Consequently, at the generational level of analysis, the ratio of help (or money) given to help (or money) received suggests the degree of reciprocity present in the relationship—as perceived by that respondent. On the lineage level, however, this logic is extended to include the perspective of both generations and permits inference of a measure of objective reciprocity.[9]

As in all of the family solidarity dimensions, the analysis of the exchange dimension retains a focus on the congruence of the measures across generations, while simultaneously attempting to maximize reliability and validity. Unfortunately, the initial conceptualization of the exchange dimension was limited in the data, with only two questions asked of each generation regarding the service assistance in the referent relationship, one question about gift exchange, and two questions about financial assistance. Thus important data regarding the specific patterns of help are not available. Nonetheless, the analytical strategy of examining both the level of exchange and the reciprocity of that exchange can be applied to data that more extensively examine the exchange process.

Consensus

The concept of consensus is an emergent aspect of family relations; it has no meaning without referent to another person and topic matter. At the generational level of analysis, the concept is one of *perceived consensus:* To what extent does the respondent attribute similar values and attitudes to the referent other? At the lineage level of analysis, both perceived and actual consensus are concepts that warrant attention. Development of the lineage-level measures requires development of isomorphic generation-level measures in order to ensure that the derived consensus measure actually taps consensus, and is not simply an artifact of poor measurement of individual attitudes and values. This is especially true because some means of assessing the differences between the generations is required, and this may be a source of error.

As a result of the emergent character of the consensus dimension, the first step in the generational level of analysis is to determine the important attitudinal and behavioral components present in the data. If the conceptualization of consensus includes an attributional component, then generational-level analysis can focus on determining perceived consensus after the common set of attitudinal dimensions is determined. This requires that the scaling models examine the congruence of measures across both generations and attributions in order to ensure that the derived lineage measures are not merely artifacts of measurement error.

Whether perceived consensus at the generational level or objective consensus at the lineage level is the focus of analysis, developing measures of consensus is difficult. Using difference scores, whether simple difference, absolute values, or Euclidian distance measures—all involve differencing, and difference scores present problems with artifactual correlations (Fuguitt and Lieberson, 1974). Computing correlations between generations across items is conceptually appealing, but may be difficult to interpret and use in subsequent analysis.[10] In short, while conceptually appealing, measurement of consensus presents a number of problems. Great attention must be given to spurious correlations, measurement error, and interpretation in developing measures of this important concept.

Conclusion

In this chapter, I have reviewed several issues involved in measuring intergenerational family relations, and have presented some strategies that are useful in analyzing three-generation data. Among these are issues pertaining to unit of analysis (generation *versus* lineage), approaches to aggregation, and general measurement theory. There are other issues as well, including problems with sampling and selecting the persons for inclusion in the study and the biases that are associated with a number of alternative approaches. Still other problems are manifest when turning from the general review, which this article has emphasized, to more specific measurement problems. For that reason, some of the problems and promises associated with the analysis of this three-generation data set are presented.

This chapter emphasizes the empirical issues in *testing* alternative measurement models in three-generation data. The remaining chapters of this book test alternative measurement models for each of the six dimensions of solidarity. Each chapter first presents descriptive statistics for the items included in the data for each chapter. Next, measurement models are tested at the generational level of analysis, and data regarding the reliability and validity of the scales are presented. Measurement models at the lineage level of analysis are then examined. Finally, each chapter summarizes the results of these analyses and presents recommendations for use of these instruments and/or recommendations for the further development of measures that tap the solidarity concepts.

Despite the fact that we emphasize the empirical testing of measurement models, the reader is cautioned against assuming that empirical data analysis can replace substantive theory (Mangen, Peterson, and Sanders, 1982). Rather, efficient testing of empirical relationships—even as part of the process of measurement—requires grounding in a substantive theory regarding the phenomenon of interest. This is certainly true when applying complex models such as LISREL that have the statistical power to address some of the complexities of three-generation data. This power is valuable, but to use it effectively requires an excellent grasp of the theoretical issues present in the research. Because of the necessity of using good theory to address the empirical issues that are germane to each concept, the analysis of each of the dimensions of solidarity is reported in separate chapters. These chapters constitute the remainder of this book.

NOTES

1. To illustrate this effect, assume a simple three-generation sample with one G1, one G2, and one G3 family member included in the triad. This yields three role relationships: G1-G2, G1-G3, and G2-G3. In a two variable, three-generation model, twelve variables must be included, two for each generation for each role relationship with which it is

involved. Because each generation is represented in two of the three role relationships, four variables for each generation must be included in the analysis.

2. The 14 direct bloodline triad combinations in Family 1 are A—those involving the grandfather: (1) A-D-I, (2) A-D-J, (3) A-D-K, (4) A-G-L, (5) A-G-M, (6) A-G-N, (7) A-G-O; and B—those involving the grandmother: (1) B-D-I, (2) B-D-J, (3) B-D-K, (4) B-G-L, (5) B-G-M, (6) B-G-N, (7) B-G-O. Note the heavy overlap in triad membership between the two sets of seven triads for grandmothers and grandfathers.

3. It is important to note that small, nonsignificant values of chi-square indicate a model that fits the data well. In practical applications with larger samples, however, it is often the case that a good model still yields a significant chi-square. As a result, the ratio of chi-square to the degrees of freedom is often used as one indicator of the adequacy of the fit (Campbell and Mutran, 1982, p. 32).

4. In actuality, most analyses of longitudinal data would probably benefit from doing an analysis such as that presented in Figure 3.2 entirely in the Λ_y portion of the model, because correlated errors across periods of measurement are expected, and could not be easily estimated using the specification presented here. The purpose here, however, is presentation of the parameters of the LISREL model, not a detailed exposition of its applicability to longitudinal analysis. Thus in order to keep the model of Figure 3.2 relatively simple, the across-period potential for correlated errors of measurement is ignored.

5. In actuality, inclusion of the affect in the G1-G3 relationship produced a covariance matrix that was multivariate nonnormal, thus invalidating the use of the LISREL maximum likelihood algorithm. As a result, the reanalysis of affect excludes these variables.

6. Only a small number of items were included in these data to assess the amount of contact the G3 had with the G1. Therefore, contrary to the other association dimensions, only a single dimension of association is noted in this relationship.

7. In fact, six dimensions were required, but these dimensions reflected method bias between the scales and the global single-item indicators.

8. While theoretically relevant, no support could be found to suggest the existence of a normative consensus dimension. The covariances are essentially random.

9. Unfortunately, only an inference of reciprocity can be derived. Because the data pertain to the frequency of service assistance or gift giving, no assessment of objective or perceived value of the assistance is available. These data would be required to develop a measure of the distributive justice present in the relationship.

10. Farber (1957) provides an example of the use of this approach in his Marital Integration Scale.

PART II

Results of the Research

4

Measuring Family Structure

KAY YOUNG McCHESNEY
DAVID J. MANGEN

One of the most easily observed and objectively determined aspects of family solidarity or cohesion would appear to be the structure of intergenerational family relations. Within this context, *structure* refers to the number and presence or absence of intergenerational family relations, together with any limiting factors, such as proximity, that may influence the opportunity for intergenerational family relations.

Nominal Definitions

Within the context of the intergenerational family system, we see family structure as an opportunity function. *Family structure* is defined as the pattern of role relationships (kinship networks), bounded by spatial constraints (proximity), that is enacted by family members over time. Kuhn, drawing on the work of Boulding (1958), defined *opportunity function* as "the set of alternatives perceived to be available in a decision situation" (1974, p. 109). How, given the disparate definitions, can we define one in terms of the other? To address that issue, we examine the concept of family structure in greater detail to illustrate how it converges with the concept of an opportunity function.

Family: When examining family structure, the first important issue concerns the definition of who is a family member: one person may include a longtime friend as "family," while another may define a biological parent as "not family," as in the case of an adopted child or an ex-husband who is excluded from contact with his children by his former wife. Illustrative of the importance of this issue is the finding that fictive kin are especially important in intergenerational family relations in some ethnic groups (Jackson, 1980). The core meaning of "family" in our society, however, seems to include a small group of people who are connected by biology, marriage, or adoption and who enact the societal roles of parent, spouse, and child. Thus, in this study, the vertical family system is defined in the sampling frame, and includes a referent person, his or her spouse (G1), their biological or legally adopted children and their spouses (G2), and their biological or legally adopted children and their spouses (G3). In practical terms, this implies that fictive kin are excluded unless a respondent self-selected to include a fictive kin member.

Structure: When patterns of interpersonal behavior, such as a woman asking her daughter to wash dishes for her, are repeated over time, these may be seen as having emergent (i.e., structural) characteristics. In this example, it becomes apparent that the relationship between this mother and daughter includes the definition that the mother has the right to request her daughter to do household chores. When similar patterns of behavior are repeated over many interpersonal dyads, for example, when it is observed that most mothers define it as their right to request their daughters to do household chores, these patterns become part of the cultural system of role relationships. If these generalized patterns are extremely pervasive throughout a society, then the mere existence of a mother/daughter dyad may be abstracted as a static indicator of this pattern. While static, it is an abstracted representation of countless repeated episodes of interpersonal behavior occurring over a whole society.

Indicators of family structure refer, therefore, to the presence or absence of family role relationships that indicate the static potential for the development of repeated patterns of interpersonal behavior. The variety of different role relationships defines, therefore, the set of available alternatives, while the proximity of the different family members defines the perception of availability of each specific alternative, thus linking the definitions of family structure and opportunity function. Family structure is an important aspect of family solidarity or cohesion because it serves to limit both the number of family members available for interaction and the difficulty, in terms of distance, time, or cost, of that interaction.

For an example of the importance of family structure as an aspect of family solidarity or cohesion, note that if a person has no living relatives, then obviously no opportunity for contact with relatives exists. On the other hand, if a person has a large number of living children and grandchildren, then the opportunity for association does exist, even if family relationships are not characterized by such association. Similarly, proximity limits opportunities for contact. If an elderly person has several living children and grandchildren, but if all of them live in another country, opportunity for contact is limited. Thus, while the number of kin and their proximity do not guarantee that association or exchange will occur, their absence or distance from the elderly relative sets a limit on some aspects of contact among family members (Lee, 1979; Marshall and Rosenthal, 1985; Sussman, 1965; Troll et al., 1979).

Operationalization of Kinship Network

One of the aspects of family structure is the vertical kinship network. In this chapter, four types of measures of kinship network were included. First, *the number of children and grandchildren,* excluding fictive kin, is included as a measure of the number of potential relationships. At the generation level of analysis, biological, adoptive, and stepchildren are included. At the lineage level, however, only biological or adopted children are included.[1]

Second, the *marital status* of members of each of the three generations in the sample was included as another measure of opportunity. Obviously, persons who have been married are much more likely to have living children or grandchildren; studies of older adults typically show that over 80% of those ever married have living children (Shanas, 1978). Thus marital status is another aspect of the potential of the intergenerational kinship network.

Third, the *gender composition* of children and grandchildren is included as a measure of family structure. The percentages of female children and grandchildren and a gender typology of the lineages are included. Gender composition of the family is considered important to intergenerational cohesion because generations are linked by female contact (Troll and Bengtson, 1979; Troll et al., 1979). Women have more contact with their own families and their spouses' families, and communicate more often with kin than do men (Lee, 1979). Mother to daughter communication is stronger than son to father communication, and both daughters and sons communicate more often with mothers than fathers (Troll et al., 1979). Further, Brody (1981) suggests that most primary caretakers of elderly parents are women.

Previous reports of gender composition of the lineage have typically been limited to gender typologies. For example, Shanas (1978) used five categories: (1) one son, (2) one daughter, (3) two or more sons, (4) two or more daughters, and (5) children of both sexes. Information on gender composition of grandchildren has not typically been collected by previous researchers (see Shanas, 1978), but is included in these data.

Fourth, measures of the *age range and age variance* of children in each nuclear family are included. Measures of age dispersion are included as measures of structure because increased age dispersion among children may increase the likelihood that at least one child has the resources to assist aging parents. This is derived from the observation of Hill and Mattessich (1979) that adult children whose families were in the "empty nest" developmental stage are more likely to have the resources of time and money necessary to become primary caretakers of aging parents. Thus, although measures of age dispersion have not been included in previous research on intergenerational family structure (see Shanas, 1978), they are included in our conceptualization.

Operationalization of Proximity

In addition to these measures of kinship structure, the residential proximity of intergenerational kin is included in these data. Proximity is expressed in two ways: (1) the actual distance in miles from the home of the respondent to the home of the referenced grandparent, parent, child, or grandchild, and (2) functional categories, indicators of how difficult or time-consuming a visit to a parent or grandparent would be.

Shanas (1978) classified proximity in six categories: (1) same household, (2) less than 10 minutes, (3) 11-30 minutes, (4) 31-60 minutes, (5) more than an hour but less than a day, and (6) more than a day's journey. In this study, a five-category functional classification is used: (1) coresidence, (2) 0-5 miles (easy driving), (3) 6-50 miles (within an hour's drive), (4) 51-500 miles (within a day's drive), and (5) more than 500 miles (an airplane flight or more than a day's journey).

Generation-Level Analysis

Findings for the four types of the kinship network measures are based on the individual-level file of this sample of 2044 respondents in three generations. Each respondent was asked the age and sex of each living child and grandchild. The findings on kinship network structure are derived from these questions.

Table 4.1 presents descriptive statistics on five indicators of the kinship network. The first measure is the respondent's marital status. Note that the large number of G3s who have not yet married (63%) is consistent with their age range of 15-27, as is the 10% of G3s who reported that they were engaged, "committed," or permanently living with, but not married to, a partner. These circumstances are not reported by G1 or G2 respondents. The high rate of married G1s (94%) is atypical of the general population. It is consistent with the selection of the sample, however, which used married male G1s as the focal point for defining the three generations. The unexpected finding that 94% of the G2s in this sample were also married, with only 4% divorced is, however, atypical of full probability samples of the approximate age range represented by this generation (U.S. Bureau of the Census, 1981).

The average number of children and number of grandchildren is also shown in Table 4.1. The small mean number of children for the G3s clearly reflects the age range of this component of the sample. The mean number of children of the G2s is larger than that of the G1s. It is likely that the majority of this difference can be accounted for by the fact that the children of the G2 generation in this sample were part of the post-World War II "baby boom." In addition, normal mortality rates among G1 children contributes to the smaller number of G1 children. As expected, the mean number of grandchildren is much larger for the G1s than for the G2s. The fact that some G2s do have grandchildren, however, supports both Hagestad's (1982) findings on the narrowing of the average number of years per generation and Shanas's (1978) data on the increase of four-generation families (Shanas, 1978).

The gender composition of the families is also shown in Table 4.1. Standard life tables show that the ratio of females to males is about 50-50 at age three. Thereafter, male mortality rates are greater than those for females, resulting in an increase in the ratio of females to males as age increases (Shryock et al., 1976; U.S. Bureau of the Census, 1981). Consequently, one would expect the percentage of female children (Row 9) of the G3 column to be about 50%, with a slight increase in the

TABLE 4.1   Descriptive Statistics of Kinship Network

Row		G1	G2	G3
Marital status:				
1	never married	0.0%	0.0%	63.2%
2	married	93.6%	94.1%	24.2%
3	divorced	1.6%	4.3%	2.3%
4	widowed	4.5%	1.6%	0.0%
5	other[a]	0.0%	0.0%	10.2%
6	missing value	0.4%	0.1%	0.1%
Number of children:				
7	mean	2.690	3.496	0.215
8	standard deviation	1.462	1.650	0.567
Percentage of female children:				
9	mean	56.760	50.026	55.133[b]
10	standard deviation	33.244	29.312	44.561
Number of grandchildren:				
11	mean	7.150	0.526	0.000
12	standard deviation	5.010	1.188	0.000
Percentage of female grandchildren:				
13	mean	50.336	55.319	0.000
14	standard deviation	24.384	40.965	0.000
15	Number of cases	516	701	827

a. Engaged, "committed," or permanently living with, but not married to, a partner.
b. For G3s, this estimate is based upon the 125 (15.1%) that have any living children.

percentage as one goes to the G2 column, whose children are mostly in the young adult age, and a marked increase as one goes to the G1 column, whose children are mostly in middle age (Shryock et al., 1976). Instead, in Row 9 of Table 4.1, the children of G3s average about 55% female, the children of the G2s average about 50% female, and the children of the G1s average over 56% female.

Additional information on the gender composition of families in the sample is provided by a three-generation typology constructed using the 522 three-generation lineages in the lineage file (described below; see also Chapter 3). Lineage types ranged from all males to all females for the three generations. As shown in Table 4.2, there are more all-female (16.5%) than all-male lineages (6.5%). Combining all the types that have female G2s (Rows 3, 4, 7, 8; 65.5%) and all the types that have male G2s

TABLE 4.2   Percentage of Distribution Lineage Gender Typology

Row	Percentage	G1	G2	G3
1	6.5	Male	Male	Male
2	10.7	Male	Male	Female
3	18.0	Male	Female	Male
4	15.1	Male	Female	Female
5	7.3	Female	Male	Male
6	10.0	Female	Male	Female
7	15.9	Female	Female	Male
8	16.5	Female	Female	Female

(Rows 1, 2, 5, 6; 34.5%), we find that there are almost twice as many lineages that have female G2s. This appears to support the finding shown in Row 9 of Table 4.1 that there are more female children of G1s than males in this sample, although we note that self-selection factors in returning the mail questionnaire may influence these findings. By combining all the types that have two females (Rows 4, 6, 7; 41.0%) and all the types that have two males (Rows 2, 3, 5; 36%), we find that there are also slightly more lineages that have two females than have two males.

The age dispersion of the intergenerational kinship system is shown in Table 4.3. The mean age range of G2 children is slightly larger than that of G1 children. This is consistent with the larger mean number of children reported by the G2s. The standard deviation of this indicator is larger, however, for G1s than G2s. Obviously, G1 respondents were more variable in the timing of their children, while the G2 had more children within approximately the same number of years. This difference is clearly shown by the larger mean age variance of children for the G1s as opposed to the G2s.

Lineage Analysis of Proximity

Measures of the residential proximity aspect of structure are available for all three role relationships from six perspectives: (1) G1 reporting on G2, (2) G2 reporting on G1, (3) G1 reporting on G3, (4) G3 reporting on G1, (5) G2 reporting on G3, and (6) G3 reporting on G2. Unlike most of the other information on family structure, the geographic proximity data are gathered for *responding children and grandchildren*

TABLE 4.3   Descriptive Statistics Age Dispersion of Children

	G1	*G2*	*G3*
Age range of children:			
mean	7.215	7.548	0.504
standard deviation	6.589	4.791	0.972
Age variance of children:			
mean	39.225	24.345	1.452
standard deviation	73.885	27.012	2.827
Number of cases	516	701	125[a]

a. For G3s, this estimate is based upon the 15.1% of the full sample that have any living children.

and do not include information about *all children*. The lineage file used in these analyses is the overlapping triads file (n = 522) discussed in Chapter 3.

The two measures of the residential proximity aspect of structure are shown in Table 4.4. The first measure, actual distance in miles, is shown in Rows 1 and 2. Because the geographic distance between the generations is reported by each pair, there are two indicators of each distance. Row 1 of Table 4.4 demonstrates that the overall averages, as reported by each generation, are quite similar. These measures of distance show that on the average G2s and G3s live within 200 miles of one another. The average distance of the G1 and G2 is over 500 miles. The distance between G1s and G3s is the largest, with grandchildren living on average about three times as far from their grandparents as they do from their parents.

Correlations between individual reports in each pair (Row 3) reflect the similarity of estimates between the generations. Correlations range from a low of 0.80 (G1-G3) to a high of 0.90 (G1-G2). The relatively low G1-G3 correlation is not surprising because generations are not adjacent. The G1-G2 correlation is quite high, as expected due to the low mobility of the older generations. The G2-G3 correlation of 0.81 seems low, because about half of the G3s were reported to be living with their parents.

An analysis of the original questionnaires of the G2-G3 pairs with substantially different distance estimates reveals a consistent pattern. G3 respondents who reported that they were attending college and living some distance from home were often likely to be reported by their

TABLE 4.4 Residential Proximity: Distance Between Generations Within Lineages

Generations	G1 Reporting About G2	G2 Reporting About G1	G1 Reporting About G3	G3 Reporting About G1	G2 Reporting About G3	G3 Reporting About G2
Distance in miles:[a]						
(1) mean	527	559	643	637	193	202
(2) standard deviation	868	911	1021	1013	600	612
(3) correlation between generation estimates						
(4)	$r = 0.8997$		$r = 0.8041$		$r = 0.8148$	
(5)	$p < 0.001$ $n = 485$		$p < 0.001$ $n = 480$		$p < 0.001$ $n = 517$	
Logarithm to the base e of distance in miles:[b]						
(6) mean	4.21	4.25	4.54	4.53	1.82	2.52
(7) standard deviation	2.38	2.41	2.40	2.38	1.93	2.56
(8) correlation between generation estimates						
(9)	$r = 0.9261$		$r = 0.9276$		$r = 0.8944$	
(10)	$p < 0.001$ $n = 485$		$p < 0.001$ $n = 480$		$p < 0.001$ $n = 517$	
Functional distance:						
(11) coresidence	0.8%	1.3%	0.4%	1.3%	55.9%	53.3%
(12) 0-5 miles	11.9%	13.0%	10.0%	12.1%	6.5%	8.0%
(13) 6-50 miles	37.9%	36.2%	35.1%	31.6%	16.3%	14.8%
(14) 51-500 miles	20.7%	21.6%	22.6%	24.5%	12.3%	14.6%
(15) more than 500 miles	24.5%	24.5%	27.8%	25.9%	8.6%	8.8%
(16) missing	4.2%	3.3%	4.2%	4.6%	0.4%	0.6%
(17) association between generation estimates						
(18)	Gamma = 0.9475		Gamma = 0.9565		Gamma = 0.9386	
(19)	$p < 0.001$ $n = 485$		$p < 0.001$ $n = 480$		$p < 0.001$ $n = 517$	

a. Rounded to nearest mile.
b. Rounded to two significant digits; distances < 1 mile recoded to 1 mile for this analysis.

parents as living at home. To the parents, this is likely a function of recent launching of this child, and she or he is still regarded as dependent. While the G3 may well continue to be economically dependent, establishing a separate residence implies independence, and is quickly internalized as an aspect of self-definition.

In order to reduce the effects of outliers and normalize the distributions, the natural logarithm of the actual distance in miles was taken, and correlations were computed between the transformed variables. As shown in Table 4.4 (Row 8), the correlations between the transformed estimates for both G1-G2s and G1-G3s are quite high, about 0.93. The comparable correlation for G2-G3s is slightly lower, about 0.89, probably still reflecting the confusion over home versus college residence for some G3s. Nonetheless, the natural log transform has increased all correlations as compared to the raw estimates.

The second measure of residential proximity—functional distance—was obtained by recoding the original distance measures into the categories shown in Rows 11-16 of Table 4.4. It is rare for a G1 respondent to live with a G2 offspring, but quite likely that residence is shared in the G2-G3 relationship. The associations (γ) between the recoded functional distance estimates all exceed 0.90, indicating the reliability of using either party as a source of information about proximity.

LISREL Analysis of Proximity

The Pearson correlations between the different indicators of proximity (Table 4.4) indicate a substantial degree of relationship. In order to assess the measurement structure of this small set of items, we use the LISREL VI measurement model.[2] A correlation matrix of the six proximity indicators, computed on the 482 cases with complete information from the overlapping triads file, is used for this analysis. The lack of independence of observations in the lineage file requires examination of potential correlated errors of measurement.

Table 4.5 presents the summary statistics for the four different LISREL models that were estimated. Each model specifies three underlying dimensions (ξ) based on the geographic proximity of that role relationship. Two variables define each ξ, with the response of the oldest generation in any of the pairs fixed at 1.0 to set a common underlying scale. All of the elements of the Φ matrix are estimated in each model.

TABLE 4.5   Summary of LISREL Measurement Models:
Geographic Proximity

Model	x^2	d.f.	Ratio x^2 to d.f.	Goodness of Fit
3 ξ Parallel measures	8.65	12	0.72	0.994
3 ξ $\lambda_{21} = \lambda_{42} = \lambda_{63}$	7.02	8	0.88	0.995
3 ξ Tau equivalence	8.14	9	0.90	0.994
3 ξ Congeneric measures	6.60	6	1.10	0.995

The first model is the model of parallel measures. This model assumes that the variables that define each dimension operate similarly in defining the measurement structure as seen in the λ coefficients and the error variances (Θ_δ). Hence, all coefficients in the Λ_x matrix equal 1.0, and $\theta_{\delta_{11}} = \theta_{\delta_{22}}$, $\theta_{\delta_{33}} = \theta_{\delta_{44}}$, and $\theta_{\delta_{55}} = \theta_{\delta_{66}}$. Conceptually, this implies that proximity is similarly viewed and defined by each member of the role relationship, and that errors of measurement are equivalent regardless of who provides proximity data.

The parallel measures model fits the data remarkably well considering the constraints placed upon the coefficients ($\chi^2 = 8.65$, d.f. = 12, p = 0.733). The goodness of fit is excellent, and the ratio of χ^2 to degrees of freedom is considerably less than 1.0, indicating a model that fits the data well. All estimated coefficients in the model are significant at $p < 0.05$ with the exception of ϕ_{31}, the covariance of G1-G2 Proximity with G2-G3 Proximity. Examination of residuals and modification indices indicates that there are no correlated errors of measurement.

The second model assumes that the younger generation in any role relationship has a similar perspective on the distance in that relationship, and that the shared status of being the younger member is central to the structure of measurement. In this model, the six elements in Θ_δ are freely estimated. In Λ_x, the constraint of $\lambda_{21} = \lambda_{42} = \lambda_{63}$ is added to the specification of $\lambda_{11} = \lambda_{32} = \lambda_{53} = 1.0$ as a constraining factor. While this model fits the data better than the parallel measures model ($\chi^2 = 7.02$, d.f. = 8), it uses four more degrees of freedom to improve χ^2 by only 1.63 ($p \simeq 0.83$), indicating a trivial improvement.

The model of tau equivalence is similar to the parallel measures model, except that it relaxes the constraints on the Θ_δ matrix and freely estimates all six parameters. Coefficients in Λ_x are fixed at 1.0. Conceptually, this model implies that the dimension of geographic proximity is similarly viewed by each member of the role relationship, but that the error variances of the measurement model are unique. This model provides an excellent fit to the data ($\chi^2 = 8.14$, d.f. $= 9$), but is only a marginal improvement over the more restrictive parallel measures model.

The congeneric measures model is the final model that is tested. It relaxes the constraints on the Θ_δ matrix and estimates the three nonfixed elements in Λ_x. This model also provides an excellent fit to the data, with the smallest χ^2 of any of the models. It also uses six more degrees of freedom than the restrictive parallel measures model, however, and, as a result, the ratio of χ^2 to degrees of freedom exceeds 1.0 with only a marginal improvement in the goodness of fit. This model does not significantly improve upon the parallel measures model ($p \simeq 0.91$).

Given this pattern of findings, we select the parsimonious parallel measures model as the model of choice. Table 4.6 presents the LISREL estimates for this model. Because all parameters in the Λ_x matrix are constrained to 1.0, the pertinent parts of Table 4.6 are the squared multiple correlations and error variances for the six items, and the Φ matrix. The model does an excellent job of explaining the stated distances in the G1-G2 relationship. This is probably a function of the low migration probabilities of both groups. The high migration potential of the G3 respondents, coupled with nonadjacent generational status, are the likely causes of the poor explanation in the G1-G3 relationship. Less than one-third of the variance in the two measures is explained by the underlying dimension. Explanation in the G2-G3 relationship is moderately strong, with the error factors probably tied to different definitions of the timing of launching.

The coefficients in the Φ matrix represent the variances, covariances, and correlations among the three underlying dimensions. The G1-G2 Proximity dimension (ξ_1) is strongly related to G1-G3 Proximity (ξ_2) but not at all to G2-G3 Proximity (ξ_3). The relationship between G2-G3 Proximity and G1-G3 Proximity is modest ($r = 0.381$, $\phi_{32} = 0.389$). It would appear that a simple causal model among the three underlying dimensions might be appropriate, with G1-G3 Proximity a function of G1-G2 Proximity and G2-G3 Proximity.[3]

TABLE 4.6   LISREL Estimates: Geographic Proximity

	Λ_x			Squared Multiple Correlations	Error Variance
	ξ_1	ξ_2	ξ_3		
G1 proximity G2	1.000	0.0	0.0	0.900	0.100
G2 proximity G1	1.000	0.0	0.0	0.900	0.100
G1 proximity G3	0.0	1.000	0.0	0.307	0.693
G3 proximity G1	0.0	1.000	0.0	0.307	0.693
G2 proximity G3	0.0	0.0	1.000	0.642	0.358
G3 proximity G2	0.0	0.0	1.000	0.642	0.358

	Φ^a		
	ξ_1	ξ_2	ξ_3
ξ_1	0.900	0.742	0.019[b]
ξ_2	0.389	0.306	0.381
ξ_3	0.015[b]	0.169	0.642

a. Variances are on the diagonal of the Φ matrix; covariances are below and correlations above the diagonal.
b. Estimated coefficient that is not significant at $p < 0.05$.

Future Measurement of Structural Characteristics

Researchers interested in including measures of intergenerational family structure can be encouraged by the findings that we have presented here. The applicability of the parallel measures model to the analysis of proximity clearly suggests that only one member of a role relationship need provide data on this facet of structure. Gathering data from only one member will yield valid estimates of the geographic distance between adjacent generations, and the inevitable errors will be equivalent regardless of who provides the data. If a three-generation design is the focus of the proposed research, we suggest that the G2 be the person to supply these data because they are adjacent to both the G1 and the G3. Prompts should be included when assessing G2-G3 distance, however, to ensure that recently launched offspring are not classified as living at home.

Assessing distance in the G1-G3 relationship is more problematic, because large error variances that will attenuate correlations are present. We hypothesize that, with increasing maturation of the G3, these problems will diminish, although competing explanations are available. Whether the problems in assessing the G1-G3 Proximity dimension obtain from the youth of the G3 or the fact that this relationship is characterized by greater age distance cannot be determined from these data. We recommend that data be gathered from both grandparents and grandchildren to allow examination of the maturation *versus* age distance hypothesis. Moreover, this will provide some consistency checks and permit use of other data if large discrepancies occur. For example, detailed maps often provide distances between locations on the map. Researchers could use these maps in conjunction with addresses on sample lists to resolve large inconsistencies. Of course, if proximity is the primary concern of the research, it may be desirable to use this technique in all circumstances.

Measurement of the other objective characteristics of structure (e.g., marital status, number of children) appear far less problematic, although our analyses did not directly address the convergence of different reports of these characteristics. We anticipate few problems in these measures because most parents certainly know the number, gender, and ages of their offspring. Two issues require some attention. First, researchers must be careful to make the distinction between *ever-born children* and *living children,* and to phrase questions so as to gather the requisite data. Second, the distinction between *biological* and *adopted* children must be made explicit.

Somewhat greater difficulty might be present with regard to the number and gender of grandchildren. Here, issues of recall (Sudman and Bradburn, 1974) are important to consider. Rather than simply asking the number of grandchildren, two strategies are possible. The more complex strategy involves use of a network methodology strategy where the number of grandchildren is derived from a complete enumeration of all of the children of the G2. This would, of course, require contact with everyone in the second generation, a fact that may preclude use in most research. An alternative strategy involves serial prompting of the G1 as to the number, age, and gender of each of their children's children. The following example assumes that the child of the G1 is female, and that her child is also female.

(1) Thinking now of your daughter ＿＿＿＿＿＿＿, did she ever have any children?

(1a) [If yes] What is the name of her oldest child?

(1b) [If not obvious] Is that a boy or a girl?
 (2)   When was she born?
 (3)   Was she adopted?
 (4)   Is she still living?
(4a)   [If deceased] When did she die?
 (5)   [If still living] In what city and state does she live?
 (6)   [If still living] Has she ever married?
(6a)   [If ever married] Is she still married to this person, or is she separated, widowed, or divorced?
(6b)   [If widowed/divorced] Has she remarried?
(6c)   [If *never married* or *separated* (6a)] Is she living with someone now as if they were married?

These questions would be repeated to the grandparent for *each* of their children, using the multiple prompts and the specificity of the questions to aid in recall. Use of a grid format for coding responses to these items is recommended, and appropriate skip patterns must, of course, be inserted into the interview schedule to facilitate the data-gathering process. An estimate of reliability could then be obtained by comparing the G1 data for a single child with that child's data on his or her children. We anticipate that this technique would yield excellent data on the number and gender composition of grandchildren, with age data being subject to greater error.

Conclusion

In summary, these data provide information on the structural aspects of this three-generational sample. They show that this heavily Caucasian sample reflects the characteristics of middle America. In other words, although it underrepresents blacks and both the extremely affluent and the extremely poor, it is an extensive sample of the intergenerational experiences of a large segment of the American population. Further, the substantial agreement between different raters of the same variables, where obtained, suggests that the items measuring family structure are reasonably reliable.

Many issues for the future measurement of family structure center on problems of conceptualization, design, and sampling procedures. For example, the finding in Table 4.1, Row 11, that some G2 respondents have grandchildren is one of the problems of generation overlap inherent in intergenerational family studies, and part of the problem in defining three-generation samples.

Clearly, the role relationship of grandparent to grandchild is present for G2s who have grandchildren, suggesting that if the meaning of "generation" is closest to "role relationship," some respondents classified as G2s in our sample might better be classified as G1s instead. On the other hand, there is also an age overlap between some of our G1s and G2s, suggesting that if our meaning of "generation" is closest to "cohort," then some of G1s and G2s might be classified differently, thus changing the sample and potentially the findings. Finally, if generation effects are the interaction of cohort and role relationship effects, this would further complicate the research design and perhaps the findings. Further conceptual clarification of the meaning of generation is needed in future research designs.

A second example centers on the implication of distance for the definition of family. The traditional nominal definition of a nuclear family, consisting of parents and children related by blood, marriage, or adoption and living under the same roof, is inapplicable in a study of the extended family in the United States. In a three-generation study, most adults will not share the same residence. In this study, however, there were two different structural types of G2-G3 relationships. For about half of these families, the G3s were still living at home (Table 4.4, Row 11). For the remaining G2-G3 families, the G3s had achieved, at least in part, the adult status concomitant with maintaining a separate residence. Thus an extension of the components of family structure might be the introduction of a new ratio variable of the number of years since establishing separate residence.

An alternative way of analyzing these data might be to divide G2-G3 families into two categories, (1) those living at home and (2) those not living at home, and apply the LISREL multiple groups model to assess if the relationships between other concepts (e.g., association and affect) is similar in the two groups. This classification would be appropriate to the hypothesis that family structure statistically interacts with the other components of intergenerational cohesion.

Given clear conceptualization, research designs, and indicators appropriate to one's theoretical model, survey research is plagued with sampling problems. In three-generation studies, sampling only a portion of the three-generation family network limits information on family structure as well as the dynamics of intergenerational relationships. In this study, the use of mail-back questionnaires also produced self-selection into the study; those with the time and inclination returned the questionnaire. This is a significant problem of sampling bias.

In summary, the operationalization of the family structure concepts used in this study is not particularly problematic, although our data could not address most issues of reliability and validity.[4] In a previous section of this chapter we detail a set of indicators that will optimize the reliability and validity of measures of family structure. Similar indicators can probably be used in other studies successfully if careful attention is given, on an a priori basis, to conceptualizing the goals of the research and the resultant implications for design and sampling. We strongly recommend, however, that researchers extend the conceptualization of a three-generation sample. Families are truly small networks, and the logic and methodology of network analysis will provide far better data on the full set of structural alternatives available *within* the family. Extension of the network methodology to include significant others *outside* the family is also required to address the full set of structural alternatives.[5] Without knowledge of the full set of potential actors and determination of the relative position of intra- and intergenerational family ties within the total family and nonfamily configuration, development of theories regarding the importance of family members will be retarded. We cannot control for the variance of other significant actors if we do not assess it,[6] and existing research—including that reported here—tends to look at some significant actors at the expense of others. While focus in research is undoubtedly necessary, the myopic application of blinders to thought processes stifles the development of comprehensive theoretical models of *social* and not just family solidarity.

NOTES

1. See Chapter 3 for a discussion of the differences between generation and lineage analysis models.

2. Version 6.3 of LISREL is used in these analyses.

3. In the LISREL model, such a causal model would entail specifying 2 ξ (G1-G2 Proximity and G2-G3 Proximity) and 1 η (G1-G3 Proximity). The Φ matrix would be a symmetric matrix with free elements, and 2 γ coefficients would be estimated to assess the structural relationships. The final coefficients include six measurement error variances ($\Theta\delta$ and $\Theta\epsilon$) and a single ξ coefficient to capture prediction error. The fit of the model would be identical to the model reported in the body of the chapter, with exactly the same

χ^2 and degrees of freedom. It would differ only in that causal relationships are assumed, likely a safe assumption because we doubt that few parents or grandparents move to get away from the G3. We do not estimate this model because our focus is on measurement, and the full information LISREL model outlined in this note would not have allowed testing for correlated errors between the η and ξ items.

4. Test-retest measures would be required for a strong assessment of reliability, and a different (e.g., network) method of gathering structure data would be required to provide evidence pertaining to validity.

5. For an application of network theory and methods, see Laumann and Pappi (1976). For a review of a number of issues in network analysis, see Burt (1978).

6. Of course, a true experimental design would simply randomize out such variance. Unfortunately, the benefits of experimental methods, even when applicable to sociological studies, are often ignored. Certainly, experimental methods cannot be applied to all or even most sociological issues; many questions of process are, however, best examined in the experimental mode.

5

Measuring Affectual Solidarity

REBECCA L. GRONVOLD

Conceptualization of
Intergenerational Affect

The construct of affect, in particular, affectual solidarity between family members, is a familiar yet a complex issue. In our day-to-day existence, all of us are touched by affect in our interpersonal relationships. Any relationship has a certain degree of affect, whether positive, neutral, or negative. Further, just as relationships are necessarily complex, so are the sentiments individuals attach to relations with others. In order to specify clearly the measurement of affectual solidarity between family members, it is necessary to trace the development of affect as a general construct of sentiment before presenting the nominal and operational definitions used in this chapter.

Feelings such as love, affection, and liking all fall under the heading of sentiment. *Sentiment* is a socially defined pattern of feeling that indicates a particular relationship to a social object and is accompanied by socially appropriate behavior (Theodorson and Theodorson, 1969). McDougall (1908) and Shand (1914) employed this concept in the early part of this century. Sentiment as defined by Pareto (1935) is a nonrational and fundamental motivating emotion. Homans (1950) posited three basic processes that characterize any human group: sentiment, interaction, and similarity. As defined by Homans, sentiment is internal to the individual (i.e., a psychological state) and the emotions found therein influence social behavior. In spite of their importance in a relationship, sentiments such as "love" or "liking" are difficult to operationalize (Goode, 1959; Rubin, 1970, 1973). It is perhaps for this reason that the affectual dimension of parent-child relationships has been neglected by contemporary sociologists and gerontologists.

There has been some effort to develop theory (Turner, 1970; Hochchild, 1975; Kemper, 1978) and measurement (Rubin, 1970, 1973) of emotions. According to Turner, love sentiment is one characteristic that distinguishes the family from other social groups (Turner, 1970, pp. 224-245). The effect of love within the family is to define the acceptable bounds and values of family relationships. The sentiment of love is enduring, pervasive, intimate, trusting, altruistic, compassionate, consensual, responsive, admiring, spontaneous, and valued (Turner, 1970, p. 243). Hence, affection between family members is a complex, multifaceted affair. The theoretical underpinnings of emotion are reflected in the love scale developed by Rubin (1970) that consists of three major components: attachment, caring, and intimacy.

The social psychological study of interpersonal relationships is the logical first step in the development of a construct of affectual solidarity among family members. First, there is a large body of interpersonal attraction literature in the realm of mate selection. The affective or emotional state is addressed in studies of individuals bonding into a family unit by Burchinal (1964), Burgess and Wallin (1953), and Reiss (1960). Conversely, studies of the vulnerability of husband-wife bonds necessarily include the affective domain (Burgess and Cottrell, 1939; Koos, 1946; Hill, 1949). Second, dynamic elements of personality structure exhibit themselves in the form of interpersonal relationships within the family. Emotional interaction between husband and wife is documented by Burgess and Wallin (1953) and Locke (1951). Love is hypothesized as a major component in a companionship marriage that is reinforced by satisfying sexual relations. Emotions are seen as a binding rather than disruptive in nature; however, this is not to deny the existence of disruptive emotions (Locke, 1951). The effect of the parental emotional state on that of the child is the major focus in studies of parent-child interaction (Macfarlane, 1941; Yarrow and Yarrow, 1964; Hoffman and Hoffman, 1964). Adams (1979) summarizes recent research that builds upon and supports the theories of the mate selection literature cited above.

Affectual solidarity is a derivative of the general construct of sentiment. Measurement of affect has largely been limited to romantic love relationships, such as the emotional bonding between husbands and wives, or interactions between parents and young children. This chapter focuses on the measurement of affect in the context of parent-child relations from adolescence through old age.

Affectual solidarity is nominally defined as the nature and extent of *positive sentiment* toward other members in the family. The kinds and amounts of positive sentiment determine the quality of relationships as perceived by each family member.

The affect dimension of family relations is multidimensional in nature (Nye and Rushing, 1969, p. 135; Brown, 1965, pp. 71-91). Nye and Rushing (1969, p. 135) identify affectual integration as "mutual positive sentiment among group members and their self expressions of love, respect, appreciation, and recognition for each other." Brown (1965, pp. 71-91) classifies relationships between two persons into five components of which relational sentiments is one. Affect, or positive sentiment, is identified as one of several dimensions that constitute family solidarity. This chapter examines the intricacies of the affectual domain between family members as one link in the chain to understanding family solidarity.

Married couples are usually the focal point in studies of the affectual dimension of family solidarity. Husband-wife dyadic studies are often expressed in terms such as adjustment (Burgess and Cottrell, 1939; Locke and Wallace, 1959; Spanier, 1976), happiness (Farber, 1957; Orden and Bradburn, 1968; Terman, 1938), and satisfaction (Blood and Wolfe, 1960; Burr, 1970; Gilford and Bengtson, 1979; Miller, 1976). The importance of the affect dimension to studies of husband-wife dyads is reviewed by Lewis and Spanier (1979).

While studies of the quality of husband-wife relations typically employ multi-item scales (Mangen, 1982), studies of affectual solidarity in the parent-child dyad typically use a single item purporting to measure the closeness within the dyad (Cantor, 1976; Jessup, 1981; Leigh, 1982). Adams (1968) assessed the concept of affectual solidarity by seven Likert-type items. Closeness in feelings toward each parent is included in these items. No summary measure for these items was constructed, however, nor were tests of validity or reliability conducted. The Family Mutual Aid and Interaction Index developed by Cantor (1976) includes three items under the heading of affectual solidarity. The closeness item used in this measurement instrument was treated as a single-item indicator.[1] Jessup (1981) was interested in the role of closeness and the general quality of parent-child relations. To measure the quality of parent-child relationships, Jessup utilized the concepts of closeness, decision making, and adolescent dependence on parental advice/guidance. In reliability testing, the closeness item had a weighted Kappa value of .23. The degree of closeness was used as an independent variable affecting kinship interaction by Leigh (1982). In regression analyses of 1964 and 1976 data, the respondent's report of closeness was a consistent predictor of interaction among kin.

Only seven studies that measure the multiple components of affect have been published, and four of these were conducted over 30 years ago. Itkin (1952, 1955) developed scales to measure family-related attitudes, in which he measured attitudes toward mother, attitudes toward father, and parents' judgment regarding a particular child. With his instruments, Itkin was tapping what we call sentiment, as 19 of the 35 items refer to closeness, respect, fairness, affection, getting along, and the like. Jansen (1952) sought to measure family solidarity using eight, five-item scales of interaction, including one for affect. Reliability was indirectly inferred by the correlations between husbands and wives on these family solidarity scores (r = .70) and scores on Marital Adjustment (r = .56). Stryker (1955) saw parent-child relations in terms of four dimensions: affection, intimacy, tension, and sympathy. There are 40 items total, 10 representing each dimension.[2] The intimacy items include closeness and the sympathy items include understanding.

There have also been attempts to develop instruments that take into account the multifaceted nature of affect. In a study of retirees, Streib and Schneider (1971) addressed affectual solidarity but made no attempt to test the adequacy of their affectual items and reported only percentage distributions. Of the nine items included in the affectual solidarity section of their questionnaire, one addressed closeness while another question on "getting along" is included in the family structure section. Cicirelli (1980) measured feelings toward family members using a summated scale of ten items, some of which are similar to those developed by Black and Bengtson (1973) and employed in this research.[3] Previous analyses of the data employed in this study (Bengtson and Black, 1973; Black and Bengtson, 1973) limited consideration of affect between generations to positive regard because in pretests the perception of affection or warmth was found more reliable than conflict items. All of the items referenced in Black and Bengtson, with the exception of quality of communication, can be found in some or all of the above-cited research.

The items employed in previous research on affectual solidarity focus on areas of positive affect as opposed to negative affect. In addition, most assessments of affect are based on the respondents' own perception of the dyadic relationship. Attribution theory (Heider, 1958; Jones and Davies, 1965; Jones and Harris, 1967; Kelly, 1967, 1971; Shaver, 1975) suggests that the attitudes attributed to another in a social relationship significantly influence the nature of that relationship. Thus, for example, if an offspring *believes* that a parent does not trust him or her, then that fact will deleteriously influence the parent-child relationship regardless of the accuracy of the perception (i.e., does, in fact, the parent not trust his or her offspring?). Studies of the attributions of affect in intergenerational relationships are, however, quite rare.

Methods and Measures

In past research, the word most often used to represent affectual solidarity is *closeness*. In the literature cited above, only Jansen (1952) does not include this item. The items of trust and fairness, on the other hand, are less frequently used.[4] Only Bengtson and Black (1973) utilize the item on the quality of communication.

The questionnaire items used in this study include all the components of affectual solidarity mentioned above. The complete set of items was asked of relationships with fathers, mothers, and children. The self-report assessments are based upon the respondents' perceptions of their relationship with each referenced relative. In the parent-child relationships, specific items addressing the degree of understanding, trust, fairness, respect, and affection are asked of each respondent. In order to tap issues of attribution in the relationship, and because relationships are not unidirectional, these five specific items were asked twice; for example, how your father feels about you, and how you feel about your father. These two sets of items reflect both attributions and self-definitions of affectual solidarity. In addition to these ten items, three indicators of the overall quality of the relationship were asked of each respondent. These indicators addressed the quality of communication in the relationship, a general statement about "getting along" with the other, and an overall assessment of the closeness of the relationship.[5] Items on the questionnaire were rated using a six-point scale, with six representing highly positive affect.

The analysis of the affectual solidarity data is conducted at two levels: generational and lineage. The generational analysis is a study between groups that compares individuals in the same role, parent or child, and uses an individual-level data file. The second analysis is at the lineage level, where members of the same family or bloodline are aggregated into an overlapping triad file (see Chapter 3).

Generational Level of Analysis

The means and standard deviations of the affect items for each generation are reported in Tables 5.1 and 5.2. All items are noticeably skewed in the positive direction.

Contrasts between adjacent generational groups are evident in Table 5.1. Looking across the rows, differences in the degree of affect by generation are observed. In every case, the older generation by role relationship reports a greater degree of affect than the younger generation. For example, grandparents (G1) report a greater degree of affect with their adult children (G2) than the adult children report to have with their adolescent-young adult children (G3).

A diagonal comparison of the mean scores can also be made. Again a similar pattern emerges across generations. In every case, the older generation reports a greater degree of affect with the younger generation than the younger generation assigns to the older generation. Gender differences are also apparent in Table 5.1. When comparing the means of the father and mother items, the G2's responses about fathers and mothers are very similar. In contrast, the youngest generation (G3) exhibits higher mean scores for mothers than for fathers on 12 of the 13 comparisons.

Univariate statistics for the grandparent-grandchild dyads are reported in Table 5.2. The positive skewness seen in Table 5.1 is again present, but not to the same degree. The role relationships represent the rows, and the responding generational groups compose the columns. In this table, the diagonal comparison shows the grandparents perceiving a greater degree of affect with the grandchild than vice versa. This is consistent with the pattern established in Table 5.1, where the older generation consistently reported higher mean scores.

Although gender differences are present in Table 5.1, the mean affect scores reported in Table 5.2 for grandmothers and grandfathers do not show this variation. An interesting finding is noted in comparing the G3's reported affect between mothers and fathers (G2) in Table 5.1 and grandmothers and grandfathers (G1) in Table 5.2. Overall, a greater degree of affect is reported by the youngest generation for their parents than for their grandparents.

TABLE 5.1   Means and (standard deviations) of the
Affectual Items by Generation

Item	Generation 1	Generation 2	Generation 3	t-Test
Child:	N = 513	N = 696		
Understands you	4.71 (1.05)	4.31 (1.07)	–	6.43***
Trusts you	5.38 (0.84)	5.11 (0.91)	–	5.26***
Fair to you	5.06 (1.07)	4.52 (1.17)	–	8.43***
Respects you	5.14 (0.94)	4.73 (1.11)	–	6.93***
Affection for you	5.05 (1.03)	4.77 (1.06)	–	4.50***
You understand him or her	4.69 (1.10)	4.33 (1.09)	–	5.62***
You trust him or her	5.35 (0.79)	5.01 (1.08)	–	6.37***
You fair to him or her	5.16 (0.80)	4.77 (0.86)	–	8.01***
You respect him or her	5.34 (0.77)	5.06 (0.98)	–	5.46***
Your affection for him or her	5.39 (0.78)	5.35 (0.90)	–	0.75
Closeness	4.68 (1.16)	4.40 (1.20)	–	4.08**
Communication	4.80 (1.23)	4.53 (1.25)	–	4.57***
Get along with	5.10 (0.88)	4.70 (0.99)	–	7.39***
Father:		N = 507	N = 537	
Understands you	–	4.03 (1.19)	3.72 (1.35)	3.96***
Trusts you	–	5.20 (0.88)	4.67 (1.35)	7.60***
Fair to you	–	4.93 (1.09)	4.58 (1.35)	4.74***
Respects you	–	5.01 (1.01)	4.54 (1.37)	6.33***
Affection for you	–	5.07 (1.11)	4.91 (1.35)	2.14*
You understand him or her	–	4.50 (1.10)	4.02 (1.23)	6.66***
You trust him or her	–	5.32 (0.97)	5.10 (1.20)	3.35**
You fair to him or her	–	4.71 (0.97)	4.29 (1.08)	6.74***
You respect him or her	–	5.12 (1.07)	5.08 (1.23)	0.56
Your affection for him or her	–	5.06 (1.14)	4.90 (1.32)	2.15*
Closeness	–	4.29 (1.38)	4.08 (1.44)	2.41*
Communication	–	5.47 (2.47)	4.34 (2.15)	7.86***
Get along with	–	4.87 (1.01)	4.51 (1.19)	5.28**
Mother:		N = 543	N = 571	
Understands you	–	4.18 (1.18)	4.08 (1.29)	1.31
Trusts you	–	5.19 (0.93)	4.76 (1.25)	6.52***
Fair to you	–	4.89 (1.17)	4.71 (1.23)	2.47*
Respects you	–	5.00 (1.04)	4.72 (1.21)	4.17***
Affection for you	–	5.14 (1.08)	5.25 (1.00)	−1.75
You understand him or her	–	4.62 (1.02)	4.31 (1.17)	4.65***
You trust him or her	–	5.26 (1.05)	5.13 (1.16)	2.04*
You fair to him or her	–	4.73 (0.95)	4.32 (1.08)	6.69***
You respect him or her	–	5.15 (1.06)	5.07 (1.13)	1.15
Your affection for him or her	–	5.04 (1.16)	5.12 (1.09)	−1.22
Closeness	–	4.44 (1.32)	4.51 (1.24)	−0.91
Communication	–	5.29 (2.27)	4.47 (1.68)	6.83***
Get along with	–	4.80 (1.10)	4.60 (1.13)	2.99**

*p < .05; **p < .001; ***p < .0001.

TABLE 5.2   Means and (standard deviations) of Affect Items
             Grandparent-Grandchild Dyad

	Generation 1	Generation 3
Grandchild Item:	N = 503	
Closeness to him or her	3.95 (1.29)	—
Communication with him or her	4.01 (1.24)	—
Get along with him or her	4.95 (0.91)	—
Understands you	4.12 (1.12)	—
You understand him or her	4.22 (1.08)	—
Grandfather Item:		N = 722
Closeness to him	—	3.45 (1.43)
Communication with him	—	3.04 (1.43)
Get along with him	—	4.56 (1.14)
Understands you	—	3.25 (1.29)
You understand him	—	3.62 (1.24)
Grandmother Item:		N = 709
Closeness to her	—	3.58 (1.47)
Communication with her	—	3.11 (1.42)
Get along with her	—	4.53 (1.15)
Understands you	—	3.26 (1.29)
You understand her	—	3.63 (1.22)

To determine the appropriateness of the items measuring affectual solidarity at the generational level, a factor analysis is computed on the ten affectual items within each generation by role (father, mother, child). The results are summarized in Table 5.3.

Examination of the first factor loadings for the G1 respondents about their adult children (G2 respondents) shows strong and positive factor-item coefficients (>.70) for all ten items. The first factor explains over 60% of the total variance of these items, with a scree test indicating that a one-factor solution is sufficient for these data. Thus self-reports and attributions of sentiment both contribute to a unidimensional affect concept. Reliability of this factor is very good.

Three analyses are conducted for G2 respondents. Strong positive factor-item coefficients are found for all three role relationships. Although there are minor differences in the factor loadings by role relationship, there are no differences in the magnitude of the self-reported affect and attributed affect loadings for the middle generation.

TABLE 5.3   Summary of Factor Structure of Affectual Items
            by Generation and Role

	Generation 1	Generation 2			Generation 3	
	Child	Mother	Father	Child	Mother	Father
Understands you	0.710	0.744	0.720	0.700	0.745	0.764
Trusts you	0.758	0.765	0.746	0.743	0.685	0.695
Fair to you	0.804	0.790	0.767	0.822	0.766	0.756
Respects you	0.818	0.813	0.810	0.855	0.773	0.809
Affection for you	0.832	0.833	0.829	0.765	0.694	0.750
You understand him or her	0.733	0.648	0.702	0.713	0.604	0.601
You trust him or her	0.773	0.814	0.804	0.784	0.769	0.746
You are fair to him or her	0.712	0.614	0.688	0.509	0.548	0.538
You respect him or her	0.796	0.816	0.827	0.815	0.775	0.792
Your affection for him or her	0.769	0.847	0.830	0.630	0.712	0.759
Eigenvalue	6.350	6.345	6.385	5.900	5.531	5.717
% Total variance	63.5	63.5	63.8	59.0	55.3	57.2
Coefficient alpha*	0.936	0.934	0.936	0.920	0.910	0.913
Number of cases	513	543	507	696	776	731

*Standardized item alpha.

Furthermore, a single-factor structure is sufficient to explain the data in all three analyses.

Mother and father relationships are represented in the G3 responses found in Table 5.3. Although a somewhat smaller percentage of the total variance is explained, single-factor structures are sufficient. Factor-item coefficients are strong and positive for all ten items and there are no substantial differences in the loadings of the self-report and attributed affect items.

The factor structures for the grandparent and grandchild role relationships (not presented; available on request) exhibit a similar pattern. The five items that address this relationship each show the same pattern of strong positive factor-item coefficients. For all three relationships, loadings exceed 0.70 and a single factor explains over 70% of the variance.

Comparison of the factor structures across the generations indicates very similar dimensions for each role relationship. While the factor structures for the G3 mother and father roles are not as strong as any of the factor structures for the G1 or G2 roles, these differences are minor. The factor structures for the grandparent-grandchild roles, on the other hand, are the strongest of all factors analyzed and reflect one underlying dimension in the limited subset of items.

Overall, these analyses indicate that there is one construct underlying each generational relationship. Explanation of total variance ranges from 55.3% to 63.8% among the father, mother, and child relationships, and from 70.2% to 74.4% for the grandparent and grandchild roles. Summaries of the factor structures indicate well-defined constructs with all the specified items contributing strongly to the construct. The factor analyses support the hypothesis of a single clear construct of affectual solidarity.

Items in each role relationship measure a single, well-defined factor, and the reliability of each set of items ranges from .893 to .936. Coefficients of congruence (Harmon, 1976, p. 343) measuring the similarity of the factor structure across generations and roles are all above .993, indicating the appropriateness of comparisons among the scales. The single-factor structure for each relationship along with the congruence across factor structures suggest construct validity.

Validity Data

Descriptive statistics for the summed affect items used in the generational scales are found in Table 5.4. Again, the skewed nature of the data is apparent. Additional factor analyses (not presented) examining possible contamination of the data due to socially desired responses indicate little contamination of the data. Thus it appears that affectual solidarity in this sample is in fact very strong and is not an artifact of socially desired response sets. Furthermore, these analyses provide some support for the discriminant validity of the scales.

In order to examine the validity of these scales further, two distinct versions of the summary scale and one single-item indicator are analyzed in depth. For each generation and relationship, a "long form" summary scale consisting of the five self-report and five attributed items is developed. This scale score is the simple unit-weighted sum of the ten items, ranging from 10-60. A "short form" scale uses only the five self-report items, and combines these into a unit-weighted summary scale ranging from 5-30.

The "get along with" single-item indicator was selected as the third measure for this validity analysis. Conceptually, the "get along with" item would appear least likely to elicit socially desired responses in that item wording implies, and hence legitimates, some of the everyday frictions common to interpersonal relationships. Legitimation of these

TABLE 5.4   Descriptive Analysis: Generational-Level Scale Scores

Generational Level	Possible Range		Observed Range		$\overline{X}$	sd	N
GI:							
child scale	10	60	16	60	51.267	7.312	513
grandchild scale	5	30	5	30	21.243	4.881	503
G2:							
father scale	10	60	10	60	48.955	8.407	507
mother scale	10	60	12	60	49.193	8.480	543
child scale	10	60	20	60	47.971	7.863	696
G3:							
father scale	10	60	14	60	45.878	9.599	731
mother scale	10	60	11	60	47.284	8.662	776
grandfather scale	5	30	5	30	17.918	5.492	722
grandmother scale	5	30	5	30	18.109	5.527	709

frictions should minimize any halo effects, and thus the item should be a good validity criterion.

The amount of information provided by the validity analysis directly depends upon generational status. This is due to the different number of scales developed for each generation. In the oldest generation (G1), the three correlations among the affect measures all address issues of convergent validity. The correlation of the "long form" with the "short form" scale provides data pertaining to the loss of information when ignoring attributed affect. The correlations of the long and short form scales with the single-item indicator provides evidence as to convergence with an outside criterion. As can be seen in Table 5.5, these correlations are quite strong for the oldest generation. Little information is lost when using the short form of the scale, and correlations with the single-item criterion are strong.

The greatest amount of validity data are available for the middle generation (G2). In this panel of Table 5.5, convergent validity can be examined for the child, mother, and father scales. In each case, little information is lost when ignoring the attribution items. Both the long and the short forms of the scales correlate substantially with the appropriate single-item indicators, indicating substantial convergent validity.

TABLE 5.5 Validity Analysis: Long and Short Affect Scales and Item, by Generation

	Child Global Item	Child Long Scale	Child Short Scale	Mother Global Item	Mother Long Scale	Mother Short Scale	Father Global Scale	Father Long Scale	Father Short Scale
G1:									
child global item	1.00								
child long scale	.77	1.00							
child short scale	.68	.95	1.00						
G2:									
child global item	1.00								
child long scale	.77	1.00							
child short scale	.71	.94	1.00						
mother global item	.14	.13	.16	1.00					
mother long scale	.12	.17	.20	.77	1.00				
mother short scale	.12	.17	.21	.75	.96	1.00			
father global item	.12	.21	.23	.69	.60	.57	1.00		
father long scale	.15	.26	.29	.59	.80	.76	.74	1.00	
father short scale	.13	.24	.29	.56	.76	.77	.71	.96	1.00
G3:									
mother global item				1.00					
mother long scale				.71	1.00				
mother short scale				.64	.95	1.00			
father global item				.66	.55	.48	1.00		
father long scale				.49	.73	.68	.74	1.00	
father short scale				.42	.67	.69	.68	.94	1.00

In addition to convergent validity, however, discriminant validity can be examined with the three role relationships. That is, the correlations of the six mother and father measures with the three child measures should be quite small: entirely different relationships and generations are being examined. The 18 correlations relevant to this analysis average only 0.19, indicating that subjects are distinctly evaluating each relationship.

Further evidence for discriminant validity is provided by examining the nine correlations of the three mother measures with the three father measures. We hypothesize that these correlations should be stronger than the parent-child correlations discussed above in that the referents for the scale share generational position. Nonetheless, these correlations should be less than the correlations *within* any of the role relationships. Examination of the correlation matrix (see Table 5.5) for the G2 indicates that this is generally the case—especially for all correlations including at least one single-item indicator. Some method bias is, however, apparent when examining the correlations involving the long and short form scales. These correlations average 0.77, suggesting that the G2 does not completely differentiate affect for mother from affect for father.

A similar analysis, restricted to the mother and father, is possible for the G3. Convergent validity appears quite good, with little loss of information resulting from use of the short form of the scale. Discriminant validity is also good, with correlations ranging from 0.42 to 0.73. In fact, the G3 more accurately differentiates mother and father affect than does the G2.

Summary of Measurement at the Generational Level

Several conclusions can be drawn from the generational analysis of affectual measurement. First, there is a strong one-dimensional structure of the ten-item scale. Second, the attributed items are often less important to the measure than the self-report items. The self-report items may be used as a short scale with little loss of information. Both the long and short scale versions have high alpha reliability. Third, construct and convergent validity appear acceptable, with reasonable discriminant validity. Some work is needed further to differentiate the parental measures from one another.

Lineage-Level Analysis

The lineage analysis of the affectual dimension utilizes a sample of overlapping triads with the G2 bloodline taken as the reference point. For each family in the total sample, there is a possibility of having no such triads (if no G2 bloodline representative responded) or as many as four triads in the lineage. There are 522 overlapping triads in this sample. (See Chapter 3 for a complete discussion of the overlapping triads file.)

In the generational analysis, the concern is with measuring the quality of some family relations separately for each group of role incumbents. In the lineage analysis, the focus is with measuring the quality of relations *between* generation role incumbents in each family.

Several indicators of the affect in each role relationship are included to allow examination of each generation's perspective on the relationship. In the G1-G2 relationship, six indicators—three from each generation—are included. The three items are (1) the "long form" of the affect scale developed in the generation-level analysis discussed previously, (2) the "get along with" single-item indicator, and (3) the single-item indicator on the closeness in the relationship. The measures assessing affect in the G2-G3 relationship are the same as those used in the G1-G2 relationship. Only two measures are used for G1-G3 relationship. The five-item scales developed for the G1 and the G3 in the generation-level analysis are included in the lineage analysis.

The means and standard deviations of the lineage measures are quite similar to those reported for the generational-scale scores (see Tables 5-1, 5-2, and 5-4), and reflect the same positive skew. Comparisons of the lineage-level means with the generational level-means reveals two exceptions. The G1 about G2 mean (52.483) is greater than the G1 child scale (51.267). In turn, the G2 about G1 mean (49.813) is greater than the G2 mother scale (49.193) and the G2 father scale (48.955). In both these cases, the standard deviation is smaller at the lineage level. This suggests that subjects in the lineage file have greater affect than the sample as a whole, although this effect is quite small.

At the lineage level, correlations between the affect scales provide evidence of the shared nature of affect. Because affect is shared between family members, strong correlations between the *same* role relationships within a family are expected. Correlations of the measures at the lineage level are presented in Table 5.6. To facilitate discussion of the correlations, Table 5.6 has been divided into two major triangles, each of which is divided into two minor triangles. Each major triangle

TABLE 5.6 Correlations of Measurement Model Indicators: Lineage Level

	G12 SCALE	G12 CLOSE	G12 GET	G21 SCALE	G21 CLOSE	G21 GET	G23 SCALE	G23 CLOSE	G23 GET	G32 SCALE	G32 CLOSE	G32 GET	G13 SCALE	G31 SCALE
G12 SCALE	1.000	0.406	0.807	0.784	0.317	0.278	0.098	0.072	0.453	0.041	0.034	0.044	0.549	0.105
G12 CLOSE		1.000	0.383	0.355	0.821	0.762	0.210	0.016	0.157	0.112	0.035	0.020	0.240	0.227
G12 GET			1.000	0.711	0.290	0.256	0.104	0.073	0.066	0.041	0.059	0.078	0.522	0.103
G21 SCALE				1.000	0.286	0.261	0.066	0.029	0.022	0.034	-0.025	0.006	0.489	0.055
G21 CLOSE					1.000	0.712	0.137	-0.003	0.127	0.073	0.035	-0.002	0.202	0.211
G21 GET						1.000	0.130	-0.015	0.090	0.113	-0.004	-0.021	0.162	0.188
G23 SCALE							1.000	0.421	0.793	0.701	0.345	0.333	0.192	0.105
G23 CLOSE								1.000	0.390	0.311	0.749	0.681	0.202	0.318
G23 GET									1.000	0.642	0.368	0.342	0.152	0.164
G32 SCALE										1.000	0.262	0.335	0.097	0.035
G32 CLOSE											1.000	0.626	0.147	0.361
G32 GET												1.000	0.094	0.234
G13 SCALE													1.000	0.374
G31 SCALE														1.000

NOTE: The scales contain ten items, except for the G13 Scale and G31 Scale, which have five items each. CLOSE is the single-item indicator on general closeness in the relationship. GET is the single-item indicator on getting along with the other in the relationship.

captures a within-phenomena block of correlations, thus providing data as to convergent validity. Each minor triangle adds a within-respondent emphasis to the convergent validity analysis. The portion of each major triangle *not* included in the minor triangles constitutes a within-phenomena, between-respondent block of correlations.

For the G1-G2 relationship, the correlations among all six indicators of affect are strong ($\bar{r} = 0.495$). The average correlation is greater for the G1 ($\bar{r} = 0.532$) than the G2 ($\bar{r} = 0.420$). Between-respondent correlations are also substantial ($\bar{r} = 0.508$), with the two ten-item scales very strongly correlated. Each of the four single-item indicators is involved in at least one correlation greater than 0.70 within the major G1-G2 triangle, suggesting that these six items are indeed measuring affect in the G1-G2 relationship.

A similar pattern characterizes the G2-G3 relationship. The correlations among the six indicators of affect are strong ($\bar{r} = 0.487$). The average correlation is greater for the G2 ($\bar{r} = 0.535$) than the G3 ($\bar{r} = 0.408$), and between-respondent correlations are strong ($\bar{r} = 0.497$). The two scale scores are strongly related ($\bar{r} = 0.701$). Here each of the four single-item indicators is involved in at least two correlations greater than 0.625 within the major G2-G3 triangle.

Examination of the between-phenomena correlations clearly reveals that affect in the G1-G2 relationship is uniquely evaluated from affect in the G2-G3 relationship. Of the 36 correlations that address this issue, only two are greater than 0.20, and most are less than 0.10. Clearly, these are distinct aspects of affect.

Only a moderate correlation exists between the two measures of affect in the grandparent-grandchild relationship. The data in Table 5.6 suggest, however, that the relationship between grandparents and grandchildren is mediated by the middle generation, especially as it is viewed by the older generation. This conclusion stems from the relatively high correlations between the G13 Scale and all six indicators of affect in the G1-G2 relationship ($\bar{r} = 0.361$) and the modest correlations between the G31 Scale and the six affect measures in the G2-G3 relationship ($\bar{r} = 0.203$). If the grandparent-grandchild relationship is distinct from other intergenerational relationships, then these correlations would be less strong, as evidenced above in the correlations of the G1-G2 measures with the G2-G3 measures.

In summary, the correlational analysis suggests that convergent validity is present in the lineage data as well. Between relationship correlations are in general trivial, with the exception noted above regarding the grandparent and grandchild relationship, suggesting discriminant validity. What is less clear, however, is the dimensional structure of the 14 affect measures included at the lineage level of analysis. The presence of strong correlations within phenomena suggests that lineage measures utilizing the responses of both generations in the relationship may be appropriate, while theory suggests that affect is an individually held cognitive phenomena, and thus generation-specific measures are hypothesized. The LISREL model is used to test these alternative theoretical structures to the data.

LISREL Analysis

In order to test the hypothesized dimensional structure, the LISREL model is used to examine different structures for the data. A covariance matrix utilizing the same items as presented in Table 5.6 is used in the LISREL analysis. LISREL is of special interest at the lineage level of analysis because we anticipate correlated measurement error between the responses of different generations in the same family.

Initially, a model including all 14 measures was examined. Including the G1-G3 measures, however, causes problems in model estimation. Consequently, this analysis uses data from the G1-G2 and G2-G3 relationship and ignores the grandparent-grandchild (G1-G3) relationship.

Because all of the scales in this analysis use the same items and have the same theoretical range, it is relevant to ask if the measurement and error structures are equivalent. To test these alternative assumptions, baseline models derived from classic measurement models are examined.

The first baseline model, a two-dimensional modified parallel measures model, is the most restrictive of the models tested and uses the fewest degrees of freedom. The two dimensions are (1) G1-G2 Affect and (2) G2-G3 Affect. All six measures within each role relationship define each dimension. The lambda coefficients and error variances for the two scale scores are equated, as are the four coefficients for the single-item indicators. As shown in Table 5.7, the value of chi-square for this model is very large.

The second model in Table 5.7 is a modified tau equivalence model, also having two latent dimensions. This model is a relaxation of the parallel measures model, with error variances freely estimated. Again there is a poor fit to the data, with a large chi-square to degrees of freedom ratio.

TABLE 5.7   Summary of LISREL Measurement Models:
Affect Dimension

Model	Model Definition	x^2	d.f.	Probability
B_1	Parallel Measures 2 Ksi	1837.38	65	0.000
B_2	Tau Equivalence 2 Ksi	1640.52	59	0.000
B_3	Congeneric Measures 2 Ksi	1594.64	53	0.000
B_4	Congruence Model 4 Ksi	100.87	54	0.000
B_5	Congeneric Measures 4 Ksi	87.17	48	0.001
M_1	One Correlated Error 4 Ksi	72.05	47	0.011
M_2	Two Correlated Errors 4 Ksi	60.46	46	0.075
M_3	Two Correlated Errors One Cross Loading 4 Ksi	48.99	45	0.353
M_4	Three Correlated Errors One Cross Loading 4 Ksi	39.61	44	0.660
M_5	Four Correlated Errors One Cross Loading 4 Ksi	34.08	43	0.833

The third baseline model is a congeneric measures model with two dimensions. All of the restrictions of the parallel measures model are removed, and all coefficients freely estimated. As in the models above, all G12 and G21 variables are assigned to one dimension and all G23 and G32 variables are assigned to a second dimension. This model is a slight improvement on the first two, but remains a poor fit.

The fourth alternative model is the cross-generation congruence model with four underlying dimensions. In this analysis, specificity is imposed on the data. Thus, for example, the affect in the G1-G2 relationship is measured by two dimensions: (1) G1's Affect for G2 and (2) G2's Affect for G1. Three items define each dimension. Congruence is imposed upon the dimensions by equating elements in the lambda matrix. For example, the lambda coefficient for the G12 Scale on the first dimension is equated to the lambda coefficient for the G21 Scale on the second dimension, and so on. This model provides a far better fit to the data than any of the two-dimension models, suggesting that affect is an individual-level phenomena anchored within the intergenerational family context.

The final baseline model tested is a four-dimension congeneric measures model with no restrictions on estimated parameters. It has the fewest constraints of the baseline models. This model provides a relatively good fit to the data, as the ratio of chi-square to degrees of freedom is approximately 2 to 1. Relaxing the specification of perfect cross-generation congruence uses six more degrees of freedom as compared to model B4, but the fit is significantly better.

Correlated errors were added one at a time to the four-dimension congeneric measures model using the modification indices as a guide. The first correlated error term added to the model (M_1) was the correlation of the G32 Get Along error with the G23 Get Along error. This correlated error term is theoretically relevant in that it taps a within-measure, between-respondent source of residual covariation, and it significantly reduces the overall chi-square for the model $(p < 0.001)$.

The second error term added to the model (M_2) addresses residual covariation in the scales as completed by the G2.[6] Error in measurement of G23 Scale is significantly correlated with error in the G21 Scale. This correlated error is understandable in that it addresses a within-respondent source of method bias associated with the scale. Inclusion of this error term significantly improves the fit of the model $(p < 0.001)$.

By some criteria, M_2 represents a sufficient fit to the data. Chi-square is no longer significant at the $p < 0.05$ level, and the ratio of chi-square to degrees of freedom is only 1.31. Examination of the modification indices, however, revealed several additional parameters that would significantly reduce chi-square if freed. The next parameter freed (M_3) a cross-loading in the lambda matrix, with the G21 Scale loading onto the dimension defined by the G1 measures. Because the G1 data address affect for the G2, this cross-loading is quite understandable. Estimation of this coefficient significantly reduces chi-square $(p < 0.001)$.

Errors in measurement of the G23 Scale are significantly correlated with errors in measurement of the G23 Scale (M_4). This within-measurement, between-respondent correlated error significantly reduces chi-square $(p < 0.001)$ and improves the fit of the model.

The final model (M_5) tested estimates the error covariance of G32 Close with G12 Get Along. This error term is *not* theoretically relevant; it crosses both respondents and measures. Nonetheless, estimation of this error term significantly reduces chi-square ($p < 0.05$).

Each consecutive model presented in Table 5.7 is a significant improvement upon the previous model. Achievement of parsimony, however, is important in selecting the model that best fits the data. Even though M_3 is an excellent fit by most standards, we choose M_4 as the best fitting model for measuring affectual solidarity. By adding the third correlated error to the model, the largest remaining modification index is only 5.33, with a normalized residual of -1.39. Also, all correlated errors are theoretically relevant in M_4. Model M_5 looses parsimony with a nontheoretical error structure and its improvement upon M_4 is minor.

The LISREL estimates of M_4 are presented in Tables 5.8 through 5.10. The squared multiple correlations are analogous to reliability coefficients, and reveal that the model explains variation in all of the measures quite well. Prediction of the scale scores is best, followed by the items on closeness, and finally by the item on getting along. Clearly, the model does an excellent job of explaining the original measures.

Elements in the phi matrix represent correlations and variances/ covariances among the underlying dimensions. The uniqueness of each generation's perspective on the affect in a relationship can be seen in two findings. First, the correlations G1-G2 Affect with G2-G1 Affect ($r = 0.349$) and G2-G3 Affect with G2-G3 Affect ($r = 0.26$) are moderately strong, but not so strong as to suggest that they are two measures of the same phenomenon. Rather, the four dimensions are obviously distinct. Second, the nonsignificant correlations of G1-G2 with G2-G3 Affect, and G2-G1 Affect with G3-G2 Affect, are theoretically expected owing to their occurrence between noncontiguous dyadic relationships. G2-G1 Affect is significantly related to G2-G3 Affect, but note that both of these dimensions use measures drawn from the G2 respondents.

Conclusions

This chapter addresses how best to measure the construct of affectual solidarity at both the generational and the lineage levels. The specific goals are to specify most appropriate long and short scale forms, as well as a best single-item indicator to use when space limitations preclude the use of the entire scale.

TABLE 5.8   LISREL Estimates: Affect Measurement
             Model—Lambda X

	G1-G2 Affect	G2-G1 Affect	G2-G3 Affect	G3-G2 Affect	Error Variance	Squared Multiple Correlations
G1-G2 Scale	6.876	0.0	0.0	0.0	5.758	0.868
G1-G2 Closeness	1.000*	0.0	0.0	0.0	0.320	0.725
G1-G2 Get Along	0.750	0.0	0.0	0.0	0.192	0.705
G2-G1 Scale	0.779	5.956	0.0	0.0	5.586	0.895
G2-G1 Closeness	0.0	1.000*	0.0	0.0	0.379	0.754
G2-G1 Get Along	0.0	0.733	0.0	0.0	0.304	0.678
G2-G3 Scale	0.0	0.0	7.700	0.0	8.022	0.860
G2-G3 Closeness	0.0	0.0	1.000*	0.0	0.294	0.692
G2-G3 Get Along	0.0	0.0	0.841	0.0	0.400	0.551
G3-G2 Scale	0.0	0.0	0.0	7.245	14.003	0.801
G3-G2 Closeness	0.0	0.0	0.0	1.000*	0.483	0.684
G3-G2 Get Along	0.0	0.0	0.0	0.771	0.452	0.572

*Indicates the fixed coefficients, used as referent.

Clearly, the best multiple-item combination to measure affectual solidarity is the original ten-item scale. In applications at both the generation and the lineage levels of analysis, these scales show high internal consistency and validity.

The best short-list combination to measure affectual solidarity is the five self-report items, or how the respondent feels toward another family member. Although the attributed items are reliable and valid, they are by definition projective and hence not as strong a measure as the self-report items.

The three single-item indicators measure affect in a reliable manner as well, and use of these items constitutes an appropriate option if space constraints preclude use of the longer scales, or if researchers prefer a more holistic as opposed to specific assessment of the affect in the relationship. If only one single-item indicator is used, we recommend use of the "closeness" item. This conclusion stems from two facts. First, the "closeness" item has been more frequently used as a single-item measure of affect in prior studies. Second, the squared multiple correlations for the "closeness" indicator are greater than those for the "get along with" measure (see Table 5.8). If, however, some considera-tion of conflict is desired in a measure of affect, the "get along with" measure may incorporate conflict more than the "closeness" item.

Although these measures exhibit high degrees of reliability and

TABLE 5.9   LISREL Estimates: Affect Measurement
Model—Phi Matrix

	G1-G2 Affect	G2-G1 Affect	G2-G3 Affect	G3-G2 Affect
G1-G2 Affect	0.823	0.349	0.071*	0.066*
G2-G1 Affect	0.345	1.192	0.180	0.003*
G2-G3 Affect	0.054*	0.165	0.701	0.426
G3-G2 Affect	0.062*	0.003*	0.368	1.063

NOTE: Variances on the diagonal; covariances below the diagonal; correlations
above the diagonal.
*Not significant at the .05 level.

validity, caution should always be used whenever measurement is
undertaken. First, this analysis is only one substantive test of these
measures, and thus reliability and validity data must be viewed as
tentative. Many replications are required for any instrument to be
regarded as reliable and valid. Second, our validity tests, while good, are
not as powerful as a multimethod-multitrait study. Third, depending on
the *theory* that underpins the hypothesis you are testing, construction of
the concepts of generational or lineage affect might occur in a different
manner. This is especially true at the *lineage* level of analysis.
Researchers might utilize the attributed items in a short scale form and
compare the self-report and attributed scales. Another approach would
be to use both the self-report scale and the attributed scale (each
consisting of five items) in place of the long scale, and no global item,
one or both global items. Theory is clearly the best guide.

Family affect has not undergone rigorous measurement analysis in
the past. This chapter is perhaps the first in-depth look at measurement
of this construct. Because of the important role affect plays in family
cohesion and because of the historical attention to its conceptualization,
attention to adequate measurement is overdue.

One disappointment of this analysis is the inability at the lineage level
to incorporate the grandparent-grandchild dyads into the overall
model. The main reason for this shortcoming is lack of data: the same
questions asked of the parent-child relationships are not asked of the
grandparent-grandchild relationships. One contribution to measurement in this area would be to collect these data so accurate comparisons
could be made and, even more important, so lineage level analysis could
be completed.

TABLE 5.10   LISREL Estimates: Affect Measurement
Model—Error Covariances and Correlations

Error Terms	Covariance	Correlation
G3-G2 Get Along with G2-G3 Get Along	0.074	0.174
G2-G3 Scale with G2-G1 Scale	2.151	0.322
G3-G2 Scale with G2-G3 Scale	2.820	0.266

NOTE: Error covariances listed in the order of entry.

NOTES

1. Cantor's (1976) Family Mutual Aid and Interaction Index can be found in Bengtson and Schrader (1982, pp. 135-136, 156-160).
2. The affect items in the Stryker (1955) instrument can be found in Bengtson and Schrader (1982, pp. 147-148, 183-184).
3. Cicirelli (1980) asked respondents to assess feelings toward family members (parents and closest siblings) using a seven-point scale ranging from "not at all" to "very, very much." The alpha reliability of this scale is .80.
4. The fairness item is used by Itkin (1952, 1955) and Black and Bengtson (1973). The trust item is used by Itkin (1952, 1955), Jansen (1952), and Black and Bengtson (1973).
5. The questionnaire items used for affectional solidarity between parents and children are

(1) How well do you feel your father(mother/child) *understands* you? (Circle the number)
  (1) not well
  (2) not too well
  (3) some
  (4) pretty well
  (5) very well
  (6) extremely well
(2) How well do you feel your father (mother/child) *trusts* you?
(3) How *fair* do you feel your father (mother/child) is toward you?
(4) How much *respect* do you feel from your father (mother/child)?
(5) How much *affection* do you feel your father (mother/child) has for you?
(6) How well do *you* understand *him* (or her)?
(7) How much do you *trust* your father (mother/child)?
(8) How *fair* do you feel you are toward your father (mother/child)?
(9) How much do you *respect* your father (mother/child)?
(10) How much *affection* do you feel toward your father (mother/child)?
(11) Taking everything into consideration, how *close* do you feel is the relationship between you and your father (mother/child)?

(12) How is *communication* between yourself and your father (mother/child)—how well can you exchange ideas or talk about things that really concern you?

(13)   Generally, how well do you and your father (mother/child) *get along* together?

Items used for grandchild/grandparent affect are

(1) Taking everything into consideration, how *close* do you feel is the relationship between you and this grandchild (grandmother/grandfather)?

(2) How is *communication* between yourself and this grandchild (grandmother/grandfather)—how well can you exchange ideas or talk about things that really concern you?

(3) Generally, how well do you and this grandchild (grandmother/grandfather) *get along* together?

(4) How well do you feel your grandchild (grandmother/grandfather) *understands* you?

(5) How well do *you* understand him or her?

6. The largest modification index for M_1 was TD (6, 5), or G21 Get Along with G21 Close. When this element was freed, the maximum likelihood estimates could not be computed. The next largest element was TD (7, 4), the error term discussed in the text. Freeing this element allowed for estimates to be calculated, and the TD (6, 5) element did not recur as a large error term.

6

Measuring Intergenerational Contact in the Family

DAVID J. MANGEN
RICHARD B. MILLER

Measuring the amount of contact between family members of different generations has been a strong substantive focus of researchers interested in the aging family (Bengtson et al., 1985). The role that family members play in the lives of the elderly is a crucial component of the socioemotional and instrumental support systems of the elderly (Lopata, 1979; Shanas, 1978, 1980; Brody, 1978, 1981).

Despite popular concern that industrialization contributes to the abandonment of elderly by their families, research consistently demonstrates that intergenerational contact is a persistent and longstanding feature of American family life (Shanas, 1962, 1978, 1980; Shanas et al., 1968; Lopata, 1979; Brody, 1978, 1981). Approximately 80% of the elderly with children see at least one of their children at least once a week (Shanas, 1978), and family members are the first choice for provision of assistance (Brody, 1978, 1981; Lopata, 1979). Clearly, the intergenerational contact and assistance are a major fact of contemporary American life.

The pervasiveness of intergenerational contact is substantiated by a great deal of empirical research (e.g., Adams, 1968; Cantor, 1976; Hill et al., 1970; Lopata, 1973; National Council on the Aging, 1975; Rosow, 1967; Shanas et al., 1968; for a comprehensive review, see Bengtson et al., 1985). Concern for the theoretical underpinnings of models of intergenerational association is less evident, however, and the reliability and validity of the measures used in this research are not well documented (Bengtson and Schrader, 1982). Studies often use data reported by only one generation, and different forms of association are assumed to be equivalent.

This chapter focuses upon two related issues. First, we examine the dimensionality of intergenerational association and document both the reliability and the validity of two techniques often used in measuring contact between parents and children. Second, we use the three-generation data to compare explicitly the degree of contact reported by each of the different generations, and examine both aggregate (generational) and within-family (lineage) differences in reported association.

Theoretical Definition

We define *associational solidarity* as the degree to which family members share activities with other family members. On a theoretical level, this definition includes both intra- and intergenerational sharing of activities, but we focus on the intergenerational component in this analysis. Because we assume that more contact implies a greater degree of solidarity in the family, this definition derives from the functionalist tradition within sociology. In the conclusion to this chapter, we discuss some of the implications of alternative theoretical perspectives for the measurement of associational solidarity.

While the degree of association between family members appears to be a relatively straightforward concept to measure, it is important to consider the dimensions and facets of the concept when employing a rational approach to measurement (Mangen, Peterson, and Sanders, 1982). The symbolic interactionist framework suggests that the meaning attached to events is an important dimension of social life. Thus we differentiate between formal, ritualistic contact at symbolic family events and informal, regularized contact as the primary dimensions of association. A further differentiation is seen in the mode of contact. Contact between family members is at times face to face, while at other times association is limited to indirect contact. The fourfold differentiation of these dimensions and facets is presented in Table 6.1.

The theoretical model presented in Table 6.1 suggests that a comprehensive measure of associational solidarity based on the functionalist tradition includes four unique scales. Much of the research on

TABLE 6.1   A Theoretical Typology of Intergenerational Association

| Meaning | Mode of Contact | |
	Indirect	Face-to-Face
Symbolic:	Sending cards or letters, or telephoning, on birthdays, to demarcate rites of passage, or in recognition of significant events and dates.	Small or large family gatherings on holidays, rites of passage, to recognize special family occasions, or attending religious services.
Informal:	Maintaining contact among family members to share confidences, discuss decisions, and "update the other."	Face-to-face contact among family members to discuss decisions, share meals, recreate, or confide in the other.

intergenerational family association emphasizes the face-to-face column of the matrix presented in Table 6.1, but does not explicitly differentiate between the formal and informal types of contact (Bengtson and Schrader, 1982). Very little research has to this time examined the indirect mode of contact as a technique of facilitating continued contact when geographic distance is great. This may, in fact, represent one of the strengths of the American family.

Operational Definition

The research strategy for measuring association emphasizes contact between generations at the level of the role relationship. The measures of association employed in this study use three distinct methods. First, the degree of association between adjacent generations (i.e., G1-G2, G2-G3) is assessed by a series of nine indicators that tap specific forms of association such as recreation, getting together for family gatherings, sharing meals, and the like. While the items do not specifically include a time referent, a one-year time frame is implicitly structured into the response options, which range from one (almost never) to eight (almost every day). Second, a general single-item indicator of the degree of association for each relationship is also included in these data. This indicator ranges from one (seldom) through six (extremely often). Finally, association in the G1-G3 relationship includes a ratio-level estimate of the number of times the grandparents and grandchildren have seen each other in the past year.[1]

Consequently, the total set of items that tap the association dimension vary depending upon the generation and the number of surviving parents. The maximum number of indicators for each generation, assuming that the family has not experienced any deaths or other disruptions in the family, is as follows:

(1) Grandparents (G1): (1) Nine scale items assessing the association with the referent child (G2) in the study; (2) one single-item indicator assessing association with the referent G2 and another assessing the relationship with the referent G3 of the study; and (3) one ratio estimate of the number of face-to-face visits with the G3. Each G1 family member is asked a maximum of 12 association items.

(2) Parents (G2): (1) Nine scale items assessing the amount of contact with the mother (G1), father (G1), and referent child (G3) for a total of 27 scale items, and (2) single-item indicators assessing the amount of contact with father (G1), mother (G2), and child (G3). The G2 provided the most information of any generation in this study, responding to fully 30 association items.

(3) Grandchildren (G3): (1) Nine scale items tapping the association with mother and father (G2) for a total of 18 items; (2) single-item indicators of contact with mother (G2), father (G2), grandfather (G1), and grandmother (G1); and (3) ratio estimates of the frequency of visitation in the past year for both grandmother (G1) and grandfather (G1). The G3 provides data on 24 distinct items.

When viewed from the theoretical model of Table 6.1, however, this broad set of data does not permit comprehensive examination of the four distinct cells of the matrix. The nine scale items ignore the joint distribution of the facets and dimensions presented in Table 6.1. Specifically, only two items address the indirect mode of contact. These items inquire about the frequency of letter writing and telephoning, regardless of the meaning of that contact. Three items address association with symbolic overtones, but these emphasize face-to-face contact and ignore the indirect mode. Three items address face-to-face informal contact, and the final item examines informal contact but fails to specify the mode of contact. Thus, while the measures address all four cells in Table 6.1, unique summary scales for each cell are not available.

The analysis of these data is conducted at two levels of analysis. The first is the generational level of analysis that employs an individual-level data file where respondents are differentiated according to the role occupied within the family. The second level of analysis is the lineage level of analysis where respondents are aggregated into direct bloodline lineage triads of grandparent, adult child, and grandchild.[2]

Generational Level of Analysis

At the generational level of analysis, there are two primary research questions. The first pertains to the overall degree or level of association between the generations. Implied within this generic research question are several additional questions comparing the degree of association reported by each generation. The second question addresses issues of measurement, including assessment of reliability, validity, and dimensional structure of the association items. All analyses at the generation level use individual-level data differentiated by ranked-generation position.

Degree of Association

The first analysis examines the degree of contact between parents and children in this three-generation sample. Table 6.2 presents the means and standard deviations, together with an F-test of significance, comparing the responses of the generations to the nine scale items.

Table 6.2 is structured such that the referent relationship defines the rows of the table, while the columns define the responding generation. The F-tests compare mean scores across generations, and test the hypothesis that there are no differences between generations in the frequency of contact with children (or mothers, fathers).

As Table 6.2 illustrates, the generation contrasts are significant for every scale item. In almost every case, the younger generation reports a greater degree of association. In general, G3 reports seeing their G2 parents more than the G2 sees their mother and father (G1). Given the age range of the G3, this is not surprising because many live at home and/or are financially dependent upon their parents.

Some exceptions are, however, apparent. For each set of association items, the amount of indirect contact reported by the younger generation is less than that reported by the older generation. This too may be understood within the context of the G3's average age. Independence usually implies separate residences, and because many of the G3 respondents still live with their parents, it is not necessary to use indirect modes of contact because face-to-face contact is possible. Once separate residences are established, however, indirect modes of contact become a more viable mechanism for maintaining intergenerational family ties.

A different form of comparison can be made from Table 6.2 by examining the mean scores diagonally. For example, if the G1 mean

TABLE 6.2   Means and (standard deviations) of the
Association Scale Items by Generation

Item	Generation 1	Generation 2	Generation 3	F-test
Child:				
Recreation	2.36 (1.29)	3.19 (1.53)	—	92.82*
Brief Visits	4.04 (2.03)	5.98 (2.06)	—	246.50*
Reunions	2.71 (1.14)	3.29 (1.41)	—	55.72*
Gatherings	2.69 (1.11)	3.36 (1.18)	—	91.99*
Talking	3.38 (1.92)	5.06 (2.10)	—	190.64*
Religious	1.78 (1.36)	2.48 (2.05)	—	41.78*
Letters	2.54 (1.85)	1.87 (1.64)	—	40.53*
Telephone	4.66 (1.99)	3.83 (2.52)	—	36.04*
Dinner	3.21 (1.57)	5.88 (2.43)	—	468.48*
Father:				
Recreation	—	2.06 (1.22)	2.85 (1.56)	87.50*
Brief Visits	—	4.05 (2.00)	5.21 (2.26)	83.28*
Reunions	—	2.56 (1.11)	2.69 (1.12)	4.29**
Gatherings	—	2.61 (1.19)	3.01 (1.17)	33.70*
Talking	—	2.85 (1.87)	3.80 (2.18)	62.84*
Religious	—	1.56 (1.17)	2.09 (1.90)	30.56*
Letters	—	2.38 (1.78)	1.78 (1.56)	38.13*
Telephone	—	4.44 (2.05)	3.19 (2.29)	95.70*
Dinner	—	3.18 (1.63)	5.09 (2.61)	210.59*
Mother:				
Recreation	—	2.14 (1.29)	2.94 (1.63)	89.58*
Brief Visits	—	4.14 (2.05)	5.63 (2.25)	150.91*
Reunions	—	2.57 (1.11)	2.77 (1.13)	10.21**
Gatherings	—	2.62 (1.21)	3.06 (1.14)	42.81*
Talking	—	3.33 (2.10)	4.67 (2.26)	118.54*
Religious	—	1.59 (1.13)	2.31 (2.00)	56.77*
Letters	—	2.49 (1.86)	1.99 (1.75)	24.74*
Telephone	—	4.90 (1.95)	4.04 (2.53)	43.86*
Dinner	—	3.17 (1.62)	5.37 (2.55)	309.46*

NOTE: All items scored from 1 (almost never) to 8 (almost every day).
*p < 0.0001; **p < 0.05.

scores on association with child are compared to the G2 responses on
mother and father association, this provides an aggregate estimate of the
comparability of the intergenerational responses to the same stimuli.
Analysis of the data in this way reveals that in 16 of the possible 18
G1-G2 comparisons, the G2 reports slightly less contact than the G1.

While these differences are small, they are nonetheless consistent. The only exceptions to this pattern concerns brief visits. G2 respondents report slightly greater contact with their mothers and fathers than the G1 report.

A similar pattern develops when extending this comparison to the G2-G3 dyad. In 16 of the 18 comparisons, the G3 reports less association with the G2 parents than the G2 parents reports with their child. The exceptions are the G3 reports of letter and telephone contact with their mothers. The differences are small but consistent on this aggregate level.

In summary, three conclusions are evident from these data. First, association between the generations is extensive. For the G1, association with children most frequently involves telephoning and brief visits. Association between the G2 and G3 is more frequent, and emphasizes brief visits, dinner, and talking over important matters. Second, association with the younger generation is more prevalent than association with the older generation, due primarily to the age range of the youngest generation in this sample. Third, in making aggregate comparisons between paired generations, there is considerable consistency between the estimates provided by each generation. One substantive exception involves an obvious role bias with respect to talking over important matters. From the perspective of the G3, discussing important issues is much more likely with mothers than fathers.

Dimensional Analysis

In exploring dimensionality, the first major issue is to determine the number of dimensions found in the nine indicators of association. Table 6.1 suggests four dimensions, although the structure of the nine stimuli are such that these are not likely to emerge. Because the development of dimensions that are maximally congruent across generations is important to this research, we conduct several exploratory and confirmatory analyses.

In order to assess the number of dimensions, a principal factoring with iterations analysis is performed for each generation and role relationship. Examination of the scree test (Cattel, 1966) reveals that only one important factor is present in the nine item analysis, with this factor accounting for between 32% (G3 responding about their fathers) to 50.9% (G2 responding about their mothers) of the total variance of the nine-item scale. In large part, this single factor is due to the mathematics of factor analysis as a variance-maximizing procedure.

There are an insufficient number of stimuli representing each cell of Table 6.1, and the stimuli are not properly differentiated from one another, and hence are correlated. With a small number of correlated items, only one dimension is required to explain the data.

A closer inspection of the magnitude of the first factor loadings revealed that two items in particular are poor measures of the factor. The items tapping indirect modes of contact are poorly explained by the factor analyses. For all of the analyses using the nine items, the letter writing variable loads negatively and often weekly on the first dimension, while the factor-item coefficient for telephoning is at times a weak negative coefficient (G2 responding about their child), at times a weak positive loading (G3 responding about their mother or father), and at times a strong positive loading (e.g., G2 responding about their mothers or fathers). These variations in the magnitude and direction of loadings present analytical and conceptual problems.

In attempting to explain these differences, we suggest that geographic distance statistically interacts with the measurement model. Several factor analyses of subsamples of the study group, differentiating respondents by both generation and geographic distance from the referent family member, reveal that distance and generational position do indeed statistically interact with the measurement structure of the association items, specifically with the two measures of indirect contact.

For the G1 respondents, contact via letters exhibits a weak negative loading in the total sample. When geographic distance is controlled through subsampling, however, the factor-item coefficient is weak and positive in the four of the five analyses. For the group that resides 81-400 miles from the referent child, the coefficient for letter writing increased in strength to 0.46. With regard to the telephoning item, the factor-item coefficient is strong and positive. The coefficient remains strong and positive in three of the five subsamples. For G1 family members who live 26-80 miles from the referent child, and for those who live over 400 miles away, the importance of telephone contact in defining the association dimension diminishes.

For each generation and each role relationship, a unique interaction effect is manifest regarding distance and the contribution of letter writing and telephoning to the associational solidarity dimension. Because the interactions are not consistent across generations or referents, the strategy of attempting to incorporate the interaction into the measurement model (Blalock, 1975) does not appear viable. It is apparent from these analyses, however, that the remaining seven items are not influenced by the distance interaction. In order to achieve maximum similarity across generations, therefore, the two measures of indirect contact are eliminated from the analysis. The dimensional structure of the remaining seven items is assessed with the LISREL multiple-groups model, with each of the six generation and role relationship item sets constituting a separate group for this analysis. Six specific covariance matrices are used as the basic data for this analysis.

We use the LISREL model (Jöreskog and Sörbom, 1979, 1984) in order to test several alternative theoretical models regarding the structure of the association data, and the similarity of that structure across generations and referents.[3] Because all seven items use the same response options, we test parallel measures, tau equivalence, and congeneric measures models for the data.[4] These models constrain or relax different parameters *within* any of the six groups. In addition, we examine the implications of setting different constraints *across* groups, including equating all parameters across the groups, constraining parameters depending upon generational position of the respondent, and constraining parameters according to the role relationship. Finally, three special models are developed based upon the results of the prior analyses. All models test a single dimension (ξ) of the data. Table 6.3 presents the summary results for these different models.

The first major set of models tests a single dimension with complete equality constraints across all six groups. In the parallel measures model, all coefficients in Λ_x are set at 1.0 and only two coefficients are estimated: (1) the variance (ϕ) of the underlying dimension and (2) a single error variance (θ_δ). The remaining error variances are constrained to equal the estimated coefficient, and all coefficients are constrained across groups. This is a very restrictive model that does not fit the data well. The tau equivalence model estimates unique error variances for each item, but equates each error variance across groups. The congeneric measures model estimates unique Λ_x and Θ_δ coefficients, which are also constrained to equality across groups. While each of these models is a significant improvement upon the parallel measures model, none fits the data very well.

The second major set of models constrains estimates within generations. Thus one set of coefficients is estimated for the G1, another for the G2, and yet another for the G3. Here, the coefficients for all three G2 groups are constrained to equality, as are the coefficients for the two G3 groups. These models are a significant improvement compared to the first set, but still do not fit the data adequately.

TABLE 6.3 Summary of LISREL Models: Generation Analysis

Model	χ^2	d.f.
I. Full equality constraints across groups		
A. Parallel measures	6510.77	166
B. Tau equivalence	3693.22	160
C. Congeneric measures	2685.19	154
II. Within-generation constraints		
A. Parallel measures	5823.08	162
B. Tau equivalence	2916.19	144
C. Congeneric measures	1702.24	126
III. Role-based constraints		
A. Parallel measures	6464.32	162
B. Tau equivalence	3583.88	144
C. Congeneric measures	2497.88	126
IV. No. constraints across groups		
A. Parallel measures	5524.11	156
B. Tau equivalence	2353.32	120
C. Congeneric measures	908.57	84
V. Special models (see text)		
A. Equal Λ_x across groups	1174.16	114
B. Constrain male-female measures	921.00	96
C. $\theta_{\delta_{43}}$	288.14	90

The three models that use role-based constraints equate parameters depending upon the role that is being measured. Here, the coefficients for the G1 Child measures are constrained to equal the coefficients for the G2 Child measures, G2 Mother equals G3 Mother, and G2 Father equals G3 Father. Once again, parallel measures, tau equivalence, and congeneric measures models are tested. These models fit the data poorly, are only marginally better than the models using full equality constraints, and are worse than the models employing within-generation constraints.

The fourth set of models removes all equality constraints across groups. In the parallel measures model, this results in estimation of 12 coefficients. For each of the six groups, all Λ_x coefficients are fixed at 1.0, and the variance of the dimension (ϕ) and a single error variance (θ_δ) are estimated. The remaining six error variances are constrained to equal the estimated coefficient. Note that this model does not explain the data well, and in fact constitutes only a slight improvement on the model of full equality constraints. In the tau equivalence model, the constraints on Θ_δ are removed and unique error variances for each item and each group are estimated. This decreases χ^2 significantly, but still does not constitute an acceptable fit to the data. Finally, the congeneric measures model removes the constraints on Λ_x and estimates a model with few constraints. This model fits the data reasonably well in comparison to the more restrictive models.

In reviewing the results of these analyses, it is apparent that the assumption of equal error variances required by the parallel measures models is the most problematic, with the assumption of equal Λ_x coefficients (tau equivalence) being less troublesome. Furthermore, comparing Model II-C to Model IV-C suggests that some constraints may be placed on the data as long as those constraints do not require equality of error variances. Examination of the Λ_x coefficients for Model IV-C suggests that these coefficients are reasonably similar across groups, but that Φ and Θ_δ coefficients are quite different across groups. Furthermore, the Λ_x coefficients for G2 Mother and G2 Father, and G3 Mother and G3 Father, are quite similar to one another.

Model V-A estimates a model with unique Θ_δ coefficients for each item and group, and unique Φ coefficients for each group. While unique Λ_x coefficients are estimated for each *item* (i.e., congeneric measures), these are constrained to equality across groups. This model fits the data better than any model except the freely estimated congeneric measures model.

Model V-B is similar to Model V-A except that it equates the Λ_x coefficients for G2 Mother and G2 Father, and G3 Mother and G3 Father. Theoretically, this model suggests that each generation has a unique perspective on association, but that the G2 does not differentiate its parents from one another, nor does the G3 differentiate its parents from one another. Estimation of this model results in a χ^2 of only 921.00. Because it estimates 12 fewer coefficients, this model is substantively equivalent to Model IV-C. We select this model as the model of choice.

Inspection of the modification indices for Model V-B reveals that one error covariance ($\theta_{\delta_{43}}$) is large and significant in all of the groups. This error covariance taps residual covariation between two items (large and small family gatherings) that are part of the symbolic dimension of intergenerational association. Estimation of these six coefficients (Model V-C) reduces χ^2 significantly, and yields a model with trivial residuals. While further improvement in the model can be obtained by estimating more error covariances, these are unique in each group and, we believe, indicative of sample-specific fluctuations in the measurement model. The detailed results of Model V-C are presented in Table 6.4.

This model fits the data reasonably well, as indicated by the GFI ranging from 0.967 to 0.986. The first panel of Table 6.4 presents the Λ_x coefficients for the six groups. These are metric coefficients, representing the contribution of that item to the underlying scale. For each of the six groups, λ_1 is fixed to 1.0 to establish a common underlying scale. This allows comparison of λ coefficients both within and across groups.

In all six groups, brief visits, talking, and dinner together contribute the most to the definition of associational solidarity. There are differences in both the magnitude and the rank order of the loadings for these three items across groups. For the G1 Child scale, brief visits are most important in defining association. Talking and dinner together are comparatively less important, while attending religious events together is least important. For the G2 Child scale and G3 Parental scales, dinner together, brief visits, and talking are almost equally important, while for the G2 Parental scales, brief visits is most important, followed by dinner and talking over important matters. On the whole, there is a remarkable degree of consistency in the λ coefficients.

Estimates for R^2 are item reliabilities. These range from 0.086 to 0.760. The *least reliable* item, on the whole, deals with joint attendance at religious events. In no case does R^2 for this item exceed 0.20. For the G3, however, attendance at reunions is even less well explained by the model, with R^2 of only 0.116 and 0.115. The total coefficient of determination for each set of items, a measure of reliability, is as follows: G1 Child (0.864), G2 Child (0.869), G2 Mother (0.883), G2 Father (0.861), G3 Mother (0.768), and G3 Father (0.753). Alpha reliability is generally adequate, ranging from 0.758 to 0.866 with these data.

Validity Analysis

The results of the LISREL analysis suggest the presence of one consistent underlying dimension with good reliability. Construct validity is suggested by the consistency of results across groups. Evidence of convergent and discriminant validity is presented in Table 6.5, together with the means and standard deviations for the summary measures of association.

TABLE 6.4 LISREL Estimates: Generation-Level Analysis

	G1 Child	G2 Child	G2 Mother	G2 Father	G3 Mother	G3 Father
	Λ_x	Λ_x	Λ_x	Λ_x	Λ_x	Λ_x
Recreation	1.000	1.000	1.000	1.000	1.000	1.000
Brief Visits	1.921	2.286	2.351	2.351	1.854	1.854
Reunions	0.842	0.820	1.079	1.079	0.439	0.439
Gatherings	0.915	0.861	1.396	1.396	0.656	0.656
Talking	1.574	2.100	1.819	1.819	1.700	1.700
Religion	0.657	0.748	0.551	0.551	0.802	0.802
Dinner	1.325	2.387	1.999	1.999	1.815	1.815
Φ	0.776	0.621	0.493	0.447	0.803	0.722
	Θ_δ	Θ_δ	Θ_δ	Θ_δ	Θ_δ	Θ_δ
Recreation	0.891	1.627	1.011	1.014	1.825	1.591
Brief Visits	1.254	1.023	1.416	1.519	2.313	2.542
Reunions	0.683	1.562	0.625	0.702	1.135	1.113
Gatherings	0.619	0.964	0.496	0.513	0.995	1.030
Talking	1.791	1.718	2.415	2.180	2.549	2.586
Religion	1.499	3.677	1.039	1.128	3.253	2.813
Dinner	0.941	2.174	0.949	0.763	3.829	4.388
$\theta_{\delta_{43}}$ Covariance	0.251	0.647	0.232	0.270	0.526	0.447
Correlation	0.334	0.564	0.342	0.379	0.505	0.427
	R^2	R^2	R^2	R^2	R^2	R^2
Recreation	0.465	0.276	0.338	0.293	0.302	0.316
Brief Visits	0.696	0.760	0.660	0.616	0.544	0.494
Reunions	0.446	0.211	0.467	0.441	0.116	0.115
Family Gatherings	0.512	0.323	0.652	0.640	0.251	0.240
Talking	0.518	0.615	0.439	0.359	0.487	0.433
Religion	0.183	0.086	0.125	0.108	0.128	0.151
Dinner	0.591	0.619	0.734	0.707	0.407	0.353
GFI	0.967	0.972	0.979	0.969	0.973	0.986

Three sets of measures are included in Table 6.5. The global single-item indicators of association constitute one set of measures. Two different techniques of scoring the scale items are used to yield the other two sets. First, the simple unit-weighted sum of the seven scale items is computed, yielding a measure ranging from 7-56 for each generation and role relationship, with high scores indicating extensive contact. Second, because Shanas (1978) and others report family association as the percentage of persons who see the referent other at least weekly, a frequency count of the number of items for which the respondent gave responses indicating weekly is computed, yielding a measure ranging from 0-7. This measure is not directly comparable to the Shanas measure for two reasons:

(1) These data focus on the *referent child* as contrasted to *any child.* This results in an underestimation of the extensivity of intergenerational contact in these data as compared to the national study of Shanas (1978).

(2) The method of scoring employed here fails to account for the distribution of joint events given the multiple indicators. To illustrate, if the respondent noted *monthly contact* to four or more of the items, then inference of *weekly contact* has some justification. This factor will also tend to underestimate the percentage of respondents reporting weekly contact.

Examination of the univariate distributions for the once-a-week variables demonstrates that underestimation vis-à-vis the Shanas (1978) data is indeed present. For the oldest generation (G1), a mean score of only 0.64 is obtained. Examination of the percentage distribution reveals that only 36.7% of the G1 respondents report weekly contact with the referent G2 by this measure. The mean scores for the G2 respondents responding about their G1 mothers (0.65) and fathers (0.56) are, as expected, similar to the G1's report. G2 family members report slightly less weekly contact with fathers (32.7%) and mothers (35.8%) than the corresponding G1 reports. A similar pattern is evidenced for the simple summary scale, with G1 respondents reporting greater contact than the G2, and G2 respondents reporting greater contact with the mother than the father.

A much greater degree of contact is reported in the G2-G3 relationship. In large part, this obtains from the fact that approximately 50% of the respondents in this role relationship share living quarters. Here, the second generation reports greater contact than the younger

TABLE 6.5 Correlations Among the Measures of Association: Generation Level of Analysis

	Child Association Scale	Child Single-Item Indicator	Child Once a Week	Mother Association Scale	Father Association Scale	Mother Single-Item Indicator	Father Single-Item Indicator	Mother Once a Week	Father Once a Week	$\bar{X}$ (s.d.)
Generation 1:										
Child scale	1.0									19.96* (7.79)
Child indicator	0.6885	1.0								2.89* (1.40)
Child once a week	0.7232	0.4260	1.0							0.64* (0.99)
Generation 2:										
Child scale	1.0									29.09 (8.90)
Child indicator	0.5833	1.0								3.44 (1.24)
Child once a week	0.8807	0.4629	1.0							2.08 (1.60)
Mother scale	0.2752	0.1506	0.2186	1.0						19.39 (7.81)
Father scale	0.2197	0.1593	0.1444	0.9175	1.0					18.81 (7.43)

Mother indicator	0.1569	0.1521	0.1136	0.7658	0.7051	1.0					2.81 (1.38)
Father indicator	0.1025	0.1592	0.1346	0.6905	0.7227	0.8511	1.0				2.63 (1.36)
Mother once a week	0.2261	0.1015	0.2259	0.7594	0.6374	0.5250	0.3850	1.0			1.83 (1.46)
Father once a week	0.1923	0.0932	0.1849	0.6411	0.7162	0.4333	0.4188	0.8642	1.0		1.50 (1.38)
Generation 3:											
Mother scale				1.0							26.71** (8.57)
Father scale				0.8647	1.0						24.70** (8.35)
Mother indicator				0.5445	0.4441	1.0					3.31** (1.37)
Father indicator				0.4630	0.5456	0.7177	1.0				2.99** (1.38)
Mother once a week				0.8690	0.7290	0.4425	0.3249	1.0			0.65** (1.03)
Father once a week				0.7693	0.8607	0.3595	0.4240	0.8227	1.0		0.56** (0.95)

*G1-G2 contrast significant at $p < 0.001$.
**G2-G3 contrast significant at $p < 0.001$.

generation, and the G3 respondents report greater contact with their mothers than their fathers.

Examination of the correlation coefficients in Table 6.5 provides evidence of the convergent and discriminant validity of the association measures. For G1 respondents, the correlations among the three indicators of contact with their children are substantial. Not surprisingly, the two methods of scoring the seven-item association scale correlate quite highly (r = 0.7232). The single-item indicator correlates more highly with the simple sum scale than the once-a-week measure, suggesting that the scoring of the once-a-week measure ignores systematic covariation in the data.

As the pivotal generation in this three-generation study, G2 respondents report the greatest amount of information. Correlations among the three measures of G2 association with their children yield a similar pattern, with substantial correlations within this one conceptual block. Again, the single-item measure correlates more highly with the simple sum scale than the once-a-week measure, and the two scale scores are highly correlated. Reported association of the G2 with their mothers and fathers correlates highly within each role relationship, thus suggesting convergent validity. However, close inspection of the correlations within the mother-father block of variables for the G2 reveals that the strongest correlations are the within-method correlations of the mother-father pair of variables. This is not unexpected, because the mother-father correlations require that both parents are living, and they are probably living together. Nonetheless, the fact that the within-method correlations are stronger than the correlations within a specific role relationship is suggestive of a potential method bias operant in these data.

The correlations between the three child indicators and the six parental indicators for the G2 provide some evidence of discriminant validity. While most of these coefficients are statistically significant, they are considerably smaller than the correlations within either the child or the parental block of variables.

The data reported by the G3 also support the validity of these measures. The three measures of contact with father correlate substantially, as do the three measures of contact with mother. Correlations between the mother and father variables are strong, and the three within-method mother-father pairs are among the strongest coefficients in the matrix.

Summary of
Generation-Level Analysis

The generation-level analysis yields several conclusions. First, the conceptual structure suggested in Table 6.1 is not substantiated, due in large part to the structure of the original items. Second, geographic distance statistically interacts with the measures of association, thus invalidating inclusion of these items in summary scales. Third, a strong single dimension of association, dominated by the face-to-face component, is present in the six role relationships analyzed here. This suggests construct validity. Fourth, the dimension exhibits reasonably high reliability as determined by LISREL modeling as well as alpha reliabilities. Finally, convergent and discriminant validity appears present, although some aspects of method bias are manifest.

Lineage-Level Analysis

At the lineage level of analysis, the responses of each member of a role relationship are analyzed with reciprocal data regarding the amount of contact in that relationship. Because of the linkage of observations and the fact that G2 family members may be represented in several lineages, the assumption of independence of observations may be violated.[5]

This, coupled with the reciprocal data of this study, requires that errors of measurement be given greater attention in this phase of the analysis. We use the LISREL measurement model (Jöreskog and Sörbom, 1984; 1979) to test alternative theoretical models of the data.[6]

The data file for this analysis is the overlapping triad file with a total of 522 lineages. Missing data on the 12 variables in the analysis reduces the sample to 338 observations. The 12 variables assessed three role relationships:

(1) G1-G2 relationship: The four variables are the G1 simple summary scale of association (G1-G2 Scale), the G1 single-item indicator (G1-G2 Item), and, after determining the gender of the G1 in this lineage, the appropriate G2 parental scale (G2-G1 Scale) and single item (G2-G1 Item).

(2) G2-G3 relationship: Included are the G2 simple summary scale of association (G2-G3 Scale), the G2 single-item indicator (G2-G3 Item), and, after determining the gender of the G2 in this lineage, the

appropriate G3 parental scale (G3-G2 Scale) and single item (G3-G2 Item).

(3) G1-G3 relationship: The four indicators of association in the G1-G3 relationship include two single-item indicators (G1-G3 Item, G3-G1 Item) and two overall estimates of the frequency of contact (G1-G3 Frequency, G3-G1 Frequency).

Interpretation of the variable labels is quite simple, with the *responding generation* listed first, and the referent generation listed second in the label.

The covariance matrix of the 12 measures is used as the basic data for these analyses. Seven different conceptual models are tested to determine the appropriate model for estimation of error covariances. The summary results of these analyses are presented in Table 6.6.

The first model (B_1) tests the hypothesis that intergenerational association is one underlying concept spanning generations and role relationships. This suggests that intergenerational families display characteristic patterns of association. One underlying dimension is used to reproduce the covariances among the items. As Table 6.6 illustrates, this model provides a very poor fit to the data.

Models B_2-B_4 suggest that intergenerational association is specific to the role relationship. The four indicators of association in each of the three role relationships are hypothesized to form one dimension, and the three underlying dimensions are hypothesized to correlate. Model B_2 is a modified parallel measures model. Because two methods of measurement are represented in the four measures for each relationship, the Λ_x and Θ_δ coefficients within each relationship for each method are constrained to equality. Model B_2 is a substantial improvement upon the single-dimension B_1 model.

The model of tau equivalence (Model B_3) relaxes the constraint of equality of error covariances and freely estimates these coefficients. This model significantly reduces χ^2, but the ratio of χ^2 to degrees of freedom and the goodness of fit index (GFI) suggest that this model does not adequately explain the data.

The congeneric measures model (B_4) relaxes the constraints on Λ_x, allowing uniqueness in the measurement coefficients. Again, this model significantly reduces χ^2 and improves the GFI, but significant residuals remain.

Model B_5 estimates a model that is generation and role specific. This model suggests that individuals have their own frames of reference when answering questions about the association in any role relationship. The

TABLE 6.6   Summary of LISREL Measurement Models:
Association Dimension

Model	Model Definition	χ^2	d.f.	Goodness of Fit
B_1	Lineage association $1\,\xi$	850.55	54	0.687
B_2	Modified parallel measures $3\,\xi$	381.34	63	0.833
B_3	Modified tau equivalence $3\,\xi$	325.59	57	0.857
B_4	Congeneric measures $3\,\xi$	299.95	51	0.864
B_5	Generation & role measures $6\,\xi$	226.28	39	0.900
B_6	Role & method measures $6\,\xi$	208.29	39	0.899
M_1	Role & method measures $6\,\xi\;\;\theta_{\delta_{4\,2}}$	161.40	38	0.922
M_2	Role & method measures $6\,\xi\;\;\theta_{\delta_{4\,2}}\;\theta_{\delta_{10\,8}}$	122.82	37	0.944
M_3	Role & method measures $6\,\xi\;\;\theta_{\delta_{4\,2}}\;\theta_{\delta_{10\,8}}\;\theta_{\delta_{8\,6}}$	100.74	36	0.952
M_4	Role & method measures $6\,\xi\;\;\theta_{\delta_{4\,2}}\;\theta_{\delta_{10\,8}}\;\theta_{\delta_{8\,6}}\;\theta_{\delta_{10\,6}}$	91.36	35	0.957
B_7	Second-order dimension (see text)	255.81	42	0.879

model postulates six dimensions. Two respondent- and relationship-specific indicators define each dimension. To illustrate, the four indicators of the G1-G2 relationship define two dimensions: (1) G1-G2 Scale and G1-G2 Item, and (2) G2-G1 Scale and G2-G1 Item. By specifying the model in this form, this analysis emphasizes both substantive variation in association as well as respondent variation in interpretation of the stimuli. This model yields a likelihood ratio χ^2 of 226.28 with 39 degrees of freedom, and is a substantial improvement on the prior models.

Model B_6 tests six role and method dimensions. This model suggests that method bias as well as true score differences in association explain the observed covariances. The six dimensions are defined by two items that are relationship and method specific. For example, the two dimensions in the G1-G2 relationship are defined by (1) G1-G2 Scale and G2-G1 Scale, and (2) G1-G2 Item and G2-G1 Item. This model implies that the respondent per se does not bias the model; rather, method bias and true score differences in the extensivity of association account for the obtained covariances. This model uses the same degrees of freedom as Model B_5 but yields a smaller χ^2.

Model B_7 is a second-order factor model with six first-order role and method dimensions (Model B_6) and three second-order role-based dimensions. This model fails to converge in 1000 iterations, regardless of specification of starting values. The summary results reported here must, therefore, be interpreted with great caution. The likelihood ratio χ^2 as well as the goodness of fit statistic indicates that this model is not acceptable. Inspection of residuals reveals that substantial covariation is not explained.

On the basis of these results, we select Model B_6 as the baseline model of choice. Theoretically, this model implies that the seven-item scales are methodologically unique and tap a different facet of association than do the single-item indicators. In part, this is due to the specificity of the scales in tapping explicitly delineated behaviors, while the single items focus on a nebulously defined "doing things together" aspect of the relationship, with response options that imply *adequacy* or *sufficiency* of the interaction. Examination of the detailed results of Model B_6 reveals that significant error covariances are present in the data. Models M_1-M_4 estimate four significant errors.

The four error covariances are substantively meaningful. The first and third coefficients address respondent- and relationship-specific residual covariation. The first coefficient includes G2-G1 Scale and G2-G1 Item, while the third includes G3-G2 Scale and G3-G2 Item. The second error covariance addresses respondent- and method-specific residual covariation, and includes G3-G2 Item and G3-G1 Item. In part, this coefficient may also result from the centrality of the G2 as a linkage between the G1 and G3. The fourth error covariance certainly addresses this aspect of the data because it crosses both relationships and methods, but includes data drawn from the G3 (G3-G2 Scale and G3-G1 Item). Estimation of these four correlated errors reduces χ^2 to 91.36 with 35 degrees of freedom, with a GFI of 0.957. While modification indices suggest that this model may be improved, inspection of residuals suggests that all of the substantial original covariances are explained, and that estimation of the next error would yield a negative covariance where the original covariance is positive. Table 6.7 presents the complete results for Model M_4.

Each dimension (ξ) is role- and method-specific, with the variable that addresses the older generations' responses in reference to the younger generation fixed at 1.0 to set a common scale. The λ coefficients for each dimension are in most cases nearly equal, suggesting that each variable contributes approximately the same to the underlying scale. In every case, however, the variable drawn from the older generation has a greater loading, and for two of the dimensions (ξ_4 and ξ_5), there is a substantial difference. Both of these dimensions address association with the G3; apparently the G3 is less extreme in its evaluation of global association measures.

Explained variation in the 12 association measures is quite good, averaging 0.61. With the exception of the two G3 single-item indicators, R^2 exceeds 0.50 in all cases, indicating that item reliabilities in these data are quite good. Overall, the total coefficient of determination for this model equals 0.999, suggesting an excellent fit to the data. The attention to correlated errors is clearly warranted, because these residual correlations are strong, positive, and significant.

Entries in the Φ matrix represent covariances and correlations among the six dimensions. Convergent validity correlations ($\phi_{12}\ \phi_{34}\ \phi_{56}$) are quite high, ranging from 0.681 to 0.905. Most discriminant validity correlations are quite low, as expected, with the exception of the four G1-G2 and G1-G3 correlations ($\phi_{15}\ \phi_{16}\ \phi_{25}\ \phi_{26}$). We interpret these as substantive correlations reflecting that association between the G1 and G3 is mediated by the G2.

Discussion

While the results of the LISREL analysis are most encouraging and suggest that these measures are reliable and valid, we note that the correlations between generations' reports of the same phenomenon (e.g., G1-G2 Scale and G2-G1 Scale) range from 0.41 to 0.75. Normally, this is quite good. Because these are measures of objective, behavioral phenomena, where each generation is responding about the *same* objective facts, however, these correlations cause some concern. In

TABLE 6.7   LISREL Estimates: Association Dimension—
Six Dimensions, Four Correlated Errors

	ξ_1	ξ_2	ξ_3	ξ_4	ξ_5	ξ_6	Θ_δ	R^2
				Λ_x				
G1-G2 Scale	1.000*	0.000	0.000	0.000	0.000	0.000	17.444	0.681
G2-G1 Scale	0.985	0.000	0.000	0.000	0.000	0.000	19.320	0.654
G1-G2 Item	0.000	1.000*	0.000	0.000	0.000	0.000	0.638	0.660
G2-G1 Item	0.000	0.924	0.000	0.000	0.000	0.000	0.977	0.511
G2-G3 Scale	0.000	0.000	1.000*	0.000	0.000	0.000	16.948	0.775
G3-G2 Scale	0.000	0.000	0.868	0.000	0.000	0.000	26.583	0.624
G2-G3 Item	0.000	0.000	0.000	1.000*	0.000	0.000	0.187	0.868
G3-G2 Item	0.000	0.000	0.000	0.617	0.000	0.000	1.662	0.230
G1-G3 Item	0.000	0.000	0.000	0.000	1.000*	0.000	0.740	0.513
G3-G1 Item	0.000	0.000	0.000	0.000	0.721	0.000	0.869	0.310
G3-G1 Frequency	0.000	0.000	0.000	0.000	0.000	0.992	108.540	0.806
G1-G3 Frequency	0.000	0.000	0.000	0.000	0.000	1.000*	202.179	0.694

	ξ_1	ξ_2	ξ_3	ξ_4	ξ_5	ξ_6
			Φ**			
ξ_1	37.271	0.905	0.202	0.169	0.790	0.675
ξ_2	6.154	1.242	0.106***	0.229	0.850	0.549
ξ_3	9.449	0.907***	58.477	0.681	0.359	0.295
ξ_4	1.142	0.282	5.759	1.224	0.352	0.200
ξ_5	4.254	0.836	2.423	0.343	0.779	0.791
ξ_6	88.205	13.102	48.357	4.741	14.947	458.184

Error Covariances and Correlations	Covariance	Correlation
G2-G1 Scale with G2-G1 Item	2.543	0.585
G3-G2 Scale with G3-G2 Item	2.439	0.367
G3-G2 Item with G3-G1 Item	0.434	0.361
G3-G2 Scale with G3-G1 Item	0.981	0.204

*Coefficient fixed at 1.0 to establish underlying scale.
**Variances are on the diagonal, with correlations above and covariances below the diagonal.
***Coefficient that is not significant at $p < 0.05$.

order to address this issue, we qualitatively analyze selected cases where the different generations' responses are *most* divergent.[7] While this analysis is selective and drawn from a purposive sample (G1-G2: n = 11; G2-G3: n = 33) that is known to disagree, we feel it provides some insight into why these discrepancies occur.

Disagreements about the degree of association in the G1-G2 dyad are associated with other tensions or disagreements in the dyad. These disagreements center on financial issues, religious differences, and grandparent "meddling" in the raising of the G2's children. The disagreements extend to other areas of the relationship. Illustrative of this cycle of progressive disenchantment is the case of a widowed G1 female who reports little association and her G2 son who reports average levels of contact. The husband she lost had been responsible for providing significant amounts of care, because she could not walk. Her son, who lives 150 miles away, reports visiting about once a month. This level of association is not reported by the G1, who further perceives the amount of contact to be insufficient. She comments: "I do not see [my] son's children enough to know their middle names."

It appears that much of the problem in this relationship stems from the widow's current financial problems and an unpaid loan made by her deceased husband to the son. When asked what things could happen that would make her happy, she comments: "To have my son pay me the money my husband loaned him before he died."

Other areas of the relationship are deteriorating as well. When asked about the affect in their relationship, both parties report a lack of trust, respect, and fairness.

Our point, however, is not to belabor the specific nuances of this or any other case. Rather, we suggest that measurement error on the association dimension is inversely correlated with the other dimensions of solidarity. This is further supported by the analysis of discrepant cases in the G2-G3 dyad.

G2-G3 disagreements on the degree of association revolve around issues of appearance, life-style, and sexuality. The G3 generally believes that these disagreements are major, while the G2 feel that they are minor problems. In large part, this is explained by the developmental tasks unique to each generation. Illustrative of this is the comment by one 36-year-old G2 female who said of her 18-year-old son: "My son is striving toward independence but is actually more dependent than he cares to admit . . . I suppose I don't really want to 'let go.' "

Issues of marriage and sexuality, especially cohabitation or early marriage plans, are present in a number of cases. At times, this gets tied into religious issues, especially pertaining to use of birth control. This factor is manifest more often when the G2 married at an early age and where that marriage is not especially happy. Interestingly, both the G2 and the G3 acknowledge their disagreements in this domain.

While the disagreements between the G2 and G3 are different than the G1 and G2 disagreements, a consistent pattern can be seen in that increased measurement error on the association dimension is apparently tied to decreased solidarity on the other dimensions.

Future Measurement of Association

The analyses we report here suggest several empirical and theoretical issues for future research using the association dimension. First, measurement of the frequency of intergenerational contact is not as simple as it appears. While respondents can readily answer questions about the frequency of contact with other family members, the nature of the stimuli used to elicit those data is extremely important to consider. Use of global single-item indicators yields substantially different data than does the use of a more detailed scale. While the two are correlated, we believe that the single item addresses the perceived sufficiency of contact as opposed to contact *per se*.

Second, when using scale items such as those included in this study, a greater degree of specificity with regard to the time referent is suggested. Our data use an implicit one-year time frame that is structured into the response options to the stimuli; we recommend that this implicit frame of reference be made explicit and structured into the introductory statement preceding presentation of the specific stimuli. If possible, a shorter time frame (e.g., two weeks) will decrease errors of recall and telescoping errors. We further recommend that the time referent in the response options be retained and made more numeric in focus. To illustrate, the response options of "several times a year" and "every other month or so" are not necessarily exclusive nor exhaustive, depending upon the respondent's interpretation of those options. While we believe that this does not present major problems for this analysis due to the ordering of the response options, the greater specificity that responses of "two to four times a year" and "five to ten times a year" provide will help to improve measurement.

Third, we recommend that future measurement of this dimension attempt to delineate specific subscales of the association dimension. Table 6.1 presents one conceptualization of association that is multidimensional. Multiple questions that focus on one cell and clearly exclude the other cells will enable greater understanding of the nature of the associational bond. To those who are uncomfortable with the functionalist overtones of the conceptualization presented in Table 6.1, we heartily encourage you to develop scales that draw on alternative theoretical frameworks. Measurement is inherently theoretical, contrary to the belief of many positivists (Mangen, Peterson, and Sanders, 1982).

One such framework that we feel can and should be examined to improve understanding of associational solidarity is exchange theory.

Emerson (1972a, 1972b) suggests that cohesion in a group is not only a function of one's ties to that group but also is a function of the *alternatives* to that group. Let us assume, for the sake of simplicity, that we wish to measure intergenerational associational solidarity, and that the alternatives we consider are intragenerational, work, and friendship structures. Thus a total of four domains are assessed, although these are certainly not exhaustive. Let us further assume that we have measured the degree of association in each of these X_i domains on comparable scales of 0-50. Cohesion to any one group (C_i) may then be defined as

$$C_i = \frac{X_i}{\Sigma X_i}$$

which ranges from zero, indicating no reliance upon the group, to one, indicating complete reliance upon that group. It is important to note that equivalent absolute levels of any one X_i may be associated with substantially different C_i, depending on the level of the other X_i.

We do not intend to suggest that this is the only way to utilize the exchange framework and measure associational solidarity, nor do we wish to suggest that exchange is the best approach to use. We encourage use of competing frameworks and competing conceptualizations within frameworks. Exchange theory is, however, one theory that allows explicit development of epistemic rules linking observed data to underlying phenomena, that is, theoretically based measurement.

The amount of contact between parents and children is one of the most frequently studied aspects of parent-child relations (Bengtson and Schrader, 1982). Our analyses demonstrate that researchers interested in measuring this important dimension can use the seven-item scale with considerable confidence in its reliability and validity. Furthermore, if space considerations preclude the use of the more extensive scale, the single-item indicator captures much of the same information as the full scale, although method bias precludes combination of the single-item into an extended and revised eight-item summary measure.

In this chapter, we have attempted to make explicit our assumptions regarding the linkage of our indicators to our concepts, and to document the empirical evidence supporting those assumptions. The analyses we report provide considerable support for our conceptualization, and point out some flaws as well. We invite others to improve upon and advance our work.

NOTES

1. The items included in the study are

Scale Items

WITH YOUR (*INSERT REFERENT*): How often do you do the following?

(1) Recreation outside the home (movies, picnics, swimming, trips, hunting, and so on)
(2) Brief visits for conversation
(3) Family gatherings like reunions or holiday dinners where a lot of family members get together
(4) Small family gatherings for special occasions like birthdays or anniversaries
(5) Talking over things that are important to you
(6) Religious activities of any kind
(7) Writing letters
(8) Telephoning each other
(9) Dinner together

The response options are

(1) Almost never
(2) About once a year
(3) Several times a year
(4) Every other month or so
(5) About once a month
(6) About once a week
(7) Several times a week
(8) Almost every day

Single-Item Indicator

(9) How often do you *do things together* with this (*insert referent*)?
(1) Seldom
(2) Not too often
(3) Some
(4) Pretty often
(5) Very often
(6) Extremely often

Grandparent Frequency Item

(10) About how many times in the past year have you seen this grandchild? _____ times

Grandchild Frequency Item

(11) About how many times in the past year have you seen these grandparents?
grandfather: _____ times
grandmother: _____ times

2. For a more complete discussion of generational and lineage analysis, see Chapter 3.

3. Version 6.9 of PC LISREL is used for the generation-level analysis.

4. See Chapter 3 for a discussion of the models of parallel measures, tau equivalence, and congeneric measures.

5. See Chapter 3 for a discussion of lineage files, especially the overlapping triads file used in this analysis.

6. Version 6.6 of LISREL is used in this analysis.

7. The qualitative analysis is based on work done by Grace Greer and Miriam Kmet. We thank them for their assistance with this effort.

7

Measuring Intergenerational Consensus

PIERRE H. LANDRY, Jr.
MARY E. MARTIN

In our conceptualization of family solidarity, various characteristics of families are examined for features that promote cohesion. One dimension of this is the degree of attitude and opinion consensus between parents and their children.

From the late 1960s through the early 1970s, many observers gave special attention to the "generation gap," the supposed disagreement or conflict between the views of adolescents and their elders. Indeed, the widespread concern over this issue was one impetus for the original survey in 1973 from which the data used in this study are drawn.

There is a substantial body of research that points to the importance of family life to most Americans (Campbell, Converse, and Rodgers, 1976; Veroff, Douvan, and Kulka, 1981). If, however, the "generation gap" continues to be as large and as pervasive in families as some authors contend, this would portend the general alienation of family generations from each other (Roszak, 1969). Such an alienation would have a profound effect on the fabric of family interaction. It seems plausible that similar views promote solidarity among family members and that dissimilar views contribute to dissension.

It is important, then, to be able to measure intrafamilial consensus on attitudes and opinions. The task is twofold: (1) to develop a measure of an individual's attitudes and opinions, and (2) to devise an appropriate summary measure that reflects the degree of similarity of views among family members across generations.

Most of the studies concerned with the similarity of views from one family generation to the next have focused on the relationship between the young and their parents (see, for example, Thomas, 1974, for a review). For the most part, these research efforts have utilized measures of self-reported opinions to compare the views across generations within families. Based on this type of measure, there is conflicting evidence regarding the similarity or differences that exist between the views of parents and their children.

There are firm advocates of what Bengtson (1970) characterized as the "great gap" hypothesis (M. Mead, 1970; Latowski and Kelner, 1970; Slater, 1970; Connell, 1972; Gallagher, 1974; Payne, Summers, and Stewart, 1973; Tedin, 1974). Roszak (1969), for one, takes the position that the young are "profoundly, even fanatically, alienated from the parental generation."

On the other hand, some research suggests generally high levels of intergenerational solidarity and, therefore, deemphasizes the generation gap (Aldous and Hill, 1965; Douvan and Adelson, 1966; Hyman, 1969; Feuer, 1969; Offer, 1969; Troll, Neugarten, and Kraines, 1969; Hill et al., 1970; Yankelovitch, 1970; Kandel and Lesser, 1972; Thomas, 1974; Bengtson, 1975; Lerner and Knapp, 1975). Writing before the major upheavals of the late 1960s, Douvan and Adelson (1966, p. 84) argued that "core values are shared by parents and peers, and conflicts center on peripheral or token issues." Seven years later, Bengtson and Black (1973) found "lineage solidarity" in their sample—more similarity than difference from generation to generation within families.

There is also considerable evidence supporting an intermediate position regarding the generation gap, suggesting that some values and attitudes (e.g., religious beliefs and practices) are more deliberately socialized than others (Aldous and Hill, 1965; Acock and Bengtson, 1975). Intergenerational differences in these areas would be less likely because of the focused effort but might be more serious whenever they did occur.

Thomas (1974) suggests that there is more support for the "no gap" position, although the studies he reviewed are far from definitive. He reminds us, however, that not all of the studies that conclude for or against the existence of a generation gap are focused on youths of the same age, so comparing empirical results is problematic.

If, instead of using self-reports from members of each generation to determine similarities or differences among them, we adopt the symbolic interactionist perspective of using attributed responses, then new insights may be gained. Symbolic interactionists suggest that it is the meaning given by a person to another's behavior that exercises greater influence over that person than whatever meaning was intended by the other (G. H. Mead, 1934; Kinch, 1963; Stryker, 1965; Burr, Leigh et al., 1979). As W. I. Thomas (1931/1972) put it, people respond according to their definition of the situation (see also Goffman, 1959). Thus, for relationships between parents and their children, some social psychologists emphasize the greater importance of attributed or perceived attitudes and opinions relative to actually held orientations (Acock and Bengtson, 1978, 1980; Jones and Harris, 1967; Kelly, 1973; Sherif, Sherif, and Nebergall, 1965).

In order to capture the benefits of both perspectives, we use both types of measures. If A is a survey respondent in a family (e.g., a father) and B is a "reciprocal respondent" (a family member to whom A has attributed some opinion, and by whom some opinion has been attributed to A, e.g., a son), then family consensus can be described in three ways: (1) the difference between the self-reported responses of A and B ("objective consensus"); (2) the difference between the self-reported response of A and the response A attributes to B (e.g., the difference between a father's actual opinion and the opinion he attributes to his son, or the "father's view of the world"); and (3) the difference between the actual response of B and the response B attributes to A (the "child's world").

Though most of the literature is concerned with similarities or differences in attitudes and opinions of parents and their adolescent children, we extend this conceptualization to middle-aged adult children and their elderly parents. In our three-generation families, then, we have actual and perceived differences regarding certain attitudes in G1-G2 and the G2-G3 dyads.

There is abundant evidence for the importance of kin networks to older people (Bengtson et al., 1985; Lopata, 1979; Shanas, 1980; Shanas et al., 1968). It is our assumption that attitude consensus across family generations contributes to family solidarity.

Generation-Level Measurement

Our focus within the consensus dimension of solidarity is on specific attitudes and opinions, and orientations to religion. Following Glenn (1980), we consider an *attitude* to be an expression of a feeling about an object, while an *opinion* is a more rationalized judgment of an object. In most instances, these terms will be used interchangeably. *Object* may apply not only to material things, but also to persons, groups, institutions, ideas, practices, and so on (Glenn, 1980). *Religiosity* is a special kind of attitude, expressing a formalized and outwardly expressed set of attitudes toward the role of religion and religious institutions in contemporary life. Finally, *consensus* refers to the degree of similarity in attitudes and opinions, with attention to perceived as well as self-reported positions. It should be noted that the attitudes measured in this study refer to specific topics, namely political conservatism, racial issues, marriage norms, and religious belief and practice.

The analysis of these data at the generational level involves two distinct stages. Because several different conceptual domains are included in the consensus construct, we first assess the dimensional structure for each conceptual domain. Many items assessing each domain are included in these data, and we will not discuss each item. Rather, because the primary goal of the analysis at this stage is to isolate conceptual dimensions that are congruent across generations and, where appropriate, congruent across self-reports and attributions, we present data pertaining only to those items that in fact meet our criteria of adequacy. Following this, we discuss the distributions of these measures in the three-generation data.

Religiosity

Two dimensions of religiosity are measured in these data. The first pertains to religious beliefs. These four items are scored on a four-point scale of agreement and disagreement with high scores indicating a stronger belief in a deity. In this sample, there is a slight decline from oldest (G1) to youngest (G3) generation in the mean scores of these measures. The items assessing religious belief focus on the self-report component; attributional data are not present.

Table 7.1 presents the factor structure, by generation, for the four items measuring religious beliefs. For each generation, a strong single factor is obtained. In each case, the factor is most strongly defined by belief in God as presented in the Bible, but loadings for all four items exceed 0.60 in all three generations. The single factor explains a minimum of 66.5% of the total variance of the four items. Reliability of the four-item factor is quite good.

TABLE 7.1   Traditional Religious Beliefs: Summary of
            Factor Structure, by Generation

Item	G1	G2	G3
Every child should have religious instructions	0.66	0.61	0.66
God exists as in the Bible	0.90	0.92	0.83
United States would be better if religion had more influence	0.79	0.78	0.74
We are all descendants of Adam and Eve	0.78	0.76	0.75
Eigenvalue	2.81	2.77	2.66
Percentage of total variance explained	70.4	69.3	66.5
Coefficient alpha	0.85	0.85	0.83
Number of cases	479	645	754

The data in Table 7.1 suggest the validity of the religious belief dimension in that the obtained factor structure is highly congruent across generations, with coefficients of congruence exceeding 0.99. Evidence of convergent validity is provided by the correlations of a single-item indicator of self-reported religiosity with the four-item unit-weighted summary scale. These moderately strong correlations (G1: $r = 0.61$; G2: $r = 0.55$; G3: $r = 0.61$) suggest a reasonably valid measure, but that additional work remains to refine this instrument.

The items assessing religious practice are a series of five dichotomous variables that assess participation in the rituals and organizational structure of a formal religious institution. For four of the five measures, G2 respondents show the greatest degree of participation in religious institutions. In only one case, that pertaining to weekly attendance at church, do proportionately more G1 respondents answer affirmatively.

Table 7.2 presents the results, by generation, of the factor analysis of these five items. Factor-item coefficients are uniformly strong across the generations, with the common definer of the dimension being weekly attendance at church. For the G2, being a member of a church group is equally important in defining the underlying dimension. Over 50% of the variance of these items is explained by the single-factor structures, with alpha reliabilities exceeding 0.75 for each generation.

Coefficients of congruence assessing the similarity of the factor structure across generation exceed 0.99, suggesting construct validity

TABLE 7.2   Religious Practice: Summary of
             Factor Structure, by Generation

Item	G1	G2	G3
Registered member: past year	0.74	0.61	0.67
Church group member	0.64	0.79	0.64
Sunday school teacher/officer	0.45	0.60	0.53
Ever attend church	0.59	0.56	0.63
Attend church weekly or more	0.82	0.79	0.72
Eigenvalue	2.70	2.81	2.63
Percentage of total variance explained	53.9	56.1	52.5
Coefficient alpha	0.78	0.80	0.77
Number of cases	495	679	816

for the derived scales. Convergent validity, assessed by correlating the simple summed scale scores with the single-item religiosity measure, ranges from 0.48 to 0.49 for the three generations. That these correlations are lower than the correlations noted above with the belief dimension is not surprising; the single-item indicator emphasizes the issues of belief, not practice.

Marriage Norms

While the analysis of the religious belief and practice dimensions was carried out independently of the remaining analyses, the first examination of the items assessing marriage norms (as well as the analysis of black demands, presented below) was pooled with the analysis of political conservatism. In part, this was due to our belief that these items assessed issues of political conservatism and, in part, due to the fact that attributional measures are included in these three domains. A total of 19 items were included in this initial analysis.

Initial examination of generation-specific factor analyses of the pooled items revealed, however, that the marriage norms and black demands dimensions confounded the analysis of political conservatism—especially when attempting to derive measures that were congruent across both generations and attributions. The rapid social change that characterized the early 1970s perhaps emphasized changes in these domains, a fact that may have resulted in a period effect on the measurement structure of these items. Stated another way, it is quite possible that separate scales pertaining to marriage norms and racial demands would not have emerged had these data been gathered in 1960, and may not emerge again in the future.

In order to simplify the analysis, therefore, we separated the item pools into the three distinct groups suggested by the initial exploratory factor analyses. For each group, therefore, a total of nine summary scales are developed. Three scales are self-report, one for each generation. For the G1, another scale is developed that emphasizes the attributions to the G2 child. For the G2, three additional scales are developed: (1) attributed to G1 father, (2) attributed to G1 mother, and (3) attributed to G3 child. Similarly, G3 scales examining attributions to both father (G2) and mother (G2) are developed.

The consequence of requiring congruence across so many comparisons is that many items were eliminated to obtain congruence, and only two items remain that measure the marriage norms dimension. The items address concern with divorce and sexuality. The G3 is the most liberal of the generations with regard to marriage norms, followed by the G2 and finally the G1. Table 7.3 presents the results obtained through factor analysis of these two items.

Factor-item coefficients are, in all factor analyses of doublets, constrained to equality because only one unique correlation is present in each analyzed matrix. The factor-item coefficients range from 0.53 to 0.68 but, due to the small number of items, reliabilities are marginal. The single factor explains from 64.0% to 72.9% of the variance of the doublets in each of the nine analyses.

Legitimacy of Black Demands

As suggested above, the black demands dimension is measured by only two items following elimination of items to achieve congruence across generations and attributions. As expected, the G1 is the most conservative on this issue, and a gradual decline is noted to the G3. Table 7.4 presents the results, by generation, of the nine factor analyses of these data.

Once again, the characteristic pattern of equal factor-item coefficients in a doublet analysis is seen in this table. Factor-item coefficients range from 0.71 to 0.87, with the single factor explaining from 75.6% to 87.8% of the variance of the two items. Alpha reliabilities are, however, greater than seen in the marriage norms dimension, ranging from 0.67 to 0.86.

TABLE 7.3 Marriage Norms: Summary of Factor Structure, by Generation

Item	G1		G2				G3		
	Self	Child	Self	Father	Mother	Child	Self	Father	Mother
Marriage can be dissolved at will	0.57	0.61	0.60	0.56	0.60	0.68	0.64	0.53	0.58
Sex should not depend on marriage	0.57	0.61	0.60	0.56	0.60	0.68	0.64	0.53	0.58
Eigenvalue	1.33	1.37	1.37	1.31	1.36	1.46	1.42	1.28	1.34
Percentage of total variance explained	66.3	68.8	68.3	65.6	67.8	72.9	70.8	64.0	67.0
Coefficient alpha	0.50	0.56	0.55	0.50	0.52	0.65	0.57	0.46	0.52
Number of cases	472	472	430	430	430	430	696	696	696

TABLE 7.4 Legitimacy of Black Demands: Summary of Factor Structure, by Generation

Item	G1		G2				G3		
	Self	Child	Self	Father	Mother	Child	Self	Father	Mother
Negroes are pushing too hard and too fast	0.71	0.81	0.78	0.83	0.79	0.83	0.77	0.87	0.85
Negroes are asking for special treatment	0.71	0.81	0.78	0.83	0.79	0.83	0.77	0.87	0.85
Eigenvalue	1.51	1.66	1.61	1.69	1.63	1.69	1.60	1.76	1.72
Percentage of total variance explained	75.6	82.9	80.6	84.5	81.5	84.5	79.9	87.8	85.9
Coefficient alpha	0.67	0.79	0.76	0.80	0.76	0.81	0.73	0.86	0.84
Number of cases	473	473	431	431	431	431	688	688	688

Political Conservatism

On the items measuring conservatism, the G3 respondents are once again the most liberal followed by the G2 and finally the G1. A total of five items measure this dimension following elimination of items to meet the constraint of congruence across generations and attributions. These items address issues of the work ethic, U.S. power, student demonstrations, law and order, and welfare. While some of these items appear to measure social as opposed to political conservatism, we treat them as measures of political conservatism in that these issues are often the focus of political campaigns or rhetoric. Table 7.5 presents the results of the factor analyses of these data.

The single-factor solution explains a minimum of 39.4% and a maximum of 51.7% of the variance of these five items. Factor-item coefficients in these analyses range from 0.32 to 0.79. In seven of the nine analyses, the law and order stimulus most strongly defines the underlying dimension. The two exceptions are both found in the G2 analysis of attributions to their G1 parents, where the item on student demonstrators defines the underlying scale. Interestingly, the factor loadings for this item in the two analyses of G3 attributions to parents are also quite strong, suggesting that the younger generation in any dyadic relationship perceives this issue to be especially pertinent for their parents. Reliability coefficients are moderately low to acceptable, ranging from 0.60 to 0.76. Indeed, the rigid constraint for congruence across generations and attributions deleteriously affects reliability. In each analysis, additional items could have been retained if this constraint were removed, and retention of these items improves the context-specific reliability while detracting from cross-context comparability.

The validity of the political conservatism scale may be seen in the congruence across generations and attributions, as well as in the correlations of the five-item simple sum scale with a global measure of political conservatism. Correlations of the self-reported scale scores with the single-item indicator are quite low (G1: r = 0.28; G2: r = 0.38; G3: r = 0.47). In part, this may be due to the differentiation of social and political conservatism, because the items included in this scale reflect traditional social issues about which political elections are often decided. If so, then these correlations suggest that the younger generation is less apt to differentiate the social and political domains.

TABLE 7.5 Political Conservatism: Summary of Factor Structure, by Generation

Item	G1		G2				G3		
	Self	Child	Self	Father	Mother	Child	Self	Father	Mother
It's a man's duty to work, a sin to be idle	0.45	0.39	0.55	0.33	0.36	0.61	0.53	0.36	0.44
United States should answer challenges to power	0.43	0.41	0.45	0.41	0.32	0.57	0.48	0.43	0.42
Student demonstrators deserve strongest punishment	0.59	0.64	0.60	0.70	0.66	0.68	0.52	0.66	0.66
Society's most important task: law and order	0.67	0.79	0.67	0.61	0.55	0.75	0.59	0.71	0.66
Most people on welfare are lazy	0.57	0.43	0.64	0.52	0.55	0.53	0.50	0.54	0.56
Eigenvalue	2.19	2.14	2.36	2.07	1.97	2.58	2.11	2.18	2.20
Percentage of total variance explained	43.8	42.9	47.3	41.5	39.4	51.7	42.2	43.7	44.1
Coefficient alpha	0.62	0.65	0.72	0.63	0.60	0.76	0.66	0.67	0.68
Number of cases	480	473	660	484	521	664	777	727	773

Scale Scores:
Univariate Statistics

Table 7.6 presents the means and standard deviations for the scales developed in each of the five conceptual domains. There are three sets of important comparisons in Table 7.6. First, comparisons across generations (i.e., within a row, across columns) provide information pertaining to the relative degree of conservatism, and so on, of the different generations. Second, comparisons of self-report scores to relevant attributed scores across generations (e.g., G1 Conservatism [self-report] with G2 Conservatism [attributed to mother and attributed to father]) provide aggregate data pertaining to the accuracy of perceptions of the other generation. Finally, within-generation comparisons of self-reports and attributions (e.g., G1 Conservatism [self-report] with G1 Conservatism [attributed to child]) provide data relevant to the perception of a "generation gap."

Marriage norms: These scale scores range from 2-8, with higher scores indicating a more liberal perspective on marriage and sexuality. With a theoretical midpoint of 5.0, cross-generation comparisons of self-report scores indicate that only the G3 is truly liberal in their beliefs about marriage norms. G1 respondents are the most traditional in their marriage beliefs, and G2 respondents—while on the traditional end of the scale—are slightly more liberal than the G1.

Examination of the accuracy of perception reveals, however, interesting contrasts. On an aggregate level, the G1 perception of the G2 is reasonably accurate, with a difference of means of only 0.11. The G2, however, believes that both their mothers ($\overline{X}$ = 3.32) and fathers ($\overline{X}$ = 3.58) are more traditional than the G1 report themselves to be ($\overline{X}$ = 3.96), implying some inaccuracy in perception of the older generation. Similarly, the G2 feels that the G3 ($\overline{X}$ = 5.29) is less liberal than the G3 reports about themselves ($\overline{X}$ = 5.67). The G3 believes that both their mothers ($\overline{X}$ = 3.68) and their fathers ($\overline{X}$ = 3.78) are more traditional than the G2 reports ($\overline{X}$ = 4.25).

Turning to the perceived generation gap comparisons, the G1 perceives only a small gap with their children—one that is smaller than the actual difference. The G2 perceives a more substantial difference with both their mothers and fathers—one that is greater than the actual difference. The G2 also believes that there is a substantial difference with their children, with the actual difference being even larger.

TABLE 7.6   Descriptive Statistics for Summated Scales

	Generation 1			Generation 2			Generation 3		
	n	$\bar{X}$	sd	n	$\bar{X}$	sd	n	$\bar{X}$	sd
Attributed to father:									
Marriage norms	–	–	–	495	3.58	1.74	737	3.78	1.72
Legitimacy of black demands	–	–	–	491	5.91	1.83	726	5.49	1.98
Conservatism	–	–	–	485	16.03	3.56	729	15.55	3.08
Attributed to mother:									
Marriage norms	–	–	–	540	3.32	1.63	782	3.68	1.72
Legitimacy of black demands	–	–	–	533	5.78	1.79	774	5.02	1.90
Conservatism	–	–	–	522	15.82	2.72	773	14.71	3.02
Self-Report:									
Marriage norms	499	3.96	1.92	683	4.25	1.95	817	5.67	1.90
Legitimacy of black demands	497	5.08	1.85	685	4.55	1.82	810	3.99	1.78
Conservatism	484	15.02	3.45	661	13.42	3.56	779	11.30	3.34
Religious practice	495	3.90	2.97	679	4.03	3.06	816	3.55	2.85
Religious belief	479	13.39	3.27	645	12.14	3.44	754	10.91	3.64
Attributed to child:									
Marriage norms	485	4.14	1.93	676	5.29	1.99	–	–	–
Legitimacy of black demands	483	5.19	1.84	675	4.16	1.76	–	–	–
Conservatism	475	15.02	3.14	665	11.61	3.53	–	–	–

Legitimacy of black demands: This scale ranges from 2 to 8, with higher scores indicating a more conservative perspective on race relations. As anticipated, there is a gradual decline in the mean scores when moving from the older to the younger generations. Note that the G1 is almost exactly at the theoretical midpoint of the scale, with the G2 and G3 moving toward the more liberal end of the continuum.

When examining the accuracy of the generations' perceptions of each other, it is clear that differences exist. The G1 believes that their children are more conservative on the issue of race relations ($\bar{X}$ = 5.19) than the G2 reports of themselves ($\bar{X}$ = 4.55). Similarly, the G2 believes that their mothers ($\bar{X}$ = 5.78) and fathers ($\bar{X}$ = 5.91) are more conservative than the G1 reports of themselves ($\bar{X}$ = 5.08). The G2 also believes that their children are less liberal ($\bar{X}$ = 4.16) than the children report of themselves ($\bar{X}$ = 3.99), although these differences are small. The G3 believes that both their mothers ($\overline{X}$ = 5.02) and their fathers ($\overline{X}$ = 5.49) are considerably more conservative than the G2 reports.

The G1 perceives little difference between themselves and their children on the issue of race relations, with a mean score difference of only 0.11. This perceived difference is smaller than the actual difference seen in the data. The G2 perceives a substantial difference with both their mothers and fathers, and some difference with their children, while the G3 perceives a major difference with both their mothers and fathers.

Political conservatism: This scale ranges from 5-20, with higher scores indicating a more conservative outlook on affairs. With a theoretical midpoint of 12.5, examination of the mean self-report score indicates that both the G1 and the G2 fall on the conservative end of this continuum, while the G3 falls on the liberal end of the scale.

A now familiar pattern is again repeated in the analysis of the accuracy of perceptions of the other generations. The G1 perceives that the G2 is more conservative ($\overline{X}$ = 15.02) than the G2 reports of themselves ($\overline{X}$ = 13.42), and the G2 feel that their mothers ($\overline{X}$ = 15.82) and fathers ($\overline{X}$ = 16.03) are more conservative than the G1 reports ($\overline{X}$ = 15.02). The G2 believes that their children are less liberal ($\overline{X}$ = 11.61) than the G3 report ($\overline{X}$ = 11.30), although this difference is not large. The G3, however, believes that their mothers ($\overline{X}$ = 14.71) and fathers ($\overline{X}$ = 15.55) are considerably more conservative than the G2 reports of themselves.

The G1 perceives no gap whatsoever with their children, exhibiting identical mean scores. The G2 perceives a significant gap with their parents as well as their children, while the G3 perceives a substantial gap with both mothers and fathers.

Religiosity: Because the measures of religious belief and practice do not include attributional measures, we discuss them together. G2 family members have the highest rate of religious practice, reflecting in all likelihood the formal outward expression of religiosity required for effective socialization of children. The G1 reports slightly lower levels of religious practice, probably due to health-related constraints on mobility, while the G3 rate of practice is the lowest of any of the three groups. Note, however, that because this scale ranges from 0-5, the G3 mean still reflects a substantial level of participation in formal religious institutions and practices.

A somewhat different picture emerges with regard to religious beliefs. This scale ranges from 4-16, with higher scores indicating a more traditional perspective on religion. While the G1 reports the highest level of traditional religious beliefs, and the G3 the lowest, note that the mean scores for all three groups exceed the theoretical midpoint of 10.0. Thus, even in the turbulent days of the early 1970s, differences between the generations in religious beliefs were not great.

Summary of
Generation-Level Measurement

Given the complex nature of the task of developing multiple scales that are congruent across generations and attributions, we believe that our efforts in developing scales that can be used in deriving measures of consensus have been successful. The measures of religious belief and practice exhibit, on the whole, the best psychometric characteristics of the many scales presented here. It is probably not coincidental that these two measures use only self-report data and ignore issues of attributions.

The marriage norms and legitimacy of black demands scales were not originally expected in the data, and as such must be viewed tentatively. Both are doublets, and as such require further work to develop an item pool that taps a broader range of the underlying concept. Nonetheless, the fact that congruent measures across generations and attributions were developed suggests some promise for further work on elaboration of these concepts.

The results pertaining to the conservatism scale are mixed. While the five-item scale exhibits a reasonable factor structure, the relatively low percentage of variance explained and the marginal alpha reliabilities clearly suggest that work is needed to improve this scale. As previously noted, however, the stringent constraint of requiring congruence across generations and attributions deleteriously affected the development of this scale. An exclusive focus upon self-reported data would improve the measurement characteristics of this scale while eliminating the possibility of exploring the theoretically interesting issues of attribution and perception of the other.

Finally, the analysis of the mean scores on the derived scales presents further support for what Bengtson and Kuypers (1971) have termed the "developmental stake" hypothesis. The G1 consistently underestimates the differences between themselves and the G2, thus promoting a belief in greater intrafamily solidarity. The G3 overestimates the differences between themselves and the G2 in the interests of promoting their independence. The G2 occupies an intermediate position, recognizing the distinctions between themselves and their parents as well as their children.

Lineage-Level Analysis

The analyses reported above focus upon individuals, differentiated according to generational position, who respond about themselves and their perceptions about other family members. When moving to the lineage analysis, we focus upon intergenerational families—individuals linked together according to their role relationships within the family.

The scales developed above measure individual attitudes and opinions. In the lineage analysis, the emphasis is on using the five scales developed in the generation-level analysis to develop measures of consensus within the lineage.

A central issue in deriving the measures of consensus pertains to how to translate the original measures, which do not address consensus per se, into measures of lineage consensus. The analysis reported above comparing mean scores on the different scales begins to address issues of consensus on an aggregate level. Here, however, we desire to focus on a micro-level analysis of the actual consensus within a specific lineage.

While several different strategies are available to examine lineage-level consensus, we elected to use the absolute value of the difference between the role occupants' scale scores. For both the G1-G2 and G2-G3 relationships, three difference scores are computed for each conceptual domain: (1) parental perception of the difference, computed by taking the absolute value of the difference between the actual score of the parent and the score attributed by the parent to the child; (2) the perception of the child, computed by taking the absolute value of the difference between the actual score of the child and the score attributed by the child to the parent; and (3) the objective difference, computed as the absolute value of the difference between the actual scores of both the parent and the child. These three scores can be developed only for those scales for which attributional data are available. Because the two measures of religiosity lack the attributional component, only the objective differences are computed.

The decision to use difference scores requires that we take into account the correlations among these indicators of consensus. Some writers (e.g., Blau and Duncan, 1967) have criticized the use of difference-score correlations, arguing that the research problems are better stated in terms of partial correlations among the component variables. A particularly thorny problem arises when the two difference scores to be correlated share a common component. It can be shown that, even when the correlations among the components are zero, there still remains a null correlation that may be expressed in terms of the variances of the components (Fuguitt and Lieberson, 1974, p. 131). If, however, the research interest really lies in the *difference* scores—as in the present case—and not in relations among the components, then the null correlations need not be considered spurious (for a more complete discussion, see Fuguitt and Lieberson, 1974, especially pp. 130-134).

Table 7.7 presents the means and standard deviations of the absolute difference measures of consensus in the G1-G2 and G2-G3 dyadic relationships. For each scale, a score of zero indicates perfect consensus, with higher scores indicating progressively more dissension.

The most striking feature of Table 7.7 is the remarkable degree of agreement between the generations. In the G1-G2 relationship, objective differences are small for all five substantive dimensions. Moreover, for the three dimensions where the parent's view and the child's view can be computed, these perceived differences are smaller than the actual differences. Note, however, that the mean scores for the G1 perspective are consistently less than the mean scores for the G2 perspective.

In the G2-G3 relationship, objective differences are once again small. In this case, however, the G2 generation consistently perceives that the differences are less than the objective differences. From the G3 perspective, however, perceived differences are greater than objective differences for the conservatism and marriage norms dimension, and less than the objective difference for the legitimacy of black demands dimension. On the whole, these data indicate a substantial level of intrafamilial agreement on attitudinal matters.

Validity of Consensus Measures

The rather complex Table 7.8 presents an array of correlations that can be used as tests of the discriminant and convergent validity of the consensus measures in the G1-G2 relationship. Six of the subtables in Table 7.8 display the correlations of the three difference scores on one scale with the three difference scores on another scale, and hence constitute tests of discriminant validity. The three subtables above the

TABLE 7.7   Means and Standard Deviations: Absolute Difference Measures of Consensus

Item (theoretical range)	G1-G2 (N = 340)		G2-G3 (N = 369)	
	$\bar{X}$	sd	$\bar{X}$	sd
Conservatism (0-15):				
Objective difference	3.53	2.45	3.44	2.49
Parent's view	1.96	1.79	2.58	2.10
Child's view	3.07	2.42	4.17	3.02
Marriage norms (0-6):				
Objective difference	1.84	1.61	1.94	1.67
Parent's view	1.13	1.35	1.74	1.51
Child's view	1.60	1.53	2.08	1.61
Black demands (0-6):				
Objective difference	1.93	1.52	1.65	1.45
Parent's view	1.11	1.17	1.14	1.21
Child's view	1.69	1.60	1.56	1.46
Religious Belief (0-12)	2.51	2.41	2.88	2.59
Religious Practice (0-5)	1.32	1.22	1.00	0.95

main diagonal present the correlations of difference scores between the male G1 and his G2 offspring, while the three subtables below the diagonal present the correlations between the female G1 and her G2 offspring. Most of these correlations are quite low, suggesting that dissension in one domain is not linked to dissension in another domain. All notable exceptions involve the G2's view of the world, suggesting that the G2 occupies a position of defining the intrafamilial context of consensual solidarity.

The three diagonal subtables in Table 7.8 contain correlations between measurements of the same phenomena, and are thus tests of convergent validity. Entries above the diagonal refer to the G1 male, and entries below the diagonal refer to the G1 female. Thus, for example, the G1 father's *objective* difference with his G2 offspring in the area of conservatism correlates only slightly with the G1's *view* of that difference (r = 0.135). While many of these correlations are higher than those in the six off-diagonal subtables, only the three correlations of the G2 perception of consensus with father and the G2 perception of

TABLE 7.8 Convergent and Discriminant Validity Tests: Lineage Differences Between G2 and G1

	Political Conservatism			Marriage Norms			Legitimacy of Black Demands		
	G1→G2	G1←G2	G1—G2	G1→G2	G1←G2	G1—G2	G1→G2	G1←G2	G1—G2
C G1→G2	.114	.063	.135	.120	-.083	.042	.077	.174	.054
O G1←G2	.128	.849	.482	-.051	.266	.079	.050	.387	.068
N G1—G2	.159	.490	.457	-.082	.343	.066	.109	.097	.125
M G1→G2	.004	-.043	.036	-.037	-.029	.368	.024	-.024	-.141
A G1←G2	.009	.231	.177	.117	.829	.307	.034	.155	-.084
R G1—G2	.107	.080	.074	.225	.227	.257	.082	.113	-.015
B G1→G2	.205	.098	.075	-.042	-.092	.040	.214	.038	.178
L G1←G2	.026	.403	.176	-.013	.089	-.112	.017	.732	.235
K G1—G2	.036	.179	.140	-.075	-.125	-.123	.231	.195	.485

NOTE: Off-diagonal tables are discriminant validity tests. Correlations with the G1 father are above the diagonal; correlations with the G1 mother are below the diagonal. Diagonal tables are convergent validity tests. Each diagonal subtable is actually three tables overlayed to make one, with G1 Father-G2 comparisons above the diagonal and G1 Mother-G2 comparisons below the diagonal. Diagonal entries compare the G1 Father-G2 measures with G1 Mother-G2 measures.

G1→G2: G1's world: the absolute difference between G1 self-report and that attributed to G2.
G1←G2: G2's world: the absolute difference between G2 self-report and that attributed to G1.
G1—G2: Objective difference: the absolute difference between G1 and G2 self-reports.

consensus with mother (conservatism: r = 0.849; marriage norms: r = 0.829; black demands: r = 0.732) are as strong as usually anticipated in tests of convergent validity.

Table 7.9 presents similar data pertaining to the G2-G3 relationship. Here, the subtables *below* the diagonal refer to the relationship of G2 family member who is the child of the referent G1 (i.e., the member of the three-generation lineage) while the subtables *above* the diagonal refer to the spouse of the member of the lineage (i.e., an in-law to the referent G1 and parent to the sampled G3).[1] Once again, the six off-diagonal subtables are generally characterized by trivial correlations, indicating that consensus in one domain in not related to consensus in another domain.

Examination of the diagonal subtables in Table 7.9 reveals a pattern similar to that found in Table 7.8. While the convergent validity correlations are in general stronger than the discriminant validity entries found in the subtables that are off the diagonal, the only convergent validity tests that approach the standards normally expected are those that look at the G3's perspective of consensus with both of his parents (conservatism: r = 0.781; marriage norms: r = 0.830; black demands: r = 0.674).

The results presented in Tables 7.8 and Table 7.9 suggest that there may be difficulties in developing a summary measure of consensus in either of the two role relationships. The different dimensions of consensus do not correlate with one another, and there are few substantial correlations within one role occupant's perspective across dimensions.

LISREL Analysis

In order to model the covariances among the 11 indicators of consensus in both the G1-G2 and the G2-G3 relationships, we use the LISREL model (Jöreskog and Sörbom, 1981) to allow for correlated errors stemming from both the central position of the G2 in both relationships as well as any artifactual correlations that result from the differencing procedure used to derive the measures of consensus.[2] Based upon the results in Tables 7.8 and Table 7.9, we elect to use the multiple-groups component of LISREL and to ignore deliberately any possible covariances between G1-G2 consensus and G2-G3 consensus. The basic statistical hypothesis, stated in its alternative form, is that the variances

TABLE 7.9 Convergent and Discriminant Validity Tests: Lineage Differences Between G3 and G2

	Political Conservatism			Marriage Norms			Legitimacy of Black Demands		
	G2→G3	G2←G3	G2−G3	G2→G3	G2←G3	G2−G3	G2→G3	G2←G3	G2−G3
C G2→G3	.166	.108	.303	.060	.062	.012	.014	.173	.114
O G2←G3	.221	.781	.514	.003	.233	.139	.090	.412	.160
N G2−G3	.358	.426	.433	-.049	.139	.051	.025	.276	.260
M G2→G3	.188	.121	.045	.201	.110	.249	.064	-.034	-.047
A G2←G3	.101	.273	.096	.269	.830	.464	-.129	.023	-.035
R G2−G3	.171	.198	.076	.430	.434	.519	.055	.025	-.008
B G2→G3	.320	.087	.108	.120	-.014	.049	-.051	.101	.253
L G2←G3	.193	.338	.087	-.026	.059	.066	.163	.674	.425
K G2−G3	.115	.089	.174	-.005	-.011	-.048	.291	.262	.282

NOTE: Off-diagonal tables are discriminant validity tests. Diagonal tables are convergent validity tests. Correlations with the G2 spouse are above the diagonal; correlations with the G2 linemember are below the diagonal. Each diagonal subtable is actually three tables overlayed to make one, with G2 Spouse-G3 comparisons above the diagonal and G2 Linemember-G3 comparisons below the diagonal. Diagonal entries compare the G2 Spouse-G3 measures with G2 Linemember-G3 measures.

G2→G3: G2's world: the absolute difference between G2 self-report and that attributed to G3.
G2←G3: G3's world: the absolute difference between G3 self-report and that attributed to G2.
G2−G3: Objective difference: the absolute difference between G2 and G3 self-reports.

and covariances among the observed indicators are due to their common source in the unmeasured construct of consensus.

Table 7.10 presents the summary statistics for the different LISREL models that were estimated. The first three models (B_1-B_3) are all variations on a basic one-dimensional model tested for the G1-G2 relationship and the G2-G3 relationship. Model B_1 specifies full equality constraints between the two groups, that is, the coefficients are constrained to be equal for both the G1-G2 and G2-G3 relationships. Model B_2 relaxes the constraints on the error variances, allowing these to be unique in each of the groups. Model B_3 further relaxes the constraints on the measurement model and freely estimates all coefficients independently in each of the two groups. While each successive model is a statistically significant improvement upon the preceding model, none of the one dimensional models constitutes an acceptable model for further analysis. In particular, many of the measurement coefficients in the G1-G2 relationship are not statistically significant.

Models B_4-B_6 attempt to improve the model by estimating domain-specific models of consensus. Four dimensions are estimated in each of these models: (1) conservatism, (2) marriage norms, (3) black demands, and (4) religiosity. Model B_4 constrains all coefficients to equality across the two groups; model B_5 relaxes the constraints on the error variances, and model B_6 freely estimates all of the coefficients in the two groups. While the four-dimensional models are an improvement compared to the one-dimensional models, and each successive four-dimensional model is an improvement upon the preceding model, the parameter estimates obtained in the four-dimensional solutions are not plausible. In particular, negative variances are estimated for two of the underlying dimensions in the G1-G2 group, and the covariances among the dimensions in the G2-G3 group imply four correlations greater than 1.0.

Models B_7-B_9 present the same trio of analyses but use three dimensions: (1) parent's view of the relationship, (2) child's view of the relationship, and (3) objective consensus. The three-dimensional models are an improvement on the one-dimensional models, but are poorer than the four-dimensional models. Relaxing equality constraints across the two groups does indeed improve the fit, but these models also yield implausible parameter estimates. In the G2-G3 group, two of the three covariances among the three dimensions imply correlations greater than 1.0.

At this point, we elected to use the LISREL model in a more exploratory fashion to see if a more realistic solution could be obtained.

TABLE 7.10   Summary of LISREL Measurement Models:
Consensus Dimension

Model	Model Definition	χ^2	d.f.
B_1	1 Overall ξ Full Equality Constraints	541.36	110
B_2	1 Overall ξ Relax Constraints on Θ_δ	364.93	99
B_3	1 Overall ξ No Constraints	306.20	88
B_4	4 Conceptual ξ Full Equality Constraints	414.43	104
B_5	4 Conceptual ξ Relax Constraints on Θ_δ	250.41	93
B_6	4 Conceptual ξ No Constraints	172.89	76
B_7	3 Role-Based ξ Full Equality Constraints	498.73	107
B_8	3 Role-Based ξ Relax Constraints on Θ_δ	334.25	96
B_9	3 Role-Based ξ No Constraints	277.69	82
B_{10}	1 ξ: 6 Measures in G1-G2; 11 Measures in G2-G3	311.42	93
M_1	1 ξ: 6 Measures in G1-G2; 11 Measures in G2-G3 $\theta_{\delta_{1\ 5\ 4}}\ \theta_{\delta_{2\ 5\ 4}}$	245.99	91
M_2	1 ξ: 6 Measures in G1-G2; 11 Measures in G2-G3 $\theta_{\delta_{1\ 6\ 4}}\ \theta_{\delta_{2\ 6\ 4}}$	194.49	89
M_3	1 ξ: 6 Measures in G1-G2; 11 Measures in G2-G3 $\theta_{\delta_{1\ 9\ 1}}\ \theta_{\delta_{2\ 8\ 2}}$	169.63	87
M_4	1 ξ: 6 Measures in G1-G2; 11 Measures in G2-G3 $\theta_{\delta_{1\ 8\ 7}}\ \theta_{\delta_{2\ 8\ 7}}$	146.15	85

TABLE 7.10 Continued

Model	Model Definition	χ^2	d.f.
M_5	1 ξ: 6 Measures in G1-G2; 11 Measures in G2-G3 $\theta_{\delta_{1\,9\,2}} \theta_{\delta_{2\,9\,7}}$	126.07	83
M_6	1 ξ: 6 Measures in G1-G2; 11 Measures in G2-G3 $\theta_{\delta_{1\,9\,7}} \theta_{\delta_{2\,2\,1}}$	108.26	81
M_7	1 ξ: 6 Measures in G1-G2; 11 Measures in G2-G3 $\theta_{\delta_{2\,6\,5}}$	99.61	80
M_8	1 ξ: 6 Measures in G1-G2; 11 Measures in G2-G3 $\theta_{\delta_{2\,7\,1}}$	91.65	79
M_9	1 ξ: 5 Measures in G1-G2; 11 Measures in G2-G3 Constrain $\lambda_{1\,7\,1}$ to zero	94.63	80
M_{10}	1 ξ: 5 Measures in G1-G2; 10 Measures in G2-G3 Constrain $\lambda_{2\,7\,1}$ to zero	97.05	81
M_{11}	1 ξ: 5 Measures in G1-G2; 10 Measures in G2-G3 Constrain $\theta_{\delta_{1\,4\,4}}$ to 5.648	97.06	82

Because only the one-dimension model yields plausible parameter estimates, albeit with many nonsignificant coefficients, we returned to that model to develop a variation. In model B_{10}, while all eleven variables are retained in the model, the five nonsignificant coefficients in the G1-G2 measurement model are fixed at zero. These five coefficients link the following variables to the underlying dimension: (1) conservatism—parental view, (2) marriage norms—objective, (3) marriage norms—parental view, (4) black demands—parental view, and (5) religious practice—objective. The remaining coefficients in the G1-G2 group, as well as all coefficients in the G2-G3 group, are identical to the specifications of model B_3. In particular, note that the *variables* are not eliminated from the model; rather, the measurement coefficients are not estimated. The error variances for the five variables are estimated, suggesting that these five variables are simply random and unrelated to the underlying dimension of consensus.

Model B_{10} fits the observed variances and covariances nearly as well as model B_3 while using five fewer degrees of freedom. We use this model as the basic model of choice to estimate correlated errors in order to improve the fit of the model. Whenever possible, we estimate the same correlated error in both groups.[3]

The summary results reported in Table 7.10 for models M_1-M_8 document the order and contribution to improvement of fit that estimating correlated measurement errors provides. A total of six correlated errors are estimated for the G1-G2 group, while eight are required for the G2-G3 group. Estimating these coefficients substantially improves the fit of the model, ultimately yielding a model with χ^2 of only 91.65 with 79 degrees of freedom.

Of the six correlated errors in the G1-G2 group, two exclusively involve the three marriage norms variables, and another two address correlated residuals among the three black demands variables. These coefficients are understandable insofar as four of the λ coefficients constrained to zero in the G1-G2 measurement model are drawn from this group of variables, and thus the correlated errors are simply tapping residual covariation that was expected. The remaining two coefficients include both the child's view variable on black demands and one of the measures of consensus on issues of political conservatism. Both the objective conservatism measure and the parental view of consensus on conservatism are significantly related to the child's view of consensus on black demands.

All three of the possible error covariances among the marriage norms variables are estimated in the G2-G3 group, and two of the three black demands errors are also significant. Another correlated error ties the objective and parental view measures of consensus together. Because these six errors are within conceptual blocks, we interpret them as tapping residual covariances not explained by the single dimension. One of the remaining correlated errors links two of the objective consensus measures: conservatism and black demands. Another links the parental view of consensus on conservatism and black demands. These, we feel, are method bias correlations.

Inspection of the parameter estimates for model M_8 revealed, however, that λ coefficients linking objective black demands to the underlying dimension of consensus were no longer significant in either group, and that the error variance of the objective marriage norms measure in the G1-G2 group was greater than the original variance, implying negative explanation of that variable. Models M_9 and M_{10} constrain the nonsignificant λ coefficients in the measurement model to zero, and M_{11} constrains the problematic error variance to equal the original variance. These steps remove parameters from the model, and doing so does not significantly harm the overall fit of the model.

Table 7.11 presents the parameter estimates for model M_{11}. While the model fits the data, it is very apparent from inspection of the results that a substantial amount of random variation characterizes these consensus measures. In particular, note that the R^2 exceeds 0.20 for only three of the G1-G2 variables and two of the G2-G3 variables. The goodness of fit of the model is quite good, however, suggesting that whatever substantial covariances are present in the data are explained by this model.

For the conservatism, marriage norms, and black demands sets of variables, we can compare the magnitude of the λ coefficients within each set because all variables are expressed on a similar underlying scale. For each of these sets, inspection of the coefficients reveals that the child's view is the most important variable in defining the underlying dimension, and that it also has the greatest explained variance. We conclude, therefore, that intergenerational consensus is primarily defined not by the parent but rather by the child.

Comparing the models for the two dyads reveals a clear pattern. First, the role relationship defines a unique model of consensus. For the G1-G2 dyad, consensus is defined by only five variables. Three of these are the *child's view* measures, while the remaining two are both measures of *objective* consensus. For the G2-G3 dyad, however, ten variables define the structure of measurement. While, as noted above, the child's view dominates in defining the structure of measurement, the other measures contribute significantly to the consensus dimension. Clearly, the dyadic relationship exerts a statistical interaction on the structure of consensus.

The error covariances presented in Table 7.11 are, with one exception, positive. This suggests that the correlated errors are simply tapping residual covariances not explained by the single dimension. The one exception is $\theta_{\delta_{1,9,1}}$, which links errors of measurement in the child's view of consensus on black demands with objective consensus on conservatism in the G1-G2 dyad. From the perspective of the G2 child, increases in perceived consensus on black demands are associated with *decreased* objective consensus on conservatism.

TABLE 7.11   LISREL Estimates

Variable	G1-G2 Dyad			G2-G3 Dyad		
	Λ_x	Θ_δ	R^2	Λ_x	Θ_δ	R^2
Conservatism—Objective	1.000*	17.067	0.392	1.000*	36.355	0.227
Conservatism—Parental View	0.000	7.663	0.000	0.664	21.342	0.175
Conservatism—Child View	1.768	23.182	0.597	2.560	21.121	0.755
Marriage Norms—Objective	0.000	5.648	0.000	0.271	9.031	0.075
Marriage Norms—Parental View	0.000	2.844	0.002	0.144	3.972	0.050
Marriage Norms—Child View	0.230	3.972	0.146	0.350	7.272	0.143
Black Demands—Objective	0.000	4.991	0.004	0.000	3.772	0.005
Black Demands—Parental View	0.000	1.376	-0.000	0.071	2.246	0.030
Black Demands—Child View	0.422	4.559	0.302	0.244	3.286	0.169
Religious Belief—Objective	0.561	39.936	0.080	0.913	44.602	0.157
Religious Practice—Objective	0.000	2.773	0.000	0.059	0.904	0.037
Φ		10.980			9.935	

Error Covariances and Correlations	Covariance	Correlation	Covariance	Correlation
Marriage Norms—Objective with Marriage Norms—Parental View	1.532	0.383	2.647	0.442
Marriage Norms—Objective with Marriage Norms—Child View	1.401	0.296	3.466	0.428
Black Demands—Child View with Conservatism—Objective	-3.164	-0.359	Not Estimated	
Black Demands—Parental View with Conservatism—Parental View	Not Estimated		2.071	0.299
Black Demands—Objective with Black Demands—Parental View	0.492	0.188	0.745	0.256
Black Demands—Child View with Conservatism—Parental View	1.143	0.193	Not Estimated	
Black Demands—Child View with Black Demands—Objective	1.124	0.236	1.035	0.294
Conservatism—Parental View with Conservatism—Objective	Not Estimated		6.696	0.240
Marriage Norms—Child View with Marriage Norms—Parental View	Not Estimated		1.119	0.208
Black Demands—Objective with Conservatism—Objective	Not Estimated		2.309	0.197
Goodness of Fit Index	0.953		0.962	

*Coefficient fixed at 1.0 to establish the underlying scale.

Summary of Lineage Measurement

The results of the lineage measurement analyses are mixed. The data clearly show that, at least as measured in these data, there is a great deal of agreement with regard to attitudinal matters. There is so little variance on most of the derived consensus measures that it is possible that this has contributed to the difficulty in modeling a higher order construct of consensus: without variance there can be no covariance. As Tables 7.8 and Table 7.9 clearly demonstrate, there is scant covariation among the different conceptual blocks of consensus measures; indeed, there is little covariation *within* each block.

Some of these difficulties may stem from the procedures used in scoring the derived consensus measures. Use of the absolute value of the simple difference implies that a ten-point difference on the component scales is only twice as important as a five-point difference. Theoretically, one may argue that families can gloss over small differences, but when these differences become larger, they exert a disproportional effect upon the underlying concept. This would suggest that simply squaring the difference term used when deriving the consensus measures might improve the models. Perhaps the differencing should occur with the *items* that are the components of the scales as opposed to the derived scales. Yet another approach would involve computing the correlation between role occupants across items (see, e.g., Farber, 1957) as a measure of consensus. Alternatively, different measurement models such as multidimensional scaling may be required.

In summary, therefore, while a measure of consensus has emerged from these analyses, it does not have the characteristics of a strong measure. The measure is not consistent across types of dyadic relationships, and the component items of the derived measure are poorly explained. While work obviously remains to be done with this measure, it is also apparent that the core concept—consensus—is present in the data. Researchers interested in using an approach similar to the one presented here should focus on the conservatism dimension to develop measures of objective and subjective consensus, or use a single-item indicator of perceived similarity of views between the generations.

Future Measurement

The preceding section makes several suggestions that might improve the quality of measurement of consensus. Implicit in those suggestions is the assumption that the basic underlying strategy—that of first measuring sociopolitical attitudes and attributions and then deriving measures of consensus—is the correct strategy for developing good measures of consensus. In this concluding section, we suggest an alternative strategy.

This chapter, and indeed this entire book, is a testament to our fundamental belief in the appropriateness of using strategies of indirect measurement. The generation-level measurement reported in the first part of this chapter is characteristic of this approach. We cannot directly measure, for example, religiosity, but we can ask several questions that address various facets of religious beliefs and from that we *infer* religiosity indirectly. Thus, as is characteristic of the scientific process, we introduce a level of abstraction into the data. When, however, we develop domain-specific consensus measures by using *any* scoring procedure, we introduce yet another level of abstraction into the data, and attempting to model an overall dimension of consensus yields still another abstraction. The point here is that perhaps we have abstracted too far; it may be necessary to return to a somewhat more direct approach.

Indeed, a more direct approach is suggested by a longstanding tradition in sociological thought—conflict theory. If we consider not consensus but dissension, then use of indirect measurement with only one level of abstraction may indeed be appropriate. Asking family members about how frequently they disagree with a referent family member about issues of child rearing, politics, sexuality, religion, and so on can provide the baseline data to infer dissension in the family. Note too that dissension in this sense cannot be equated with the absence of affect. One may trust, respect, understand, and care about another while still *disagreeing* with them about many matters.

In summary, therefore, we suggest that other researchers approach the measurement of consensus with a careful eye to some of the problems that our analysis has uncovered. We were not as successful as we had hoped, although we believe that our measures begin to address the core of the consensus concept. Both methodological and theoretical work remains to be done in order to develop sound measures of intergenerational family consensus.

NOTES

1. Table 7.9 is arrayed in this way to match as closely as possible the parents' genders used in Table 7.8. That is, G2 linemembers are disproportionately female, by a factor of about two to one. Thus in comparisons between Table 7.8 and Table 7.9, child-to-mother

relationships are for the most part in the lower-left and child-to-father relationships in the upper-right portions of the table. Because the G2 lineage members were not uniformly mother or father, and because later analyses will use only linemembers, we found it necessary to array the data for this table in this rather complex manner.

2. Version 6.9 of PC LISREL was used to estimate these models.

3. In Table 7.10, models M_1 through M_{11} include references to specific coefficients that are estimated or constrained in the LISREL solution. These parameters include three subscripts. The first subscript refers to the *group* for which the coefficient is estimated or constrained. Group 1 is the G1-G2 dyad, while group 2 is the G2-G3 dyad. The second and third subscripts refer to the specific parameter in the LISREL model for that group.

8

The Exchange
Dimension of Solidarity

Measuring Intergenerational
Exchange and Functional Solidarity

PAULA HANCOCK
DAVID J. MANGEN
KAY YOUNG McCHESNEY

The exchange of money, goods, and services is a key aspect of family solidarity. Historically, families have played a major economic role in the lives of individuals. Up until the time of widespread industrialization, the family was the unit of production; the individual's survival was dependent upon economic cooperation and coordination within the family unit. As the production of goods and services within the home and on family property was taken over by factory production, wages replaced family production as the source of survival.

In present times, economic cooperation among family members is no longer the vital element in individual survival. Individuals, however, do depend to a degree on exchanges of goods and services with others. Often this occurs within the family. Family members share goods and services and serve one another as reliable sources of continuing human contact, emotional support, and confidant relationships (Hagestad, 1981). Shanas (1978) found that over 80% of the bedfast elderly at home depend primarily on family members for meals, housework, and personal aid. Sussman (1965) and Blenkner (1965) point out that individuals and nuclear families exist in a *network* of kin relations and that the major activities of this network are mutual aid and social activities.

Conceptualization

In this research, *exchange* is defined as the giving and receiving of assistance among family members of different generations. While conceptually appealing, intragenerational support is *not* included in this definition. The focus is on the amount of assistance people give to and receive from the intergenerational family system. Giving and receiving is an aspect of interdependence among family members. Thus exchange is a component of family solidarity that is both a cause and consequence of other aspects of family dynamics. Power, equity, and justice in families are all intertwined with issues of exchange (Nye, 1979).

Emerson (1972b) views exchange relationships in terms of power and dependence, and looks to alternative resources as one mechanism that balances these relationships over time. An unequal power distribution in exchange relationships is unstable—implying a lack of cohesion—and individuals utilize alternative resources to gain or restore a balance of power. Other mechanisms include withdrawal, status giving, and coalition formation. All of these mechanisms involve the manipulation of resources and alternatives in the exchange relationship. Thus the notion of power and alternative modes of action is central to the exchange framework. Power may be a determinant in the beginning of an exchange relationship, but through the balancing mechanisms available to the dependent person, power dissipates over time.

Implicit to Emerson's (1972b) discussion of exchange processes is a focus on voluntary relationships among persons. Relationships among family members are not always characterized by this voluntary component. This is clearly evident in the relationship of young children to their parents, but is also seen in the relationships among adult family members. Cromwell and Olson (1975) identify normatively prescribed rights as a structural component of power in families. The norms governing family relationships influence the operation of Emerson's (1972b) balancing mechanisms. While adult family members may, for example, form coalitions or disown another family member, the social consequences of taking these actions are significant.

Thus power is an important process to be explained within families in order to analyze fully the exchanges of goods, services, and money that take place. Need for exchanges does not in and of itself explain why assistance is provided; other factors operate as well.

Exchange theory highlights two other aspects of relationships, reciprocity and distributive justice, that require attention when examining intergenerational exchanges of assistance and support. Gouldner (1960) states that if a social system is to be stable, there must be "mutuality of gratification." In other words, stability or solidarity depends on reciprocity. The norm of reciprocity in its most general form implies that people should help those who have helped them, and should not injure those who have helped them. Thus reciprocity does not imply equality in exchange. Reciprocity simply means that some amount is given and some amount is received; these amounts are not necessarily (or even usually) equal. The rough equivalence found in exchange induces a certain amount of ambiguity that over time generates doubt as to who is indebted to whom. This ambiguity contributes to the cohesiveness of the relationship.

Distributive justice (Homans, 1974) is an acknowledgment of fairness in reward allocations. It is a comparison of one's own situation with a referential structure, and addresses the issue of the equality of exchanges. In families, perceptions of fairness may be based on the normative structure of that family, that is, what family members should in general do for each other. Individuals compare their own situations with the generalized other's family situation to determine if fairness exists. The absence of justice causes strain, which causes pressure to correct the situation. Thus the greater the feelings of distributive justice, the greater the family solidarity.

When looking at exchanges between generations within families, it is complicated to assess equity objectively. Stage of life must be considered. The ability to give and the need to receive is largely contingent on life cycle stage. As Hill et al. (1970) found, the middle generation is the donor generation in terms of money. This is the time of life when earnings reach their peak; the family member at this stage of life is most able to assist financially other family members whose earnings are declining due to aging and retirement (G1), or whose careers have not yet stabilized (G3). Money may implicitly or explicitly be given in exchange for services, while services may be given in exchange for future benefits (e.g., inheritance, for other services, or to pay off a past debt).

Previous literature suggests that reciprocity takes place over the life cycle rather than immediately. When parents become aged, children fulfill the filial role by taking responsibility for the physical needs of their parents (Blenkner, 1965). Hagestad (1981) also suggests that the balancing of exchanges must be viewed across generations and over time.

To summarize, *exchange* is nominally defined as the giving and receiving of assistance among family members of different generations. While need and interdependence play an important role in the content and direction of exchanges, family power, reciprocity, and distributive justice also influence the nature and duration of the exchanges.

Operational Definitions

With the data included in this study, power, and individuals' perceptions of fairness and justice cannot be assessed. Measures of the overall frequency of service and gift exchanges, and the degree of financial support, however, can be assessed. Thus this study can only inferentially address the degree of reciprocity between the generations in their exchanges.

In assessing the degree of solidarity within families, three criteria can be examined: (1) Is any assistance taking place? (2) Is the assistance reciprocated? (3) What is the level or degree of balance in the exchanges?

Operationally, *intergenerational exchanges* are defined in material terms as the exchange of gifts, services, and money within three-generation families. This definition is consistent with past research that has examined family support systems, although not exhaustive of the range of possibilities. Adams (1968) defines *exchange* in terms of advice, money, gifts, services, and help in job placement. Cantor (1975, 1976) and Mayer (1976) see exchanges as consisting of money, gifts, services, and advice. Hill et al. (1970) look at exchanges of money, goods, services, and advice within families. The National Council on Aging's (1975) definition is congruent with all of the above, with the added component of providing shelter. Finally, Streib and Schneider (1971) use exchanges of money, advice, services, and providing shelter.

Because data are available from three generations regarding the frequency of exchanges and, for the items referencing financial assistance, the degree of financial support provided, the degree of assistance can be directly assessed. The degree of reciprocity and justice are inferred from the frequency measures through analysis of correlational patterns among the indicators.

Generational-Level Analysis

At the generational level of analysis, each generation is asked five questions about the referent role relationship(s). The eldest generation (G1) is asked five questions about the referent child (G2). The G2 is asked thirteen questions, three each in reference to the G1 father and mother, two questions with regard to the G1 marital dyad, and five questions with reference to the child (G3). The G3 is asked three questions each regarding the G2 mother and father, and two regarding the couple, for a total of eight questions. The questions address the following subjects: (1) giving financial assistance, (2) receiving financial assistance, (3) giving service assistance, (4) receiving service assistance, and (5) exchange of gifts. The financial assistance items are scored on a four-point ordinal scale ranging from (1) not at all to (4) regular, primary source of support. The service assistance items are scored on an eight-point ordinal scale of frequency ranging from (1) almost never to (8) almost every day.[1]

Table 8.1 presents the univariate statistics and correlations for G1 males and females on the five exchange items referencing the G2 child. For both grandfathers and grandmothers, the giving and receiving of financial assistance is rare. The mean scores indicate that financial assistance does not flow between the generations. There is little variation as well, reflecting the overall financial well-being of this middle-class sample. Slightly more than 60% of both males and females in the G1 report that they never give money to the G2, and approximately three-fourths report that they never receive money from the G2.[2] This group of elderly is more likely to report giving rather than receiving financial assistance from their children. Both male and female G1 family members report approximately the same amount of financial assistance.

Reported instances of service assistance are somewhat more prevalent, but still suggest a high level of independence. Both males and females report that they are slightly more likely to be the recipient rather than the provider of instrumental assistance, and these exchanges occur slightly more than once a year. Using the ratio of the provider means to the recipient means as indicators of aggregate perceived reciprocity gives ratios close to 1.0, indicating balance. The differences between giving and receiving, as well as the differences between males and females, are quite small. Again, these data do not support an image of the older generation as dependent upon their children for assistance. Rather, a high level of independence with substantial perceived justice is the norm.

TABLE 8.1   Correlations, Means, and Standard Deviations of
Individual G1 Reports of Money, Help, and Gifts
Exchanged with Children (G2) by Gender

	EXCH5	EXCH6	CAS11	CAS12	CAS10	Females $\overline{X}$ σ
Give Money Child (EXCH5)		−.0176	.2289**	.1837*	.0605	1.226 0.465
Receive Money Child (EXCH6)	_.0495		.0456	.0237	.0058	1.024 0.179
Give Help Child (CAS11)	.1572*	−.0047		.6692**	.3908**	2.014 1.538
Receive Help Child (CAS12)	.0602	.1755*	.6029**		.3043**	2.223 1.577
Exchange Gifts Child (CAS10)	−.0029	.0301	.1783*	.1860*		2.802 0.747
Males: $\overline{X}$	1.286	1.034	2.071	2.170	2.619	
σ	0.531	0.221	1.536	1.545	0.822	

NOTE: This table is based on 516 G1s: 250 females (above diagonal) and 266 males (below diagonal). Due to missing data, correlations are based on a minimum number of 218 and a maximum number of 247 cases for females and on a minimum number of 223 and a maximum number of 261 cases for males.
*Correlation significant at the $p < 0.05$ level.
**Correlation significant at the $p < 0.001$ level.

The correlations among the five indicators of exchange in the G1 reveal gender variations. For males, the giving of financial assistance is weakly related to giving service assistance, and receiving financial assistance is weakly related to receiving instrumental aid. Giving and receiving service assistance is strongly correlated (r = 0.6029), though the two service assistance variables display weak but statistically significant correlations with gift exchange. All significant correlations are positive, suggesting a pattern of reciprocity.

For G1 females, giving financial assistance to the child is weakly correlated with both giving and receiving service assistance, but receipt of financial assistance is not related to any of the other exchange indicators.[3] The giving and receiving of service assistance are strongly correlated ($r = 0.6692$), and these are moderately related to gift exchange. The relatively greater strength of the female gift exchange correlations suggests a greater integration of the G1 female into the intergenerational family system. Again, all significant correlations are positive.

Table 8.2 presents the univariate statistics and bivariate correlations among the 13 measures of exchange for the G2 males and females. For both men and women, the G2 report giving and receiving very little financial aid with the G1, and the mean scores approximate the means reported by the G1 (see Table 8.1).

With regard to instrumental assistance, G2 males and females report that they give slightly more than they receive from their parents, although the differences are small. In this sample, service exchanges are relatively rare. Means for the G2 range from 1.917 to 2.811, indicating an average range of once a year to approximately four times a year. Recall that the G1 family members in this study are relatively well off; they are not the frail elderly. G2 females are more involved in giving and receiving than are their male counterparts. Male G2 family members give service assistance equally to their mothers and fathers, while the G2 females are more likely to give and receive service assistance in their relationships with their mothers. The G2 male is more likely to receive assistance from his father than his mother. On the whole, these data demonstrate that the G2 male is involved in the support network of his parents, but at a lower level than the G2 female (e.g., Brody, 1978, 1981).

Gift exchange between the G1 and G2 occurs on average less than every other month (X range of 2.454 to 2.774) and the G1 concurs in the frequency of gift exchanges (see Table 8.1). G2 females exchange more frequently than do G2 males. Exchanges with mothers are more frequent than exchanges with fathers, although these differences are small.

The correlations among the eight G2 items regarding the G1 demonstrate small gender variations. For the G2 females, giving financial assistance to parents is not related to any of the other measures of exchange. For G2 males, however, giving financial assistance to parents is positively correlated with giving instrumental assistance to both mother and father. For both males and females in the G2, the receipt of financial assistance from parents is positively correlated with the giving *and* receiving of instrumental services to both parents. Interestingly, the correlations are marginally greater for the G2 males than the G2 females.

When examining the correlations among the four service assistance variables, a clear pattern of relationship is demonstrated for both males and females. The average correlation for the males is 0.699, and 0.634 for females. These strong correlations suggest that G1 and G2 family members in this sample develop strong patterns of reciprocity with regard to service assistance.

The correlations of the four service assistance variables with the two gift exchange variables in the G1-G2 relationship are moderately strong and positive for both males and females. If the G1-G2 relationship is characterized by patterns of service assistance, it will likely be characterized by gift exchange as well. As expected, the giving of gifts to a father is strongly correlated with giving gifts to a mother.

The data in Table 8.2 demonstrate that financial and instrumental exchanges are much more prevalent in the G2-G3 than in the G1-G2 relationship. Financial assistance is likely to be asymmetrical: G2 parents give money to their adolescent or young adult children, but are unlikely to receive much financial assistance. Service assistance is also more prevalent in the G2-G3 relationship, because a substantial percentage of the G3 still live with their parents. Balance characterizes the instrumental exchanges, with approximately equal mean scores reported by the G2 females, and the G2 males reporting slightly greater receipt of services from their offspring. More assistance is given and received by the G2 mother, however, illustrating the greater importance of the maternal role in the family.[4]

Providing greater financial assistance to children is moderately related to giving and receiving increased service assistance for both males and females. Receiving financial assistance from the child is weakly related to instrumental aid patterns, although these correlations are statistically significant. The two measures of service assistance are strongly correlated, suggesting instrumental reciprocity. Gift exchanges are moderately correlated with service assistance for both males and females. For G2 males, providing financial assistance is slightly related to the frequency of gift exchange. This relationship is not noted for the G2 females.

TABLE 8.2 Correlations, Means, and Standard Deviations of Individual G2 Reports of Money, Help, and Gifts Exchanged with Parents (G1) and Children (G3) by Gender

	EXCH1	EXCH3	MAS11	MAS12	FAS11	FAS12	MAS10	FAS10	EXCH5	EXCH6	CAS11	CAS12	CAS10	Females Mean s.d.
Give Money Parents (EXCH1)		-.045	.087	-.002	.070	-.084	.064	-.018	.036	-.044	-.055	-.067	.000	1.088 / 0.323
Receive Money Parents (EXCH3)	-.011		.124*	.131*	.154*	.123*	.053	.074	-.029	-.048	.010	-.004	.066	1.168 / 0.404
Give Help Mother (MAS11)	.228**	.204**		.646**	.778**	.563**	.303**	.307**	.085	.015	.161*	.126*	.114*	2.811 / 1.834
Receive Help Mother (MAS12)	-.012	.327**	.658**		.495**	.649**	.308**	.320**	.135*	.060	.224**	.217**	.124*	2.525 / 1.754
Give Help Father (FAS11)	.162*	.143*	.904**	.579**		.670**	.294**	.311**	.017	-.044	.099*	.078	.099*	2.413 / 1.712
Receive Help Father (FAS12)	-.016	.218**	.635	.692	.723		.175	.212**	.073	.024	.090	.110*	.019	2.235 / 1.618
Exchange Gifts Mother	.071	.086	.333**	.190*	.361**	.265**		.824**	.077	.014	.095	.121*	.281**	2.774 / 0.625

Correlation matrix (above diagonal = females, below diagonal = males):

	MAS10	FAS10	EXCH5	EXCH6	CAS11	CAS12	CAS10	Female Mean	Female s.d.
(MAS10)		.218**	.358**	.224**	.388**	.303**	.843**	2.681	0.636
Exchange Gifts Father (FAS10)	.097		.047	-.056	.224**	.518**	.553**	2.944	1.174
Give Money Child (EXCH5)	.040	-.008		.039	.168*	.153*	.096*	1.089	0.346
Receive Money Child (EXCH6)	.048	.098	.212**		.114	.387**	.844*	5.108	2.361
Give Help Child (CAS11)	.053	.020	.162*	.150*		.783**	.263**	5.194	2.361
Receive Help Child (CAS12)	.037	.007	.237**	.117*	.257**		.269**	2.986	0.559
Exchange Gifts Child (CAS10)	.017	.050	.142*	.151*	.027	.325**		2.777	0.628

Males:

	MAS10	FAS10	EXCH5	EXCH6	CAS11	CAS12	CAS10
Mean:	1.174	1.124	2.310	1.917	2.307	2.108	2.472
s.d.	0.495	0.342	1.464	1.320	1.508	1.468	0.675

Additional means/s.d. printed: 2.454 / 0.694, 2.969 / 1.152, 1.069 / 0.289, 3.959 / 2.242, 4.300 / 2.379, 2.777 / 0.628.

NOTE: This table is based on 701 G2s: 379 females (above diagonal) and 322 males (below diagonal). Due to missing data, correlations are based on a minimum number of 249 and a maximum number of 370 cases for females and on a minimum number of 180 and a maximum number of 318 cases for males.

*Correlation significant at the $p < 0.05$ level.
**Correlation significant at the $p < 0.001$ level.

165

To this point, the analysis of Table 8.2 has examined only those relationships, from the perspective of the G2, *within* the G1-G2 or G2-G3 role relationships. A substantial proportion of Table 8.2 presents correlations *between* the measures of the two relationships. Most of these correlations are trivial; however, several patterns are manifest.

The first pattern concerns service assistance. For both males and females in the G2, the giving and receiving of assistance with a G1 mother is moderately correlated with giving and receiving assistance with the G3 child. To a lessor extent, this is also true of assistance to and from the G1 father.

The second pattern concerns gift exchanges. If a family is characterized by gift exchanges with parents, it is also likely to give gifts to its children. Giving instrumental assistance to parents, although not receiving assistance from the parent, is positively correlated with gift giving to the child.

Finally, two interesting correlations are present in the male portion of the matrix. Receipt of financial assistance from the child is moderately correlated with giving ($r = 0.224$) and receiving ($r = 0.212$) instrumental assistance with the G1 mother, although not the father.

Table 8.3 presents similar data for the eight G3 questions asked in reference to the G2.[5] As expected, the G3 provides very little financial assistance to the G2, while the G2 provides substantial financial assistance to the G3. Service aid is frequently exchanged by both generations, with G2 mothers being the most frequent providers and recipients of such assistance. Both male and female G3 family members concur in this perception. Gift exchange between the generations occurs regularly. Indeed, a review of the mean scores for all the gift exchange variables in Tables 8.1 through 8.3 reveals that generational position influences gift giving very little; all of these mean scores are in the range of 2.5 to 3.0.

Analysis of the correlations in Table 8.3 reveals a now-expected pattern. For both males and females, the correlations among the service assistance variables are very strong, suggesting a pattern of perceived reciprocity between the generations. Gift giving to one parent is strongly related to giving to the other parent, and moderately related to the provision of service assistance. For the G3, however, the frequency of receiving financial assistance is more strongly correlated with service assistance than is true in any of the other generations, and stronger here for G3 females than males. In part, this is due to the presence of some variability in the financial assistance measures for the G3 that is lacking

TABLE 8.3 Correlations, Means and Standard Deviations of Individual G3 Reports of Money, Help, and Gifts Exchanged with Parents (G2) by Gender

	EXCH1	EXCH3	MAS11	MAS12	FAS11	FAS12	MAS10	FAS10	Females $\bar{X}$ σ
Give Money Parents (EXCH1)		.0024	.1504**	.0943*	.0968*	.0969*	.0774	.0736	1.220 0.447
Receive Money Parents (EXCH3)	.0104		.5115**	.4605**	.4436**	.4023**	.0863*	.1362*	2.698 1.226
Give Help Mother (MAS11)	.1627**	.3897**		.7468**	.6966**	.5283**	.2227**	.1536**	5.498 2.326
Receive Help Mother (MAS12)	.1275*	.2654**	.7323**		.5377**	.6098**	.2582**	.1554**	4.973 2.488
Give Help Father (FAS11)	.1796**	.3184**	.7429**	.5840**		.7231**	.1976**	.2520**	4.138 2.337
Receive Help Father (FAS12)	.1272*	.1631**	.5538**	.6424**	.7362**		.1696**	.3027**	3.833 2.255
Exchange Gifts Mother (MAS10)	.0904*	.0447	.3132**	.3039**	.2760**	.2965**		.6099**	2.842 0.744
Exchange Gifts Father (FAS10)	.0115	.0658	.1915**	.1492*	.2348**	.2846**	.6465**		2.694 0.756
Males $\bar{X}$	1.283	2.574	4.956	4.320	4.524	3.897	2.725	2.578	
σ	0.496	1.126	2.352	2.446	2.231	2.280	0.913	0.807	

NOTE: This table is based on 827 G3s: 442 females (above diagonal) and 385 males (below diagonal). Due to missing data, correlations are based on a minimum number of 373 and a maximum number of 428 cases for females and on a minimum number of 324 and a maximum number of 372 cases for males.
*Correlation significant at the $p < 0.05$ level.
**Correlation significant at the $p < 0.001$ level.

for the G1 and G2. In addition, many of the G3 are still dependent upon their parents and share their homes.

Analysis of the correlation matrices presented in Tables 8.1 through 8.3 clearly indicates that financial assistance, service assistance, and gift giving are phenomenologically different aspects of the exchange process within generations. Moreover, financial assistance in the G1-G2 dyad, and G2 receipt of financial assistance from the G3, are extremely rare. Therefore, we restrict the analysis of the measurement structure at the generational level to the correlational analysis presented, recognizing that factor analysis is not justified with the limited item pool and the lack of variance in the financial assistance measures. Moreover, reliability analysis is redundant given the greater detail of information presented in the correlation matrices (Mangen, Peterson, and Sanders, 1982).

Analysis of validity is, however, a different matter. Given the lack of variability in the financial assistance measures, two conclusions are possible. First, and we believe most likely, financial assistance is rare in this middle-class sample of predominantly young-old G1 family members. It is plausible that significantly different results would be obtained with an older sample when using the same items. Second, it is quite likely that the items assessing financial assistance are too restricted in that these items focus upon financial *support* and do not assess emergency assistance and the like. Of course, by its very definition, emergency support is presumed to be intermittent, and thus would also manifest small variances.

With regard to service assistance, the limited set of items used in this study are clearly insufficient to assess the range of possible supports that might occur. Recall error tends to decrease with added prompts (Sudman and Bradburn, 1974), and detailed prompts were not used in this study. We discuss the issue of content validity in greater depth later in this chapter following the lineage-level analysis of the current data.

Lineage Analysis of Service Exchange

The lineage analysis of exchange emphasizes the service assistance component for two reasons. First, the absence of variance in the financial exchange measures (except for the G3 receipt of assistance) and covariation among them yields data that are not amenable to dimensional analysis. Second, the gift exchange data are eliminated because the questions do not specify the directionality of gift giving, and as a result are not as specific as the service assistance measures. The data in the exchange analysis are drawn from the overlapping triads file with a total sample size of 522; after elimination of missing data, the covariance matrix used in the LISREL model is based on 405 lineage triads with complete information.[6]

Movement to the lineage analysis requires minor redefinition of the variables. Rather than looking at the amount of assistance given to a mother, father, or child, the variables in the lineage file are linked to the other members included in that lineage. For example, if a triad includes a G1 female, a G2 male, and a G3 female, we include G1 items addressing the relationship with the referenced G2 male, G2 items about his relationship with his G1 mother and the referenced G3 child, and G3 items on service assistance with her father. Thus the analysis focuses on the referenced role relationships within the lineage under examination.

The LISREL analysis examines six primary, theoretical models for explanation of the covariances among the eight indicators. These models are labeled M1-M6 in Table 8.4. The first model suggests that exchange is a lineage-level property. If one relationship is characterized by exchanges, so too will the others, with the result that only one dimension (ξ) is required to explain the data. Table 8.4 presents the summary results for the 1 ξ and other models. As anticipated, this model fits the data poorly ($\chi^2 = 1188.83$, d.f. = 20).

The second model examines the data from the perspective of each *respondent* providing data about each relationship. The Respondent-Based Measures model requires 4 ξ to explain the data, with each ξ defined by the items of one respondent in reference to another member of the lineage. Thus ξ_1 is defined by the G1 items about *giving to* and *receiving from* the G2, with the three other dimensions examining the G2 perspective on the G1, the G2 perspective on the G3, and the G3 perspective on the G2. This model explains the data quite well ($\chi^2 = 96.91$, d.f. = 14).

The third model also requires 4 ξ to explain the data, but the items defining each dimension suggest that it is more appropriate to refer to this as the Role-Based Measures model. In this model, each dimension is defined by the *exchanges received by each generation*. In short, this model theorizes that exchange is an objective, observable phenomenon, evaluated unidirectionally in each role relationship. Two variables define each dimension. For example, the *G1 Receives Assistance* dimension is composed of two items: (1) how often G1 says she or he

TABLE 8.4 Summary of LISREL Measurement Models:
Service Exchange Data

Model		x^2	d.f.	Ratio x^2 to d.f.	Goodness of Fit
M1.	1 ξ	1188.83	20	59.44	0.587
M2.	4 ξ Respondent-based measures	96.81	14	6.92	0.942
	One correlated error $\theta_{\delta_{43}}$	50.24	13	3.86	0.970
	Two correlated errors $\theta_{\delta_{43}}$ $\theta_{\delta_{65}}$	21.65	12	1.80	0.987
M3.	4 ξ Role-based measures	369.07	14	26.36	0.844
M4.	2 ξ Parallel measures	496.42	31	16.01	0.773
M5.	2 ξ Tau equivalence	456.91	25	18.28	0.783
M6.	2 ξ Congeneric measures	386.77	19	20.36	0.836
	One correlated error $\theta_{\delta_{76}}$	177.82	18	9.88	0.907
	Two correlated errors $\theta_{\delta_{76}}$ $\theta_{\delta_{32}}$	102.02	17	6.00	0.939
	Three correlated errors $\theta_{\delta_{76}}$ $\theta_{\delta_{32}}$ $\theta_{\delta_{43}}$	54.22	16	3.39	0.967
	Four correlated errors $\theta_{\delta_{76}}$ $\theta_{\delta_{32}}$ $\theta_{\delta_{43}}$ $\theta_{\delta_{87}}$	27.05	15	1.80	0.984

receives from G2, and (2) how often G2 says she or he *gives* to G1. Other dimensions include G2 Receives from G1, G2 Receives from G3, and G3 Receives from G2. This model uses exactly the same degrees of freedom as the Respondent-Based Measures reported above, but fits the data less well (x^2 = 369.07, d.f. = 14). Inspection of the parameters in this model revealed extremely large covariances among the underlying dimensions in the Φ matrix. Specifically, the *giving* and *receiving* dimensions in each of the two examined role relationships were highly related to one another.

The large covariances among the dimensions suggest a set of three additional models that are presented in Table 8.4. In each of these models, 2 ξ are used to explain the data. Four variables define each dimension, with both generations' reports of giving *and* receiving to the other generation included. Thus the dimensions are (1) frequency of G1-G2 exchange (1), and (2) frequency of G2-G3 exchange (ξ_1). Note that the *direction* of the service assistance is irrelevant to the construction of these dimensions, implying reciprocity although not necessarily distributive justice.

The different two ξ models differ in assumptions regarding coefficients in Λ_x and Θ_δ. The Parallel Measures and Tau Equivalence models equate nonzero coefficients in Λ_x within any ξ, in this case equal to 1.0 because one coefficient is set to 1.0 for definition of a common scale. The Parallel Measures model adds the constraint of equating the error variances as well. Thus because X_1 through X_4 define ξ_1 and X_5 through X_8 define ξ_2, then $\theta_{\delta_{11}} = \theta_{\delta_{22}} = \theta_{\delta_{33}} = \theta_{\delta_{44}}$ and $\theta_{\delta_{55}} = \theta_{\delta_{66}} = \theta_{\delta_{77}} = \theta_{\delta_{88}}$. The Congeneric Measures model removes both of these constraints, and freely estimates the coefficients in Λ_x and Θ_δ. (See also the discussion of these models in Chapter 3 of this book.)

The summary statistics for the three variations of the two ξ model are presented in Table 8.4. The restrictive Parallel Measures model uses very few degrees of freedom, but fits the data poorly ($\chi^2 = 496.42$, d.f. = 31) in comparison to the four models. The Tau Equivalence model relaxes assumptions about Θ_δ and uses six more degrees of freedom to reduce χ^2 by 39.51. While this is a significant improvement (p $<$ 0.001), the ratio of χ^2 to degrees of freedom and the Goodness of Fit Index clearly suggest that improvements are possible. Indeed, relaxing the constraints on Λ_x for the Congeneric Measures model reduces χ^2 substantially while again using six degrees of freedom ($\chi^2 = 386.77$, d.f. = 19).

Determining the best model among the six major variations requires examination of a number of statistics for the different models. Of the two ξ models, the Congeneric Measures model is clearly best at explaining the data by virtue of its lower χ^2 and higher Goodness of Fit index. Comparison to the four ξ models is less clear, however. The values of χ^2 are lower for each of the four ξ models, and the Goodness of Fit indexes are higher. The four ξ models, however, each use five more degrees of freedom due to estimating more coefficients in the Φ matrix.

Inspection of modification indices and first-order derivatives suggests that the Congeneric Measures model can be substantially improved by estimating correlated measurement errors, with some improvement possible for each of the four ξ models. Given these conflicting data, we elect to examine further modifications for two models: (1) the 4 ξ Respondent-Based Measures model (selected because χ^2 is lowest), and (2) the two ξ Congeneric Measures model (selected because several modification indices are large).

Two correlated errors are estimated for the four ξ Respondent-Based Measures model. Both are theoretically relevant. The first is the error covariance of *G1 Receives from G2* with *G2 Gives to G1* ($\theta_{\delta_{43}}$). The second error covariance relates *G2 Receives from G3* with *G3 Gives to G2* ($\theta_{\delta_{65}}$). Estimating these coefficients is clearly tapping residual covariation across people in the lineages with respect to receipt of assistance by the *older generation* in the role relationship. Each coefficient is significant, and the χ^2 for the model is substantially reduced ($\chi^2 = 21.65$, d.f. = 12, p = 0.042). While this model fits the data very well, estimation of λ_{82} would reduce χ^2 significantly. It is difficult, however, to interpret this cross-loading.

A total of four error covariances are estimated for the two ξ Congeneric Measures model. Once again, all are theoretically relevant and address either within-person or within-phenomenon residual covariation. The first error covariance is a within-person covariance that involves the two G3 items regarding patterns of assistance with the G2 ($\theta_{\delta_{76}}$). Estimating this coefficient substantially improves the fit of the model, reducing χ^2 by over 200 and improving the Goodness of Fit statistic.

The second within-person error covariance involves the two G1 items on assistance with the G2 ($\theta_{\delta_{32}}$). Estimating this coefficient reduces χ^2 to 102.02 and improves the Goodness of Fit statistic to 0.939. While the model is clearly better, analysis of residuals and the ratio of χ^2 to degrees of freedom suggest that the model can be improved.

The third and fourth error covariances are across-people but within-phenomena. The first ($\theta_{\delta_{43}}$) addresses the amount of assistance received by the G1. Estimating this coefficient reduces χ^2 significantly and improves the goodness of fit to 0.967. The final error covariance added to the model addresses the G3's receipt of assistance ($\theta_{\delta_{87}}$). Estimating this error term reduces χ^2 to only 27.05 with 15 degrees of freedom (p = 0.028). The goodness of fit is excellent (0.984), and the ratio of χ^2 to degrees is only 1.80. Examination of the residuals reveals that the original covariances are explained by this model.

Few statistical criteria are available to guide selection between the four ξ, two θ_δ model, and the two ξ, four θ_δ model. Both provide an excellent fit to the data. On balance, virtually the only difference between the models involves parsimony: the two ξ, four θ_δ use three fewer degrees of freedom.

Table 8.5 presents the LISREL estimates for the two ξ, four θ_δ model. In the two ξ models, the λ coefficients for the G2 report of service received is set to 1.0 for each of the dimensions. This constitutes the reference point for comparison of the other parameters in the Λ_x matrix. All estimated coefficients in Table 8.5 are statistically significant ($p < 0.05$).

The model does an excellent job of explaining the four G2 items, with squared multiple correlations exceeding 0.60 for all of the items. In part, this may be due to the dominant position of the G2 in defining the overlapping triads file (see Chapter 3). This is further supported by the magnitude of the estimated G2 coefficients (λ_{41} and λ_{82}). These parameters are larger than any of the G1 or G3 coefficients in the Λ_x matrix. The poorest explanation is of the G1 or G3 reports of service received from the G2, with λ coefficients less than 0.50 for both of these parameters and explained variance less than 0.22.

Because each ξ has as its reference variable a *G2 Receives* item (X_1 and X_5), and because all items are measured on the same underlying scale, comparison of the magnitude of λ coefficients may be interpreted as an index of overall reciprocity in the sample. From the perspective of the G2, the ratio of coefficients $\lambda_{11}/\lambda_{41} = 1.21$ or $\lambda_{52}/\lambda_{82} = 1.11$ suggests perceived reciprocity in that these ratios are close to 1.0. Note, however, that in both comparisons the relative advantage is toward greater receipt of assistance of the G2.

From the perspective of the G1, the ratio $\lambda_{31}/\lambda_{21} = 0.82$ suggests broad-based reciprocity as perceived by the G1. Here, too, the relative advantage is toward greater receipt of assistance by the G2.

Turning to the G3, the ratio $\lambda_{62}/\lambda_{72} = 0.74$ suggests reciprocity, although once again the relative advantage favors G2 receipt of assistance.

While the magnitude of loadings *within* any one generation for any one role relationship is approximately equal, the across-generation comparisons suggest an absence of reciprocity. In the G1-G2 relationship, the ratios $\lambda_{11}/\lambda_{21} = 1.75$ and $\lambda_{41}/\lambda_{31} = 1.76$ both suggest the relatively greater involvement in the relationship by the G2. A similar

TABLE 8.5   LISREL Estimates: Exchange Analysis

Variable	Λ_x ξ_1	ξ_2	Squared Multiple Correlations	Error Variances
G2 Receives G1	1.000	0.0	0.877	0.301
G1 Gives G2	0.573	0.0	0.337	1.390
G1 Receives G2	0.468	0.0	0.199	1.919
G2 Gives G1	0.826	0.0	0.613	0.929
G2 Receives G3	0.0	1.000	0.926	0.419
G3 Gives G2	0.0	0.677	0.455	2.884
G3 Receives G2	0.0	0.499	0.218	4.692
G2 Gives G3	0.0	0.904	0.751	1.424

	Φ		Θ_δ Correlated Errors	
	ξ_1	ξ_2	Covariance	Correlation
ξ_1	2.152	0.725	$\theta_{\delta_{76}}$ 2.488	0.676
ξ_2	0.216	5.247	$\theta_{\delta_{32}}$ 0.812	0.497
			$\theta_{\delta_{43}}$ 0.449	0.336
			$\theta_{\delta_{87}}$ 0.543	0.210

NOTE: Entries on the diagonal of the Φ matrix are variances. The covariance is above and the correlation below the diagonal.

pattern characterizes the G2-G3 relationship, where $\lambda_{52}/\lambda_{62} = 1.48$ and $\lambda_{82}/\lambda_{72} = 1.81$, again suggesting the greater investment by the G2.

Entries in the Φ matrix are the variances (diagonal), covariance (top), and correlation (bottom) of the two ξ. These indicate that service assistance between the generations is related within a family, with the frequency of service assistance in the G1-G2 dyad moderately correlated with assistance in the G2-G3 dyad (r = 0.216).

The final part of Table 8.5 presents the error covariances and correlations (Θ_δ). As noted above, the four correlated errors have substantive meaning in addition to improving the empirical fit of the model to the data. The positive error covariances suggest that these terms are indeed capturing residual within-person or within-phenomenon covariation that the two ξ do not capture by virtue of being too broad.

Discussion

The generation and lineage analysis of patterns of exchange between the generations reveal several points about this aspect of family relations. First, financial assistance between the generations is not very great, except in the case of the G3's receipt of financial aid. This in large part is due to the adolescent ages of the G3, and in part may be due to the relative youth and financial well-being of the G1 in this sample.

Second, service assistance is much more pervasive, regardless of generational position. Service assistance is a reciprocal pattern, and is not linked to patterns of financial assistance in the G1 and G2.[7] With the G3, receipt of financial assistance is related to patterns of service aid (Table 8.3). This is due to the shared residence of the G2 and G3.

Third, in this sample, gift giving is a reasonably regular phenomenon apparently tied to birthdays and holidays.[8] While positively correlated with service assistance, it is a distinct aspect of the relationship.

Finally, the analysis reported here illustrates the complexity of the exchange process within families and the deficiencies of the data used to measure exchange in this study. While summary measures of the frequency of exchange are valuable in describing intergenerational relations, the limited set of items lack specificity as to the circumstances surrounding the exchange of service or dollars. Hence understanding of the dynamics of the exchange process is limited.

Future Measurement of Exchange

In order to improve the future measurement of intergenerational exchanges, several steps are required. The *conceptualization* of the dimensions of exchange must be broadened. The specificity of items tapping the components of each dimension must be increased. Response options must be improved. Finally, it is necessary to broaden the methods employed to tap the dimensions of exchange.

Table 8.6 presents one reconceptualization of the exchange construct using the rational approach to measurement (Strauss, 1964; Mangen, Peterson, and Sanders, 1982). This conceptualization derives four dimensions of exchange (frequency, value, reciprocity, and justice) from exchange theory. These dimensions are conceptualized as operating within five facets or areas of possible exchange. The facets of financial assistance, services, goods, advice, and gifts represent areas of exchange

TABLE 8.6 Rational Approach to Measurement: Elaboration of the Concept of Exchange

			Facets		
Dimensions	Financial Assistance	Services	Goods	Advice	Gifts
Frequency of exchange:	The frequency of actual cash transfers. Prompts to use include payment of medical expenses, housing costs, utility and telephone expenses, groceries, car payments, gasoline expenses, and various taxes. Use budget categories.	The frequency of service aids given and received. Aids to recall include transportation, car repairs, home repairs, shopping, yard work, child care, aid during illness, and housekeeping.	Assesses how often products exchange hands in this relationship. Prompts to aid recall may include groceries, clothing, household appliances, car, airplane tickets, housing if property is owned by provider, and prescriptions.	How often do individuals give and receive advice in the relationship. Prompts include: legal, financial, job, or business, marital and personal problems, running a home, child rearing, and cutting red tape.	Symbolic emphasis in this facet to differentiate it from others. Birthdays, Christmas, and Hanukkah, weddings and anniversaries, graduations, and religious rites of passage are possible aids to recall.
Value of the exchange:	If cash transfers have occurred, tap the amount of money that has been expended for each of the items. Use of receipts is	If service aids have occurred, conduct an economic analysis of the market costs of the services. May also assess the	If goods have changed hands, determine the market value. If possible, receipts are ideal but not necessary. Will require	Determine the market value of the advice if provided by a lawyer, accountant, or professional in that field. Must	Actual receipts provide the best data but subject provided estimates are sufficient. Categories ranging from less

	ideal but difficult. Response options must be unique for each prompt.	rewards forgone by the provider as well as the market analysis of costs.	substantial detail in describing product (e.g., square feet of dwelling unit).	gather data on the amount of time spent on advising to assess value.	than $5 to over $1000 are probably necessary to assess full range.
Exchange reciprocity:	Objective measure examines the ratio of the frequencies of financial aid given to received in that relationship. Perceptual measure is assessed for each relationship.	Objective measure examines the ratio of the frequencies of service aids given/received. Perceptual data from each actor in the relationship are also gathered.	Objective measure comprises ratio of frequencies of goods exchanged. Perceptual measure included in interviews to assess the perspective of each individual in the transaction.	Ratio of frequencies of advice given/received is objective measure. Assess perspective of each actor in the transaction for a perceptual measure.	Ratio of frequencies of gift-giving in the relationship is an objective measure of reciprocity. Perceptual measure included for each person in the relationship.
Exchange balance or justice:	Objective measure derived from the ratios of the value of financial aid given/received. The perceptual measure assesses fairness from the perspective of each actor.	Objective measure compares the ratios of the values of services given and received in that relationship. A perceptual measure of fairness as perceived by each actor is also used.	Ratio of the value of goods given and received is an objective measure. Assess fairness from the perspective of each person in the transaction.	Ratio of the value of advice given and received constitutes the objective measure, with perceptual data on fairness of the transactions included for each member of the relationship.	Ratio of the value of gifts given and received is an objective measure. Self-response items on fairness asked of each person in the relationship.

often examined in research on the content of intergenerational exchanges (Bengtson and Schrader, 1982).

Frequency of Exchange

The frequency of exchange represents the dimension that is typically examined in intergenerational research. The emphasis of this dimension is on how often people give and receive in their relationships with other family members. Frequency data are easily gathered by classic survey methods. Improvement of measures is possible, however, by using extremely detailed prompts to aid in recall and decrease telescoping errors (Sudman and Bradburn, 1974, 1982). Specification of the five facets of exchange aids recall to a degree, but improvement in measurement can be obtained with even greater detail. To accomplish this, each facet must be clearly distinguished from the others and specific prompts *within* each facet must be developed.

Facet differentiation is crucial because aspects of exchange may be interpreted uniquely within each family. For example, G2 families that periodically bring several bags of groceries to a G1 family member may, without detailed prompts, consider this exchange as financial assistance, goods, or gifts depending upon their orientation to the exchange process. Indeed, this exchange may not be recalled without prompts. Thus gift giving is restricted to *symbolic occasions* and financial assistance to *actual cash transfers* in order to differentiate these from provision of goods. Note, however, that a wedding gift of money appears to cross facet boundaries. The symbolic emphasis is most important here, warranting coding as a gift exchange. Similar problems are possible in differentiating services from advice. Consider a family with a G1 attorney. In this measurement schema, counseling a son or daughter on the legal ramifications of declaring bankruptcy is considered *advice* while preparing the legal documents is a *service*.

The prompts that are suggested as indicative of specific exchange components within facets are largely drawn from other research on intergenerational relationships (Adams, 1968; Cantor, 1976; Hill et al., 1970; Lopata, 1979; see Bengtson and Schrader, 1982, for an extended discussion). By making the prompts as detailed as possible, the probability that respondents will recall exchanges that have occurred is enhanced. Financial assistance prompts that cover most major categories of a budget are desirable, and service categories that address areas of assistance often provided by family members are needed.

Questions can be developed for each prompt, and detailed response options provided. Data on the frequency of exchanges are enhanced when responses are anchored within a fixed temporal referent (e.g., within the past year) and when response options use numerically as opposed to verbally oriented responses. For example, numerically oriented response options to assess yearly frequencies are (0) never, (1) once or twice a year, (2) 3-6 times a year, (3) 7-11 times a year, (4) once a month, (5) 2-3 times a month, (6) weekly, (7) 2-4 times a week, and (8) daily. While this detail may be considered excessive for some research endeavors, the point here is that data are improved when clear, comprehensive, and nonoverlapping response options are provided to respondents.

Value of the Exchange

As conceptualized here, value is an economic concept based on market costs. For the financial assistance facet, assessment of dollar values is not problematic unless respondents are unwilling to divulge sensitive financial data. In collecting income information, the use of income ranges is known to improve response rates (Sudman and Bradburn, 1982), and should assist in determining the value of financial exchanges as well. While this results in a loss of information, the benefit of minimizing missing data in all likelihood offsets the loss of precision. In limited circumstances, it may be possible to examine receipts to determine value; if so, this is the optimal strategy.

Determining value for the other facets is less straightforward and will certainly include measurement error. The strategy suggested for these facets is to determine the equivalent costs of purchasing these goods or services in the market economy (Greenberg, 1984). If, for example, a G2 father prepares his son's income tax report, then the cost of having a tax service prepare that report is the value of this exchange. As anyone who has ever shopped around for tax services knows, however, the costs vary tremendously depending upon the provider. This is the case with determining the market value of all of the specific exchange items noted in Table 8.6. Determining market value will require estimation of the average cost of providing that service in the geographic area under examination.

To complicate estimation of value further, the concept of cost as an opportunity forgone may significantly affect the value of any given exchange, especially with regard to provision of services. To illustrate, a physician who spends one day assisting an aged parent with home maintenance loses a day that could be spent serving patients and generating $1000 in revenue, while a neighborhood youth might gladly perform the same services for $50. Is the value of this exchange the large sum that the physician has forgone by spending his time with a parent and neglecting his patients or the smaller amount that would hire the neighborhood youth? The opportunity cost more accurately reflects the *cost to the provider* if he or she directly provides the service. This perspective on costs is even more complex than the accountant perspective discussed above, in that the value of exactly the same service is different contingent upon the characteristics of the provider. Regardless, either perspective will likely require an economist to permit determination of value.

For those who are not inclined to examine value within an economic perspective, the *perceived value* or importance of the exchange can be directly assessed using survey research methods. For each of the areas of possible exchange referenced in the frequency dimension, questions pertaining to the importance of such exchanges can be asked of respondents, and Likert-type response options employed. If this perspective is used, however, recognize that some exchanges may have negative value to givers and receivers of an exchange. For example, an adolescent may well resent mother's "interference" when she stops by and cleans the apartment, or a G2 daughter may not appreciate having to counsel an aged parent on the nuances of managing relations with governmental bureaucracies.

An alternative strategy for measuring perceived value is through the use of ipsative measures requiring respondents to rank in order of importance each of the areas of exchange within any one facet. This strategy is isomorphic with a theoretical perspective on values as a preferential ordering of outcomes. Ranking is, however, difficult if a large number of items must be ordered.

Reciprocity and Justice

In this reconceptualization of exchange, the concepts of reciprocity and distributive justice are not measured directly. Rather, these measures are derived from the frequency and value measures discussed above. Measuring reciprocity and justice involves similar logic and procedures. Consequently, the future measurement strategies for these dimensions are discussed together in order to simplify presentation.

Reciprocity and justice are emergent concepts that apply to the role-relationship level of analysis; as such, they are dyadic measures. Assume for this discussion a simple two-generation study that emphasizes financial exchanges. The logic we present is generalizable to multiple generations and facets. We use $G1:FG_i$ to refer to the i variables assessing the frequency of G1 provision of financial assistance to G2 as stated by G1 (i.e., data are gathered from *G1* respondent, *FG* refers to "finances given"). $G1:FR_i$ refers to the G1 items on receipt of financial assistance from the G2. $G1:VG_i$ refers to the G1 items on value given to the G2, and $G1:VR_i$ refers to the G2 items on value received. Four similar sets of measures are available for the G2 ($G2:FG_i$, $G2:FR_i$, $G2:VG_i$, and $G2:VR_i$).

Using these data, measures of reciprocity and justice are derived from the comparisons of the different sets of measures. Two measures of reciprocity that use data from both generations include

$$R_i = \frac{G1:FG_i}{G1:FG_i + G2:FG_i}$$

$$R'_i = \frac{G1:FR_i}{G1:FR_i + G2:FR_i}$$

Thus R_i equals the proportion of times that the G1 gives financial assistance in the G1-G2 relationship, and R'_i equals the proportion of times that G1 receives financial assistance in the G1-G2 relationship. Note that the two sets of i-derived reciprocity measures are based on distinct measures. The R_i measures emphasize each generation's reports of the frequency of *giving* in the relationship, while the R'_i emphasize the frequency of *receiving* in the relationship. Because the perspectives of both generations are used in constructing these measures, we refer to these sets as *objective reciprocity* measures. Note also that two measures could be computed to reflect the G2 proportion of times that the G2 gives or receives in the G1-G2 relationship; these simply equal $1-R_i$ and $1-R'_i$.

Perceived reciprocity (PR_i) measures are derived from the responses of only one generation:

$$G1\text{:}PR_i = \frac{G1\text{:}FG_i}{G1\text{:}FG_i + G1\text{:}FR_i}$$

$$G2\text{:}PR_i = \frac{G2\text{:}FG_i}{G2\text{:}FG_i + G2\text{:}FR_i}$$

In this formulation, reliance is placed upon a single generation's report of what they give and receive in that relationship. Perceived reciprocity equals frequency of giving divided by the sum of frequency of giving and frequency of receiving, computed for each of the i-specific areas of possible financial assistance and for each generation.

These four sets of measures have theoretical ranges of 0-1, with item-specific reciprocity indicated if the R_i, R_i', $G1\text{:}PR_i$, and $G2\text{:}PR_i$ equals 0.50. Movement to the extremes indicates an absence of reciprocity.[9] Convergent validity is indicated if parallel derived measures (e.g., R_2 and R_2') are strongly correlated.

Similar measures are derived from the variables assessing value to derive measures of distributive justice (J_i, J_i') and perceived justice ($G1\text{:}PJ_i$, $G2\text{:}PJ_i$):

$$J_i = \frac{G1\text{:}VG_i}{G1\text{:}VG_i + G2\text{:}VG_i}$$

$$J_i' = \frac{G1\text{:}VR_i}{G1\text{:}VR_i + G2\text{:}VR_i}$$

$$G1\text{:}PJ_i = \frac{G1\text{:}VG_i}{G1\text{:}VG_i + G1\text{:}VR_i}$$

$$G2\text{:}PJ_i = \frac{G2\text{:}VG_i}{G2\text{:}VG_i + G2\text{:}VR_i}$$

These four measures are proportions of value received or given, with the "objective" measures using data drawn from both generations in the denominator, and the "perceived" measures using data from only one generation in both the numerator and the denominator. Again, the measures have theoretical ranges of 0-1, with item-specific justice indicated if the J_i, J'_i, $G1:PJ_i$, and $G2:PJ_i$ equal to 0.50. Movement to the extremes again indicates an absence of justice.[10] Here, too, convergent validity is indicated if parallel derived measures are strongly correlated.

Is it reasonable to suggest that reciprocity or justice is present if and only if each of the i-derived measures approximates 0.50? If this is necessary, it implies that exchanges occur on a "tit-for-tat" basis without regard for the resources available to each generation. It is more likely that reciprocity and justice are manifest *across* the range of i exchange domains. If this is true, then correlations among the i items within any one block of derived measures will not be uniformly high. Yet many mathematical procedures used to analyze the structure of measurement assume a pattern of substantial correlations across items to justify development of summary measures.

The derivation of higher-order measures of reciprocity or justice that incorporate each generation's resources is straightforward. The procedure is applicable to each of the eight sets of derived measures presented above, but is demonstrated with the R_i to simplify discussion. Specifically, the arithmetic average of the R_i is an indicator of the reciprocity across the exchange domains. The range of $\overline{R}$ is 0-1, with exactly the same interpretation as that given the R_i except that it incorporates each generation's resources and ability to contribute to a pattern of intergenerational exchange.

The averaging procedure may be applied to each set of derived measures to obtain four summary measures of reciprocity ($\overline{R}$, $\overline{R}'$, $\overline{G1:PR}$, and $\overline{G2:PR}$) and distributive justice ($\overline{J}$, $\overline{J}'$, $\overline{G1:PJ}$, and $\overline{G2:PJ}$). At this point, application of measurement models is warranted because the multiple indicators of reciprocity and distributive justice should be strongly correlated.

Other strategies and procedures are also available in attempting to measure these complex and challenging concepts. Recent work with the concept of distributive justice has frequently used a magnitude estimation approach to measurement (see, e.g., Lodge, 1981; Rossi and Nock, 1982; Hamblin, 1974); much can be gained by careful use of this complex measurement procedure.

Conclusion

In sum, while the measures of exchange employed in this three-generation data set yield important information about patterns of assistance within families, it is apparent that the conceptualization of exchange in this study is quite narrow. Recent advances in both theory and methodology need to be effectively incorporated into future research on exchanges of assistance and support. In the presentation of strategies for future measurement, we present some approaches that may be useful for future researchers.

It is important to recognize, however, that use of the extended conceptualization presented in Table 8.6 will virtually require that the research examine *only* patterns of exchange in families. If we assume a simple three-generation study, examine all three vertical role relationships, and include variables for each of the exchange domains suggested in Table 8.6, each generation must provide data for over 450 variables.[11] It is likely that most researchers will find their budgets stretched too tight to permit inclusion of the full range of dimensions and/or facets.

Moreover, we are convinced that the focus on intergenerational exchanges within the family is too narrow; intragenerational exchanges—especially those between spouses, siblings, and in-laws—must be included in our conceptualizations. Finally, an exclusive focus upon family exchanges is also too narrow. While the family is without doubt the crucial component of personal support systems, others also provide support. Friends, neighbors, and even voluntary associations provide important forms of assistance. A comparative perspective suggests the relevance of examining the relative contribution of different forms of social support, especially for those without proximal family members.

Service exchanges are a crucial element of intergenerational solidarity, and perhaps reflect the dimension of greatest concern to those in the helping professions. The wide-ranging suggestions for conceptual expansion suggested above are useful in further specifying the concept of exchange and thus improving its utility for researchers and practitioners alike. Nonetheless, the analysis that we report suggests that simply determining the overall frequency of service assistance does indeed tap the core of the service exchange concept, and validates the use of these measures as broad-based indicators of intergenerational aid. Such measures are especially important when service exchange is an ancillary and not primary focus of the research.

Intergenerational exchanges are a complex phenomenon, and it is readily apparent that no research endeavor can comprehensively examine all of the germane issues suggested by the reconceptualization that we advance. We hope, however, that our efforts to analyze this construct and further its conceptualization will benefit others exploring the dynamics of exchange processes.

NOTES

1. The exact wording of the items and the response options are:

Financial Assistance

A.   In the past year have you given your parents (child) any financial assistance?

    1.   No, not at all
    2.   Infrequently
    3.   Regularly—I partially support them
    4.   Regularly—they get most of their support from me.

B.   In the past year have you received any financial assistance from your parents (child)?

    1.   No, not at all
    2.   Infrequently
    3.   Regularly—They partially support me
    4.   Regularly—I get most of my support from them

Service Assistance

How often do you do the following?
A. Your helping him (her) out with chores or errands
B. Him (her) helping you out with chores or errands

    1.   Almost never
    2.   About once a year
    3.   Several times a year
    4.   Every other month or so
    5.   About once a month
    6.   About once a week
    7.   Several times a week
    8.   Almost every day

Gift Exchange

How often do you do the following?
A. Gift exchange

    1.   Almost never
    2.   About once a year
    3.   Several times a year
    4.   Every other month or so
    5.   About once a month
    6.   About once a week
    7.   Several times a week
    8.   Almost every day

2. Note that over 20% of the G1 sample refused to provide data on financial exchanges.

3. All correlations with the financial assistance measures must be interpreted with caution. The small amount of variation in these items will, on an a priori basis, result in diminished correlations.

4. This may be changing over time, what with increasing female labor force participation and changing sex-role ideology. We suspect, however, that this pattern is still true today.

5 The G3 was not asked any questions about assistance to the G1.

6. Version 6.3 of the LISREL program is used in this analysis.

7. Note, however, that this may be due to a lack of variation in the G1 and G2 financial assistance measures. See note 2 above.

8. This was derived from an analysis of written-in comments on the questionnaires.

9. If an absence of exchange is indicated for a specific item, the derived measures are defined as 0.50 to avoid division by zero errors.

10. Once again, exchange values that sum to zero require that the derived justice measures be defined as balanced and equal to 0.50.

11. A total of 38 exchange domains are listed in Table 8.6. Gathering data on exchanges given and received doubles this number, and three role relationships result in 228 variables to assess the *frequency* of exchange. Inclusion of data for the value dimension results in another doubling of the number of variables.

9

Measuring Intergenerational Norms

DAVID J. MANGEN
GERALD JAY WESTBROOK

Conceptualization

Norms are the "socially defined rules or standards of behavior [that] provide guidelines to the range of attitudes and behaviors appropriate to roles and social situations" (George, 1980, p. 140). This definition incorporates the idea of expectations. In any culture, behavior can be judged by its adherence to norms, as well as by its logic and reasonableness (Harris and Cole, 1980). In large part, this is due to the fact that norms are emergent properties of the social structure, and thus are shared by members of the social group.

Although norms set standards for behavior and establish the expectations that guide behavior, they are not uniformly applied. Different norms may be operant for certain individuals, or the same norms may be differentially applied, depending upon the individual's ascribed and attained status within the group. Gender, age, and occupational status are three characteristics that influence how norms will be applied.

Understanding the content, prescriptions, and proscriptions of the prevailing norms can facilitate adherence to acceptable social behavior. The heterogeneity of today's norms (i.e., some rigid, some transitional, some ambiguous, and some contradictory), however, has produced disagreement regarding the *behavioral consequences* of these norms for the lives of older people. On the one hand, rigid norms may deter finding appropriate strategies in a shifting social context (Troll, Miller, and Atchley, 1979). In a rapidly changing society, rigid norms may be difficult to follow because they hinder utilization of innovative coping strategies. On the other hand, norms in transition produce a lack of clear expectations about our own roles and behaviors as well as those of others. As a result, standards for conforming are absent. The ambiguity of the age norms in contemporary American society often results in anxiety or alienation because consistent expectations are not present (Rosow, 1974). Further, changes over time in the structure, composition, and even the concept of "family" have forced even those most stable of norms, familial norms, to undergo accompanying changes.

Theoretical Definition

Familial norms can be defined as those *standards of behavior that govern and mediate intrafamilial interactions and expectations of the family as a social system.* Because of the importance of norms in guiding people's behavior, family sociologists have been investigating the role that familial norms play in the support systems of family members. Such norms shape expectations and attitudes and define proper and equitable behaviors regarding the type and degree of filial obligations. As components of family solidarity, *familial norms* may be conceptualized as addressing the degree of perceived filial responsibility (familism), while *normative solidarity* may be viewed as addressing the degree of intergenerational consensus regarding filial responsibility.

Seelbach and Sauer (1977) identify filial responsibility as referring to the obligations of adults to meet the basic needs of their parents, while elsewhere, Seelbach (1977) includes in his definition of filial responsibility, the "emphasizing [of] duty, protection and care."

Bengtson, Cutler, Mangen, and Marshall (1985) note that the conceptual bases underlying the study of parent-child relations are underdeveloped, and that the entire area of normative solidarity deserves greater attention. Hagestad's (1982) review of the research in this area concurs, as she identifies the paucity of research investigating norms. Theoretical development, together with specification of the process of norm formation and enforcement, clearly require greater attention. There are some data available, however, regarding the norms of familism.

Kerckhoff (1966a, 1966b) reports that the America family is characterized by norms of *assistance,* but that *proximity* is not expected. Although family members expect familial aid in times of need, they do not expect family members to live close to other family members. Shanas (1980) saw both aged parents and their middle-aged children identifying privacy and independence as high priorities, and observed that older adults' living arrangements reflect these priorities. Seelbach (1977) confirms the elderly's penchant for independence, as well as their expectations of aid from their families if and when self-management is no longer possible. He points out that G2 children perceive extensive obligations toward their aging parents. Blenkner (1965) discusses normative solidarity as filial maturity, a concept that is individualistic in orientation. She argues that filial maturity involves a shifting in roles such that middle-aged children help their aging parents. Shanas (1980) implied the existence of norms of reciprocity as she reported that 70% of those 65 years old and above gave aid to their children and grandchildren, as well as receiving aid from their children. She concluded that "help and service across the generations is a continuing feature of family life" (1980, p. 13).

Treas (1977) places the norms of filial responsibility in a historical perspective, noting that children served as resources against the trials of old age in developing societies, and that last wills and testaments in colonial America often "stipulated the conditions of support for the surviving widow" (Treas, 1977, p. 489).

Norms, however, are not static; they change, as do the way in which they are enforced. Influences such as demographic change, changes in society, family structure, and status, as well as the increasingly multicultural nature of our population all contribute to the shaping and changing of familial norms.

Bengtson, Burton, and Mangen (1981) examined ethnic variations in norms of familism and found that Mexican Americans were more likely to express a familistic perspective. Seelbach and Sauer (1977) report a conditional relationship between older persons' morale and their expectations of filial responsibility, when controlling for race. That is, for blacks there was a moderate negative relationship (p < 0.01) between morale and expectations, whereas for whites the relationship was very weak, insignificant, and positive. When controlling for socioeconomic status, the racial differences disappeared, suggesting that SES might explain a greater amount of the variance than did race. These subcultural variations in family norms will likely become increasingly important in our society as it becomes increasingly heterogeneous (Gelfand, 1982).

Cantor (1975) views basic service provision to aging parents as having changed over time from being the family's responsibility to being a responsibility shared by the family and the government. Family members retain responsibility for basic human and social needs—those that are more personal in nature, while the government is seen as responsible for health, income maintenance, and transportation needs. With increasing industrialization, traditional norms appear inflexible, and thus may begin the change (Seelbach and Sauer, 1977). This change results in a system where social and psychological concerns become the focus of responsibility, in contrast to the economic orientation of a more traditional period (Treas, 1977; Cantor, 1975).

Demographic changes have consequences for norms of familism. With the aging of the population, and decreases in both birth and death rates, there is a greater drain on the resources that families can provide. With increased life span, fewer children, and the tendency for an elderly surviving G1 parent to be a very old widow whose children are among the young-old, there is decreased potential aid and increasing competition for available aid.

Familial expectations are related to characteristics of the older person. In general, the parent's marital, health, and financial status influence the degree of perceived obligations (Lopata, 1973, 1979; Houser, Berkman, and Long, 1981; Adams, 1968). Not surprisingly, widowed parents, those in poor health, and those with lower income levels expect greater assistance from their adult children. Some characteristics of offspring are also important to consider. Greater numbers of children (Houser, Berkman, and Long, 1981) and geographic proximity (Townsend, 1968) tend to be related to greater parental expectations.

Because of the importance of norms in molding expectations and shaping standards of behavior, and because of the complexities brought on by the transitional nature of norms, it is becoming increasingly important to develop sensitive indicators of norms of familism. The purpose of this chapter is to analyze in detail the measurement of normative solidarity in three generations and within family lineages.

Generation-Level Analysis

The research employed a 10-item modification (see Appendix A) of Heller's (1970) 15-item familism scale. Half of the items on our scale (items 3, 4, 7, 8, and 9) are similar or identical to items on the Heller scale. The remaining 5 items were developed specifically for this research in order to increase the efficacy of the instrument in tapping familial norms across a broad age range. Responses for each item were scored on a four-point Likert scale of agreement and disagreement.

This instrument was presented to respondents in all three generations (516 G1s, 701 G2s, and 827 G3s). Because the instrument was implicitly a familism scale, it was neither designed nor able to capture information about the expectations of middle-aged children or their older adult parents regarding geographic proximity of the older parents to their G2 children, or provision of support and/or assistance *to* the G2 children *by* their G1 parents. In short, the scale taps broad issues of familism, not specific expectations of appropriate behavior. The generation level of analysis, however, enabled an examination of perceived normative content on a global basis, without reference to any specific actor.

Table 9.1 presents the means and standard deviations, by generation, of the 10 normative items. Items 1, 3, 4, 6, 7, and 9 are worded such that the higher the score, the greater the familistic orientation. On all six of these items, the G1 had higher mean scores than did either of the other two generations. Item 2 addresses freedom of choice regarding one's manner of dress, with higher scores indicating a greater individualistic orientation. Here, the G3 had higher mean scores than the other two generations, with the G2 exhibiting the lowest mean score. Item 5 addresses issues of communication within the intergenerational family system. While this item does not readily lend itself to a familistic versus individualistic interpretation, G1 and G3 family members agree that the rapid pace of social change has resulted in problems with communication. G2 family members also feel that this is true, although less strongly than the G1 and G3. Items 8 and 10 both deal with financial assistance from the G2 to the G1 (item 8) and G3 (item 10). It is interesting to note that the recipients of the suggested financial assistance have the lowest mean scores for both of these items.

In order to assess the dimensional structure of these items, a series of principal factoring analyses were conducted for the total sample and for each generation. For these analyses, we recoded all items so that high scores indicated familistic responses.

The results of these analyses indicated that the 10-item version of the Heller scale did not possess a consistent dimensional structure across the three generations. In the oldest generation, a total of three factors, explaining 43.9% of the total variance, had eigenvalues greater than 1.0.

TABLE 9.1   Means and Standard Deviations: Norms of Familism

Items		Total Sample	G1	G2	G3	Probability
Take on household	X̄	3.38	3.49	3.38	3.33	< .001
chores	sd	0.69	0.68	0.69	0.70	
Own choice in style	X̄	2.99	2.78	2.56	3.47	< .001
of dress	sd	0.89	0.87	0.81	0.71	
Talk over important	X̄	3.23	3.40	3.37	3.00	< .001
decisions	sd	0.79	0.73	0.66	0.86	
Share activities	X̄	2.66	2.95	2.48	2.63	< .001
	sd	0.92	0.92	0.89	0.90	
Problems with	X̄	2.99	3.05	2.88	3.04	< .001
communication	sd	0.83	0.80	0.88	0.81	
More weight to	X̄	3.08	3.36	3.08	2.91	< .001
family opinions	sd	0.83	0.75	0.78	0.87	
Marriage extends	X̄	2.77	3.06	2.71	2.63	< .001
families	sd	0.97	0.94	0.95	0.98	
Family should pay	X̄	2.49	2.25	2.73	2.42	< .001
parental debts	sd	1.02	1.13	0.96	0.94	
Conflict of life	X̄	2.24	2.75	2.36	1.81	< .001
styles	sd	0.95	0.92	0.86	0.86	
Parents finance	X̄	2.32	2.65	2.36	2.07	< .001
education	sd	0.99	1.03	0.95	0.92	

Examination of the scree test (Cattel, 1966) indicated that only one factor, explaining 21.2% of the total variance, was present in the 10-item scale. A similar pattern is evidenced in the second and third generations. Three factors explaining 44.6% of the total variance emerge in the G2 analysis. Again, the scree test indicates that only one factor, explaining 22.2% of the total variance, is present. In the G3, four factors that explain 56.2% of the total variance have eigenvalues greater than 1.0, but the scree test again indicates the presence of only one underlying trait. The first factor for the G3 explains 21.8% of the total variance.

These analyses clearly indicate that the 10 items measure only one dimension. Use of all 10 items, however, *is not* recommended due to the low explanatory power of the first factor as well as the discrepancies of item loadings across both factors and generations. These results led us to try to determine a single factor across each of the generations that was simultaneously internally consistent and congruent across the three generations. In order to attain these twin goals, a series of parallel analyses were conducted where items were dropped one at a time, and the shortened set of items was reanalyzed. Whenever possible, items were trimmed from the scale if the loading of that item on the first factor was, across generations, consistently low. If that item had a factor loading greater than 0.35 in any of the generations, then the item was retained until all items that did have low loadings on the first factor were eliminated. When all items with consistently low loadings were eliminated, then the items that were low on at least two of the generations were eliminated. This process ultimately yielded an abbreviated five-item version of the Heller scale that was both maximally internally consistent and congruent across generations.

To illustrate this process, in the initial analysis of the 10-item version of the scale, item 5—a double-barreled stimulus linking the quality of intergenerational family communication with the pace of social change—consistently yielded factor-item coefficients less than 0.20. This resulted in the decision to eliminate this item. Furthermore, upon retrospective inspection, the content of this item appears ambiguous to the concept of norms of familism.

Table 9.2 presents the factor structure for each generation for the revised scale. This shortened scale is congruent across generations. These items all reflect a familism content, and are all worded such that agreement indicates a familistic response. Even this trimmed version, however, does not reflect alpha reliabilities of the magnitude that allow complete confidence in the scale.

In spite of these concerns with the factor structure and the internal consistency of the scale, the five items that remain in the abbreviated version of the familism scale do share an underlying content of global familistic obligations. Items that are specific to any one generation or intergenerational relationship are excluded, and the ambiguous communication-social change item was eliminated. Measurements of the familism concept under conditions specific to direct financial exchanges (items 8 and 10) were also systematically eliminated. As a result, the shortened scale was consistent across the generations.

Lineage-Level Measurement

At the lineage level of analysis, conceptualization of normative solidarity suggests two analyses. The degree to which norms of familism

TABLE 9.2   Factor Matrix: Norms of Familism

Items	Total Sample	G1	G2	G3
Talk over important decisions	0.471	0.378	0.446	0.481
Share activities	0.515	0.529	0.558	0.519
More weight to family opinions	0.523	0.508	0.512	0.440
Marriage extends families	0.507	0.536	0.417	0.513
Conflict of life styles	0.508	0.421	0.459	0.423
Eigenvalue	2.02	1.90	1.92	1.90
Total variance explained	40.4	38.1	38.3	38.1
Coefficient alpha	0.63	0.59	0.59	0.59
Sample size	1922	482	665	775

are held by family members constitutes one analysis. This is similar to the generational analysis reported above, but is conducted within the LISREL model to permit examination of correlated errors of measurement resulting from aggregation into lineage units. On the lineage level, the emergent concept of normative consensus becomes a property of role relationships. An examination of the existence and degree of normative consensus present within these relationships is also conducted.

The sample of families employed for these analyses is an overlapping triads file (see Chapter 3) with a total of 522 cases. Each family is potentially represented in from one to four lineages. Thus this analysis is role relationship based. After eliminating missing data, the multivariate analyses reported here use a sample of 441 lineages with complete information.

Table 9.3 presents the means and standard deviations for the different measures of normative solidarity examined at the lineage level of analysis. The first three columns of Table 9.3 summarize lineage-level responses to the five items that exhibited a congruent structure in the generational analysis. When examining the familism measures, two results are apparent. First, the redefinition of the sample from a generational sample to a lineage sample has changed the familism

TABLE 9.3   Means and Standard Deviations:
Lineage Level of Analysis

Items		G1 Familism	G2 Familism	G3 Familism	G1-G2 Euclidian Distance	G2-G3 Euclidian Distance	G1-G3 Euclidian Distance
Talk over important	X̄	3.43	3.35	3.00	0.88	1.15	1.50
decisions	sd	0.71	0.66	0.88	1.33	1.67	2.18
Share activities	X̄	2.98	2.56	2.61	1.69	1.44	1.65
	sd	0.92	0.89	0.88	2.01	1.88	2.05
More weight to	X̄	3.39	3.03	2.83	1.30	1.37	1.65
family opinions	sd	0.75	0.80	0.86	1.84	1.83	2.05
Marriage extends	X̄	3.11	2.80	2.60	1.66	1.95	1.89
families	sd	0.93	0.94	0.96	2.23	2.41	2.39
Conflict of life-styles	X̄	2.78	2.29	1.77	1.73	1.61	2.47
	sd	0.93	0.84	0.83	2.14	1.95	2.70

NOTE: N = 522. No more than 26 cases are missing on any familism measure or 33 cases in any consensus measure. All the familism variables are scored 1-4, with higher scores indicating greater familism. Euclidian distance measures of consensus range from 0-9, with high scores indicating lack of consensus.

measures very little. Mean scores for all variables are within the $+/-0.10$ points from the generational means presented in Table 9.1. Most of the scores exceed the theoretical midpoint of 2.5, thus indicating a high degree of familism. Indeed, only two of the mean scores suggest nonfamilistic responses. For both the second and third generations, the issue of "changing one's life-style to fit in with the family" evokes a slight degree of disagreement.

The other three columns of Table 9.3 report the average Euclidian distance between generational pairs on the five familism measures. The Euclidian distance measures address normative consensus in the lineage, and yield measures ranging from 0 (indicating complete agreement) through 9 (indicating maximum disagreement). The squaring term in computation of the distance measure gives disproportional weight to greater disagreement.

The most striking feature of the mean disagreement scores is the remarkable degree of consensus. In only one case is the mean score greater than 2.0, and that refers to the differences between grandparents and grandchildren with regard to "changing one's life-style." Recall that these data were collected when visible life-style symbols such as dress or hair length were likely to cause conflicts. Examination of the percentage distributions (not presented) for the 15 Euclidian distance measures further substantiates the high degree of consensus. For the five G1-G2 difference measures, a minimum of 73.4% of the cases fell within the range of 0 to 1 indicating only one point of disagreement on the original measures. For the G2-G3 relationship, a minimum of 69.6% of the families fall within the 0 to 1 range, and that on the issue of "marriage as extending families." The greatest degree of disagreement is present in the G1-G3 relationship. Here, with regard to the "changing life-style" issue, only 61.8% of the lineages fall within the 0-1 range on the difference measure.

On the whole, these findings indicate a very high degree of consensus, much more than originally expected. It is important to recognize, however, that a purely random pattern of responses in a generational pair would yield 62.5% of the cases in the range of 0-1 on the Euclidian distance measure. Of the 16 possible combinations of two items with four responses each, 10 are either exact matches or within one point. This is, of course, part of the problem in any differencing procedure, and one that is accentuated when the range of responses is small.

The univariate analysis of normative solidarity indicates two primary trends. First, the overall high degree of familism noted at the generational level of analysis continues to be manifest at the lineage level. Second, these measures reflect a high degree of normative consensus. As we shall demonstrate, however, it is questionable as to whether this concept emerges in the lineage analysis.

Measurement Analysis of
Normative Consensus

The lineage analysis of normative consensus did not substantiate our hypothesis that an emergent property of normative consensus exists. While the data in Table 9.3 refer to Euclidian distance measures of disagreement between the generations, we also examined simple differences and the absolute value of simple differences. Regardless of the scoring procedure employed, correlation analysis indicated a random pattern of association among the 15 difference scores.

A principal factoring analysis of the difference scores was undertaken to examine the dimensional structure of the derived consensus measures. Plotting the scree test of the eigenvalues obtained by the factor analysis yielded a straight line, as would be expected by purely random data. Again, this analysis was conducted with three different ways of scoring consensus, and all three resulted in the characteristic pattern for random data. If the concept of normative consensus exists, it is not captured by these data.

Measurement Analysis of
Norms of Familism

The second analysis examines the degree to which the different generations report familistic norms. This analysis is similar to the generational analysis in that the original untransformed items are analyzed. It differs from the generational analysis in that a total of fifteen variables (i.e., five variables for each of three generations) are included in the analysis, and because the analysis is conducted on a lineage file.

Because of the lack of independence of observations within the lineage file, we employ the LISREL VI measurement model to estimate the structure of the 15 familism measures. Input to the LISREL model consisted of a variance/covariance matrix based on 441 cases after elimination of missing data.

Table 9.4 presents a summary of the different measurement models. The first model (B_1) tests one general dimension of norms of familism throughout the lineage. This model posits a single underlying dimension that explains the covariances among the 15 variables, and theoretically argues that familism is an emergent lineage property that spans generations. In our analysis, this represents a baseline model. While the model yields a reasonable goodness of fit statistic, the likelihood-ratio chi-square of 421.64 with 90 degrees of freedom is highly significant. Moreover, the ratio of chi-square to degrees of freedom is 4.68, indicating a poor fit to the data.

The second model (B_2) uses five dimensions to examine method bias in the data. Each dimension is defined by the same conceptual item drawn from each generation, that is, three items define each dimension. Chi-square for this model is 390.49 with 80 degrees of freedom, indicating a poor fit to these data.

Model B_3 is a parallel measures model with three generation-based dimensions. Due to the constraints on the measurement coefficients and the error variances, this model uses the fewest degrees of freedom of any of the models tested. While the parallel measures model fits the data better than any of the previous models, the likelihood ratio chi-square remains highly significant.

The model of tau equivalence (B_4) relaxes the constraints on the error variances and freely estimates these coefficients. This substantially reduces chi-square, yielding a ratio of chi-square to degrees of freedom only slightly greater than 2.0. Inspection of residuals reveals, however, that a substantial portion of the original covariances are not yet explained.

TABLE 9.4   Summary of LISREL Measurement Models:
Normative Dimension

Model	Model Definition	x^2	d.f.	Goodness of Fit
B_1	Lineage Familism $1\,\xi$	421.64	90	0.870
B_2	Method Bias $5\,\xi$	390.49	80	0.880
B_3	Parallel Measures $3\,\xi$	348.66	111	0.907
B_4	Tau Equivalence $3\,\xi$	204.60	99	0.941
B_5	Perfect Congruence $3\,\xi$	185.36	95	0.946
M_1	Perfect Congruence $3\xi\ \theta_{\delta_{10\ 9}}$	164.55	94	0.953
M_2	Perfect Congruence $3\xi\ \theta_{\delta_{10\ 9}}\ \theta_{\delta_{10\ 2}}$	153.19	93	0.956
M_3	Perfect Congruence $3\xi\ \theta_{\delta_{10\ 9}}\ \theta_{\delta_{10\ 2}}\ \theta_{\delta_{4\ 1}}$	142.20	92	0.959
B_6	Congeneric Measures $3\,\xi$	175.20	87	0.949

Model B_5 relaxes in part the constraints on coefficients in the lambda matrix. The cross-generation congruence model equates factor loadings for the same item across generations. Thus four more coefficients are estimated in this model, reducing chi-square by almost 20. This is a significant improvement on Model B_4.

The final major variation is a congeneric measures model (B_6). The partial constraints on the lambda coefficients are removed. Relaxing these constraints reduces chi-square by 10.16 but uses eight more degrees of freedom ($p > 0.20$).

These findings indicate that the model of perfect cross-generation congruence (B_5) is the appropriate broad theoretical model to use in explaining the data. Inspection of the modification indices and residuals for B_5 indicate, however, that significant covariation remains. In particular, correlated errors are present.

Model M_1 adds a correlated error term between two G2 items, those regarding the extending of families and changing of life-styles. Estimating this coefficient reduces both chi-square and the ratio of chi-square to degrees of freedom, and the goodness of fit for the model improves.

The second error term (Model M_2) suggested by the analysis crosses generational boundaries. The error variance for the G2 item on changing life-styles is significantly related to the error variance for the G1 item on sharing activities ($r = 0.175$). Estimating this coefficient improves the fit of the model.

The third correlated error (M_3) involves two G1 items. Errors in measurement of the extending families and discussing decisions items are negatively correlated. Estimating this coefficient reduces chi-square by 10.99 and improves the fit of the model.

To this point, specification of the next parameter to be freed had been clearly indicated by modification indices and analysis of the residual covariances. Analysis of residuals and modification indices for M_3 is less straightforward. The maximum modification index suggests that the constraint of perfect congruence should now be relaxed in order to improve the fit of the model. Inspection of the residuals reveals that virtually all of the substantial covariances in the original matrix have indeed been explained, and that *negative residuals* remain. Because most of the original covariances are positive, and because relaxing the constraint of the perfect cross-generation congruence does not make conceptual sense, we select M_3 as the model of choice for the normative dimension. Table 9.5 presents the LISREL estimates for this model.

Table 9.5 is divided into three panels. The first panel presents the primary information on the measurement model for the perfect congruence model with three correlated error terms. The regression coefficients relating the items to the three underlying dimensions are represented in the first three columns. These metric lambda coefficients are similar to factor loadings in that they define the structure of the measurement. For each generation, the coefficient for the discuss decisions item is fixed at 1.0 to set a common scale for all of the underlying dimensions.

The lambda coefficients reveal that the items on sharing activities and extending families contribute most to defining the underlying scales, followed by the changing life-style measure. The family opinions and discuss decisions items are comparatively less important in defining the structure of measurement. In many respects, these findings suggest that the important normative context involves traditional behavioral outcomes, with less concern for processual issues.

TABLE 9.5   LISREL Estimates: Familism Measurement
Model—Three Dimensions and Three Correlated Errors

Lambda X:	G1 Familism	G2 Familism	G3 Familism	Error Variance	Squ Mul Correl
G1 Discuss decisions	1.000	0.0	0.0	0.369	0.
G1 Share activities	1.313	0.0	0.0	0.601	0.
G1 Family opinions	1.020	0.0	0.0	0.441	0.
G1 Extending families	1.272	0.0	0.0	0.621	0.
G1 Change life-style	1.151	0.0	0.0	0.705	0.
G2 Discuss decisions	0.0	1.000	0.0	0.282	0.
G2 Share activities	0.0	1.313	0.0	0.561	0.
G2 Family opinions	0.0	1.020	0.0	0.463	0.
G2 Extending families	0.0	1.272	0.0	0.762	0.
G2 Change life-style	0.0	1.151	0.0	0.568	0.
G3 Discuss decisions	0.0	0.0	1.000	0.645	0.
G3 Share activities	0.0	0.0	1.313	0.590	0.
G3 Family opinions	0.0	0.0	1.020	0.646	0.
G3 Extending families	0.0	0.0	1.272	0.704	0.
G3 Change life-style	0.0	0.0	1.151	0.538	0.

Phi Matrix:	G1 Familism	G2 Familism	G3 Familism
G1 Familism	0.123	0.222	−0.010*
G2 Familism	0.027	0.121	0.147*
G3 Familism	−0.001*	0.017*	0.111

Correlated Error Terms:	Covariance	Correlatic
Error Terms		
G2 extending families with G2 change life-style	0.165	0.251
G2 change life-style with G1 share activities	0.102	0.175
G1 extending families with G1 discuss decisions	−0.097	−0.203

NOTE: Variances are on the diagonal of the Phi matrix; covariances are bel
diagonal and correlations are above the diagonal.
*$p > 0.05$.

It is important to recognize, however, that while this model ex
the covariances of the measures quite well, only a moderate amo
the variance of each item is explained. The squared multiple correl
range from 0.118 to 0.313, and average only 0.22. Clearly, further
is needed in developing a strong measure of the norms of familis
   The second part of Table 9.5 presents the phi matrix, para
estimates of the variances and covariances of the underlying dimen

As suggested by the univariate data, the diagonal elements in the phi matrix indicate little variance in the three generations. The covariances (below the diagonal) and the correlations (above the diagonal) indicate some degree of relationship between the three dimensions. Only one of the three covariances, however, is statistically significant at the 0.05 level. G1 and G2 norms of familism are significantly related (r = 0.222).

The third part of Table 9.5 presents estimates of the error covariances and correlations. These are listed in the order of entry into the model. The error variance for the G2 item on changing life-styles is involved in the first two error terms, suggesting that this visible component of the normative dimension is particularly salient, and has not been adequately explained in the primary measurement model. One component of changing life-styles involves the size of the family—a factor very similar to the issues involved in the extending families domain. Location of family members is often a component of changing life-styles as well, and this may render problematic the sharing of activities with the G1. Finally, the negative correlation for the two G1 items in the third correlated error term suggests that a strong concern with extending families is, after controlling for the primary measurement model, related to little concern for the processual issues involved in discussing decisions. This suggests a traditional mode for the G1. Alternatively, the negative relationship for this final coefficient may indicate that too many coefficients are being estimated in the model.

Summary and Recommendations

In the generational analysis, initial assessment of norms of familism is plagued by an inconsistent factor structure across generations. When consistency is obtained by deletion of items, the abbreviated scale exhibits marginal psychometric characteristics (see Table 9.2). The short five-item scale displays marginal reliability, and the necessity of deleting items from the scale to achieve cross-generation congruence diminishes from the construct validity hypothesized in this set of items.

At the lineage level of analysis, a LISREL measurement model of three dimensions and three error terms provides a reasonably good fit to the covariances of the items. While the model fits, the covariances among the items are not strong. As a result, measurement of familism is less than ideal, with squared multiple correlations ranging form 0.118

through 0.313. This indicates a substantial degree of error variance in the overall model. Moreover, contrary to expectations, only one of the three correlations among the dimensions of familism is significant. All of these suggest less than optimal measurement of norms of familism at the lineage level.

Further evidence of the limitation of the Heller scale is found in the analysis of normative consensus. In these data, it is not possible to find an emergent property of normative consensus. It is important to note, however, that the dimension may have not emerged in the analysis solely because of the high degree of consensus among family members regarding familism (see Table 9.3).

In summary, the adequacy of measurement of norms of familism in this study is less than ideal. In part, this may be due to the general orientation of each of the items. Because all items were phrased in a somewhat nebulous, general family content area, responses can be given in the abstract without regard for germane issues within that family. Because norms are group properties, and intergenerational norms typically vary by age and/or generational position, it seems reasonable to hypothesize that accurate assessment of norms of familism requires specification of the role relationship. Stated another way, the behaviors expected from other family members are in part conditioned by the other, and expectations vary for sons versus daughters, for older versus younger offspring, and for parents versus children. In short, it is necessary to focus the measurement on a specific role relationship as opposed to the more global orientation used here. Attribution of norms to the other is a logical extension of this idea as well, because both actors in any relationship have expectations of the other. This would permit operationalization of normative solidarity within an exchange theory framework because the relative expectations vis-à-vis one another would be addressed, allowing operationalization of the concept of dependence (Emerson, 1972a, 1972b).

Second, it is likely more specific aspects of familistic behavior must be assessed in future measurement. It is relatively easy to agree in the abstract that one has responsibilities to one's family; the acid test comes when a family member attempts to invoke the norm. Specification of circumstances likely to evoke normative content is needed to improve the measurement of familism.

On a more technical level, operationalization of both familism and normative consensus will be aided if increased variability of responses is obtained. We believe that utilization of items specific to the role and expected behavior, as suggested above, will assist in this goal. In addition, response options need to be further distinguished. While we assume in this analysis that the distance between "disagree" and "agree" equals the distance from "strongly agree" to "agree," this is likely questionable. Scaling norm items in an ipsative framework, or using magnitude estimation procedures (Hamblin, 1974), will assist in enhancing the variability of responses.

Finally, further elaboration of the concept of familism is clearly required. This chapter addresses the perception of norms of familism, but ignores central issues in normative research. Several issues await examination in the literature on norms with families. The process of norm formation is rarely examined. Research typically assumes the development of the norm, and examines the outcome of an unknown and unspecified process. This constitutes an excellent opportunity for the application of experimental studies. The entire area of normative sanctions deserves greater attention. While a norm may be expressed, it has little credence if violations of the norm are ignored, or adherence taken for granted. Under what circumstances, for example, is it legitimate to terminate (e.g., disown) the social aspects of an involuntary, biologically based relationship? The norms governing financial and service exchange clearly require greater examination. This is central to future measurement of familism, especially as it pertains to family relations in the later years. Norms of reciprocity (Gouldner, 1960) and distributive justice (Homans, 1974) require attention within this framework.

Given these considerations, we used the rational approach to measurement (Mangen, Peterson, and Sanders, 1982; Strauss, 1964) to attempt to explicate the concept of normative solidarity. The results of this effort are presented in Table 9.6, where we have specified four facets of social relations that have normative content, and three dimensions of norms that we see as central in groups. Each cell of this typology constitutes a dimension to be measured in intergenerational relations.

Most of the cells, especially those in the *financial aid* or *instrumental* rows of the matrix, are relatively straightforward, and have been implicitly considered in much of the normative research currently available. More interesting, however, are the *social* and *affective/emotional* rows of the matrix. In part, this stems from the difficulty of defining fairness or equity in a social or affective setting. If a mother reveals an extramarital affair to her adult daughter, what response of the daughter balances the exchange relationship?

TABLE 9.6 Conceptual Elaboration of Normative Solidarity

	Familism	Distributive Justice	Reciprocity
Financial Aid Expectations	The degree to which specified family member is expected to provide financial assistance under specified circumstances.	The degree to which equity of value is expected in patterns of financial assistance between family members.	The degree to which an act of financial assistance legitimates expectations that the act will returned in kind if not value.
Instrumental Expectations	The degree to which other family members are expected to provide service assistance under specified circumstances.	The degree to which equity of value is expected with regard service assistance.	The degree to which service aid provided yields expectations that aid will be returned.
Social Involvement Expectations	The degree to which specified family members are expected to involve one another in social affairs.	The degree to which equity of perceived value is expected in shared social relations.	The strength of expectations regarding the legitimacy of sharing social events.
Affective/Emotional Expectations	The strength of expectations that other family members be available for socioemotional support.	The degree to which family members are expected to share equally revealing confidences.	The degree to which sharing a confidence yields expectations that other will return the trust.

NOTE: This model does not include specification of the role relationship, and should be repeated for each role relationship under examination in the research. This model does not specify the referent behaviors for any of the analytical cells. Multiple indicator measures should be developed for each cell.

Specification of the range of different behaviors relevant for this typology is clearly beyond the scope of this chapter, and has not been included in the elaboration presented in Table 9.6. We also note that the typology, as presented in Table 9.6, does not include the further elaboration of the nature of the role relationship. If, as recommended, this additional feature is included in the conceptual elaboration, the full matrix would have to be replicated for *each* role relationship under consideration in the research.

Conclusion

Considerable work is needed in the measurement of the normative component of solidarity. This analysis clearly indicates that developing measures of normative solidarity that are congruent across generations is difficult; perhaps this is due to generation-specific expectations of what the family "ought" to do in relation to that generation.

Our analysis of the ten-item modification of the Heller scale suggests that the five items that exhibit cross-generation congruence do tap a common underlying concept of familism, and that researchers interested in a broad-based familism measure may profitably use the abbreviated scale as an exploratory vehicle to guide future research. To measure familism, additional items need to be developed, and we suggest some possible areas to explore in expanding the conceptualization of normative solidarity.

Future refinements of this measure may also benefit by increasing the specificity of the items in order to reduce ambiguity and maximize face validity. We expect that this will increase variability and also improve the reliability of the scale. Increasing the specificity and focusing the items on behaviors that the respondent expects of his or her parent or child may also improve the measurement of normative consensus, a concept that does not emerge in this research. Significant work remains to be done with the measurement of the normative dimension of solidarity, and we encourage others to build upon the foundation presented here.

Appendix A

The items included in the revision of Heller's (1970) scale used the following format for eliciting responses:

Disagree 1 2 3 4 Agree

1. The young person who lives at home should take on many of the everyday household chores and responsibilities.
2. The way a person dresses should be entirely his own choice and not a family matter.
3. A person should talk over important life decisions (such as marriage, employment, and residence) with family members before taking action.
4. As many activities as possible should be shared by married children and their parents.
5. Different generations within the same family have problems communicating today because of the rapid change in values in our society.
6. Family members should give more weight to each others' opinions than to the opinions of outsiders.
7. Marriage should be regarded as extending established families, not just creating new ones.
8. If an old man has a medical bill of $1000 that he cannot pay, his son or daughter is morally obligated to pay the debt.
9. If a person finds that the life-style he has chosen runs so against his family's values that conflict develops, he should change.
10. Even though it means considerable sacrifice, a parent should finance his or her child's education all the way to completion (through graduate school if necessary).

PART III

Summary and Conclusions

10

Intergenerational Cohesion

A Comparison of Linear and
Nonlinear Analytical Approaches[1]

DAVID J. MANGEN
KAY YOUNG McCHESNEY

The preceding chapters of this book emphasize the measurement of one of the several concepts in the global family solidarity construct. In these chapters, the data analysis focus is on simplifying the number of variables in the data array by determining if a limited number of underlying dimensions (i.e., factors) are present in a given set of items. By contrast, this chapter focuses on simplifying the number of objects (i.e., cases) in the data array to determine if a smaller number of family types adequately describes the data.

Typological construction is, therefore, another way of examining the structure of a data set in that types emerge from similar patterns among the variables of interest. Most studies examining the relationship among various aspects of family life in the later years focus on a linear additive conceptualization of the relationships among components of intergenerational cohesion. Alternatively, bivariate relationships are often analyzed (Bengtson et al., 1985). The LISREL and factor analysis models of the preceding chapters exemplify use of the multivariate linear model as applied to the measurement of one underlying dimension.

In this chapter, we focus on the relationships among several of the dimensions of family solidarity as defined by Bengtson and Schrader (1982) and analyzed extensively in this book. By examining several components simultaneously, our work begins to address the oft-debated question of the degree to which the American family system is characterized by extended versus nuclear family patterns (Kerckhoff, 1965, 1966a, 1966b; Rosow, 1965; Litwak, 1960, 1965; Sussman and Burchinal, 1962). It is only a beginning, however, because horizontal as well as vertical kinship relations are of concern to that debate. We focus on the vertical kinship tie, and examine family patterns across two generations.

Two approaches are used to analyze the data. First, a simple bivariate correlation framework that explores the linear additive relationships among the cohesion concepts is employed. A pattern of correlations that is uniformly high suggests that the family solidarity construct is a higher order linear and additive concept composed of the individual dimensions measured. This is the model implicitly assumed in research. In direct terms, the model states that families are more cohesive if they (1) live proximally, (2) associate frequently, (3) assist one another, and (4) care for one another.[2]

The second analytical model employs a hierarchical cluster algorithm that examines the unique patterns or clusterings of families in multi-dimensional space.[3] If the linear and additive model is the more appropriate model, then the clustering procedure will yield a limited number of types characterized by parallel patterns of mean scores plotted across the types. That is, families giving a highly cohesive response on one dimension would also give highly cohesive responses to the others. Similarly, a moderate or even a noncohesive response on one dimension should result in a similar response for the other dimensions. If the linear model is inappropriate, then intersecting patterns of mean scores plotted across types will be manifest. This would suggest that the family solidarity construct is not a simple higher order construct; rather, many families may be characterized by complex configurations of the different concepts. Stated another way, some families may well be cohesive on one dimension but fragmented on others.

These methods indirectly compare two theoretical models of inter-generational cohesion as outlined above. Because our measures focus on measuring solidarity in the role relationship, we apply these methods to only one relationship in this three-generation study: the grandparent (G1) and adult child (G2). A sample of 254 G1-G2 dyadic lineages for whom complete data are available is used in this analysis. The dyads are a subset of the overlapping triads file (see Chapter 3).

The six dimensions of family solidarity that are examined in these dyads are (1) the affect that G1 expresses toward G2, (2) the affect that G2 expresses toward G1, (3) the amount of service assistance that G1 receives from G2, (4) the amount of service assistance that G2 receives from G1, (5) the geographic proximity of G1 to G2, and (6) the amount of contact between G1 and G2. Because previous analyses reveal that the different generations' reports of geographic proximity and inter-generational contact (association) are highly correlated, the reports of the generations are averaged to yield only one variable for this analysis. Furthermore, if all variables are to be given equal weight in the analysis, it is necessary to equate the variances of the variables (Anderberg, 1973; Tryon and Bailey, 1970). Consequently, all variables are standardized to a mean of zero and unit variance.[4]

Correlation Analysis

The first analysis explores the correlations among the six dimensions of cohesion. Thus the focus is on the linear additive relationships among the concepts of interest. If the construct of family solidarity is indeed characterized by a simple linear additive function, then uniformly high correlations should be present. Table 10.1 presents the Pearson product moment correlations among these variables.

Examination of the zero-order correlations among these variables reveals many substantial and some trivial correlations. Not surprisingly, the geographic proximity of the generations to one another is strongly related to the amount of association between the generations ($r = -0.627$), with increasing distance between family members resulting in decreased interaction. This suggests that geographic proximity may be viewed as an opportunity function (Kuhn, 1974) in the intergenerational family system. Geographic proximity strongly influences the amount of service assistance provided by each generation to the other ($r = -0.4046$; $r = -0.3513$), but virtually no effect is noted on either measure of affect.

Generational position appears to have little effect on the giving and receiving of service assistance. Not only are the unstandardized mean scores for service received approximately equal, the zero-order correlation relating the service assistance variables is quite strong ($r = 0.8071$), suggesting a high degree of service reciprocity between genera-

TABLE 10.1   Correlations Among the Six Solidarity Measures

	G12 Affect	G21 Affect	G1 Receives from G2	G2 Receives from G1	G1-G2 Proximity	G1-G2 Association
G12 Affect	1.0000					
G21 Affect	0.4738	1.0000				
G1 Receives from G2	0.1748	0.1719	1.0000			
G2 Receives from G1	0.1992	0.2394	0.8071	1.0000		
G12 Proximity	−0.0339	−0.0549	−0.4046	−0.3513	1.0000	
G1-G2 Association	0.3347	0.3622	0.7063	0.6654	−0.6270	1.0000

tions in the family. The giving and receiving of services is strongly related to the level of interaction in the family, but only moderately related to the measures of affect.

Surprisingly, the two measures of the affect expressed by each generation are not as strongly correlated as hypothesized (r = 0.4738). This suggests that the perception of affect is not an emergent property of the family. Rather, these data suggest that intergenerational affect is an individual-level property that is anchored and evaluated within the family context. Obviously, the members of intergenerational dyads do not evaluate the emotional context of that relationship similarly. Furthermore, affect cannot be equated with association. The zero-order correlations relating these variables are moderate in size (r = 0.3347; r = 0.3622) and in the expected direction, but clearly too small to consider one of the concepts a proxy for the others.

What is noteworthy about the correlations among these six indicators, however, is the presence of two conceptual blocks among these measures. The first block includes the behavioristic indicators: proximity, association, and the giving and receiving of assistance. The second block includes the two measures of affect. Examination of the correlations within each block reveals sufficiently strong relationships to suggest the appropriateness of conceptualizing family solidarity as a higher order linear additive construct. The correlations between the blocks, however, are—with the exception of the association, affect correlations—quite low, suggesting that at least two family solidarity constructs exist.

Hierarchical Cluster Analysis

Given these data, it is hypothesized that family solidarity is not a simple unidimensional second-order construct composed of the six concepts outlined by Bengtson and Schrader (1982).[5] Rather, the exigencies of modern industrial life as well as the variable nature of intergenerational relationships lead to the development of unique patterns of cohesion within families. This suggests, however, that a simple linear additive approach to analyzing intergenerational relationships ignores some important facets of the data. Nonlinear regularities in the data become outliers in a standard correlation procedure. In order to explore more fully possible nonlinearities among these concepts, a hierarchical cluster analysis based on the Ward (1963) criterion is used to determine if groupings of the lineages (i.e., the cases) more effectively explain the variances of these measures than simple correlation techniques.[6] Given the strong relationship of the two components of service exchange (see Tabled 10.1), however, we eliminate the G2 Service Received variable from this phase of the analysis and employ the G1 Service Received variable as a proxy for both.

Clustering cases requires that some measure of similarity or dissimilarity between objects, and some criterion for evaluating cluster structure, be chosen. The measure of dissimilarity employed is the squared Euclidian distance between the cases, computed as

$$d^2 = \Sigma \left(X_{i,j} - X_{i,k}\right)^2$$

where the subscript i refers to the variables, and the subscripts j and k refer to the cases being clustered. For each pair of cases, we take the difference on variable i, square that difference, and sum across the i variables in the analysis.

The criterion for evaluating the cluster structure and determining which cases to merge at each step is that the merger should result in the minimum increase in within-group sum of squares, which is proportional to squared Euclidian distance. Table 10.2 presents the summary results of the grouping procedure for the final 13 stages.

Examination of the nominal typological structure produced by the hierarchical cluster analysis at each step of the grouping procedure suggests that 13 clusters are required to explain the structure of these data. While determining the number of clusters to retain is indeed problematic, analysis proceeds by looking for the stage in the clustering

TABLE 10.2 Within-Group Sum of Squares for the Total
Cluster Structure and Proportion of Unexplained
Variance for Each Variable: Selected Stages of
the Hierarchical Clustering

Stage	Within-Group Sum of Squares Total	G1 Affect	G2 Affect	G1 Receives from G2	G1-G2 Proximity	G1-G2 Association
1	0.0	0.0	0.0	0.0	0.0	0.0
2	0.0	0.0	0.0	0.0	0.0	0.0
.	.	.	.	.	.	.
.	.	.	.	.	.	.
.	.	.	.	.	.	.
241	276.48	0.2371	0.2756	0.2355	0.1662	0.1784
242	293.67	0.2719	0.2757	0.2529	0.1727	0.1875
243	311.31	0.2743	0.3410	0.2547	0.1729	0.1876
244	330.16	0.3025	0.3468	0.2839	0.1736	0.1982
245	354.56	0.3869	0.3576	0.2848	0.1739	0.1982
246	389.52	0.4539	0.3909	0.2962	0.1812	0.2174
247	424.56	0.5155	0.4368	0.2963	0.1945	0.2350
248	469.43	0.5231	0.5548	0.3345	0.1957	0.2475
249	520.12	0.6841	0.5819	0.3346	0.2015	0.2538
250	578.15	0.7607	0.5918	0.3732	0.2040	0.3556
251	688.09	0.7658	0.6293	0.7098	0.2040	0.4108
252	853.59	0.8588	0.7856	0.7156	0.5899	0.4240
253	1265.00	1.0000	1.0000	1.0000	1.0000	1.0000

NOTE: Stage number refers to the number of hierarchical merges that have taken place. The number of clusters remaining is equal to the number of cases (254) minus the number of stages. Column entries for the variables indicate the proportion of the variance that is within group as a function of the total variance of that variable.

process where the within-group sum of squares and the proportion of variance not explained by the typological structure increases sharply. This is analogous to the scree test often used in factor analysis. For the first 47 mergers, *exactly identical* cases are merged together. It is not until merger number 213 that the proportion of the variance of any one variable not explained by the typological structure exceeds 0.100. Retaining 13 types (stage 241) results in a typological structure that explains 78.14% of the total variance of the variables, and over 70% of the variance of each indicator of intergenerational cohesion.

The dominant variable in describing the typological structure of intergenerational relationships in the later years is the geographic proximity of the G1 and G2, with 83.38% of the variance of proximity explained by the 13-type structure. The contact between generations is also a central variable in the typological structure. Fully 82.16% of the variance in the amount of contact between the generations is explained. Close inspection of Table 10.2 reveals that the service assistance variable is of somewhat less importance in describing this intergenerational typology, with only 76.45% of the variance explained. The two affect variables are least important, and indeed somewhat dormant in describing and defining the typological structure. While less important in defining the typological structure, over 70% of the variance of each affect measure is explained by this grouping of cases. Overall, the within-group homogeneity of the 13-type cluster structure is very high.

While the preceding discussion illustrates that an adequate typological structure is present in the data, it says very little about the score profiles of the families that are members of each type. Table 10.3 presents the means and standard deviations of each of the 13 types, together with the correlation ratio (eta) relating the type structure to each of its component parts.

In discussing the mean score profiles across types, recall that all variables are Z-scores with a mean of zero and a standard deviation of one. Also, all variables *except* G1-G2 Proximity are scored so that a high score indicates the cohesive response; the proximity variable is scored so that a high score indicates substantial geographic distance between the generations.

For purposes of discussion of the characteristics of the types, we examine the hierarchical tree describing the final 13 mergers to determine if some additional groupings could be placed upon the structure to facilitate discussion of the characteristics. Examination of the tree reveals that four superordinate types can be defined. We use this classification system as a heuristic device to aid our presentation; we explicitly *do not* use this classification as an empirical model because within-type homogeneity at this level is very poor (see Table 10.2).

Type Characteristics

The moderates: Types 1-4, containing 135 (53.1% of the sample) family lineages, are all characterized by moderate scores on the five variables used in the grouping procedure. Mean scores on each of the dimensions are within one standard deviation of the overall mean in all

TABLE 10.3 Means and Standard Deviations of
Cluster Dimensions for Each Type

Type	G12 Affect	G21 Affect	G1 Receives from G2	G1-G2 Proximity	G1-G2 Association
1	0.7636	0.8835	−0.5296	−0.1397	−0.4061
n = 20	0.4082	0.3207	0.4931	0.4014	0.4335
2	−0.7527	0.3251	−0.5347	−0.4206	−0.1017
n = 22	0.5586	0.4618	0.4694	0.3112	0.5026
3	−0.0178	−0.0078	0.2131	−0.5428	0.3485
n = 33	0.5068	0.5894	0.4185	0.0417	0.4489
4	0.7372	0.6018	0.3369	−0.5387	0.8940
n = 60	0.3878	0.4948	0.6335	0.0719	0.4814
5	0.3851	1.0110	2.5149	−0.5795	1.5202
n = 13	0.5820	0.2608	0.3816	0.0036	0.4579
6	0.2948	−0.9319	1.1092	−0.5570	0.6717
n = 14	0.4580	0.4516	0.5675	0.0223	0.2653
7	−1.2510	−1.0210	2.2016	0.1124	1.4648
n = 5	0.9412	0.5637	0.9827	1.5427	0.4643
8	−0.7617	−0.6050	−0.9127	2.4077	−0.6931
n = 15	0.3656	0.8668	0.1947	0.4067	0.1874
9	0.5277	0.5078	−0.8574	1.8092	−1.0038
n = 25	0.5299	0.4848	0.2042	0.6907	0.4004
10	−2.4177	−3.9597	−0.3350	−0.3413	−1.2750
n = 3	0.5814	0.5963	0.5754	0.4039	0.6162
11	−2.9527	−1.1547	−0.8016	−0.4703	−1.2029
n = 7	0.6993	0.6362	0.4271	0.1873	0.4632
12	0.3551	−1.3752	−0.5154	0.0507	−0.7521
n = 16	0.4729	0.7259	0.3944	0.5889	0.3962
13	−1.1783	−0.8266	−0.6760	−0.0384	−0.7873
n = 21	0.6069	0.5374	0.5315	0.6148	0.3935
eta	0.8734	0.8511	0.8743	0.9131	0.9064
$F(12, 241)$	64.624	52.790	65.185	100.759	92.498
	$p < .0001$	$p < .0001$	$p < .0001$	$p < .0001$	$p < .0001$

NOTE: Entries in the first row for each type are arithmetic averages; entries in the second row are standard deviations.

instances. The standard deviations are all substantially less than 1.0, illustrating the within-type homogeneity of the derived groups. Important differences are manifest, however.

Type 1 (n = 20) is characterized by average geographic proximity. Despite this, they associate with one another less than the statistical norm, and are less likely to engage in service exchanges. Members of the dyad feel positively about each other, as indicated by the reports of affectual solidarity. Both members report closeness above the norm, although in neither case is the affect more than one standard deviation above the overall mean.

Type 2 (n = 22) families are somewhat closer geographically than is the norm, and are about average in their frequency of contact. They tend not to engage in service exchanges. This type is intriguing, however, in that the affect in the relationship is not reciprocated. Note that G1 reports an average affect of -0.7527—fully three-quarters of a standard deviation below the mean—while G2 reports affect slightly above the overall mean of zero.

Type 3 (n = 33) families are reasonably close geographically and in relatively frequent contact with one another. They are somewhat more likely than the norm to engage in service exchanges, although this is a weak tendency. The intergenerational relationship is characterized by average affect; both members of the dyad report affect virtually at the overall mean.

The most numerically frequent type is Type 4 (n = 60). They live relatively close together, and are in frequent contact with one another. They help each other, although this is not a striking feature of the type. Furthermore, both parties report a warm, affectually close relationship, with mean scores considerably above the overall mean.

These four types are all characterized by moderate behavioral and affectual responses toward one another. In no instances are the mean score profiles substantially different than the mean; rather, shades of differentiation as opposed to stark contrast characterize these groups.

Types 5, 6, and 7 are labeled *The Exchangers*. While numerically infrequent (only 32 lineages; 12.6% of the sample), these types share the feature of being well above the average in the amount of service assistance provided to the G1 family member.

Type 5 (n = 13) families live somewhat closer to each other than is the norm, and they are much more likely to visit one another. The G1 family member receives substantially more service assistance from the G2 than is the norm, as the mean score of 2.5149 indicates. The G2 feels very positive about the relationship, but this is reciprocated only in part by the G1.

While Type 6 (n = 14) families live, on average, the same distance from each other as the Type 5 families, they are only somewhat more likely than the norm to be in contact with each other. They are, however, substantially more likely than the norm to engage in service exchange, although again this assistance pales beside the frequent assistance provided by Type 5 families. A distinguishing feature of the Type 6 lineages is with regard to the affect. The G2, in spite of (or perhaps because of) the frequent contact and service assistance, scores substantially below the mean on affect while the G1 reports slightly higher affect than the overall norm.

Type 7 (n = 5) families are relatively rare; one might even consider them outliers. They are about average in geographic proximity, although note that the standard deviation of 1.5427 is substantially above the overall standard deviation of 1.0. Type 7 families are in frequent contact with each other, and extremely likely to engage in service exchanges. Neither party cares much for the other, however, as illustrated by mean scores more than one standard deviation below the overall mean.

Types 8 and 9 (40 lineages; 15.7% of the sample) have been labeled *The Geographically Distant*. Both types live a considerable distance from one another, and because of this score low on the frequency of contact measure. Both types are characterized by low levels of service exchange as well. The two types are differentiated from one another in one way: Type 8 families (n = 15) do not particularly care for one another while Type 9 families (n = 25) report a positive affectual tone to the relationship.

In contrast to the geographically distant, Types 10-13 (47 lineages; 18.5% of the sample) are identified as *The Socially Distant*. These four types are characterized by geographic proximity that is approximately average. In all cases, however, the level of association between the generations is substantially lower than the overall norm, and service exchanges are not prevalent. In no instance does the G2 feel particularly close to the G1 and generally this absence of affect is reciprocated by the G1. Only Type 12 G1 family members (n = 16) report a level of affect above the overall mean, and that is only slightly higher. Service exchange and association scores are, however, somewhat low.

Type 10 (n = 3) is a minor type, and is distinguished by the extremely low affect reported by the G2 and the G1. On the other three measures, however, this small cluster is moderate. The lineages live somewhat closer together than the average, but they are somewhat below the mean on contact and service exchange.

Type 11 (n = 7) is also a small cluster, and is quite similar to Type 10.[7] While geographically closer than average, this group is substantially below the mean on association and service exchange. The G1's affect toward the G2 is almost three standard deviations below the mean, and the G2 reciprocates, although not as vehemently.

Type 13 (n = 21) families are nearly identical to Type 11 families on the behavioristic measures of solidarity. Both members of the dyad report negative affect, however, although not as strongly as Type 10 or Type 11 families.

Discussion

These findings suggest that the relationships among the different dimensions of family solidarity in later years are not as simple as has been typically assumed in gerontological studies of the family in later life. The linear additive model, implying that families are more cohesive if they (1) live proximally, (2) are in frequent contact, (3) assist one another, and (4) care for one another, is not the only regularity in the data. Interactions are clearly present. While the linear additive conceptualization of family solidarity does indeed apply within some dimensions, the relationships among variables between conceptual areas are better explained by the nonlinear typological structure. Examination of the score profiles for the 13 types reveals that only three types (numbers 4, 5, and 8), constituting 34.6% of the sample, have profiles purely consistent with the linear additive conceptualization. An additional three types (numbers 10, 11, and 13: 12.2%) are consistent on all dimensions except proximity. Using a liberal definition of consistency, it is nonetheless clear that the linear additive model holds for less than one-half of the sample; the remaining seven types display patterns that are inconsistent on at least one of the measures. These findings clearly suggest that a better explanation of each of the solidarity concepts is achieved by taking into account the pattern of relationships across all of the variables.

What are the main deviations for consistent profiles? As noted above, proximity issues constitute one deviation. Recalling that the dominant variable defining the cluster structure is proximity and the role that physical separation plays in allowing interaction or service exchange, it is not surprising that this tendency occurs. Whatever family members feel about one another, physical separation limits the opportunities for contact and the face-to-face assistance that service exchange implies. It is for this reason alone that Types 10, 11, and 13 are included under a liberal definition of consistency: they live as close as average or closer, but see each other less, help out less, and don't care for one another. They are consistent in behavior and affect, but inconsistent in their choice of residence.

Another deviation from purely consistent profile involves un-reciprocated affect. While one of the members of the dyad likes the other, she or he does not return the affect. Types 2 (G1 dislikes), 6, and 12 (G2 dislikes), amounting to 20.5% of the sample, display this pattern. Type 2 also displays a second inconsistency in that association and service exchange are infrequent despite closer than average geographic proximity. Type 1 is the pure type on this deviation. While they live relatively near one another, association and service assistance are low. Type 1 affect remains high for both individuals, however, thus warranting description as nucleated. Type 9 families share the positive affective tone, but their large physical separation yields low interaction and assistance scores. In short, the relationships among these five variables are much more complex than implied in the linear additive model.

It is possible that the typological model is more effective than the correlational model at explaining the joint distributions of the variables because of bias in either the original sample or the lineage file. Because this sample reflects a particular region of the country and is also subject to self-selection in return of the original questionnaires, some amount of bias is undoubtedly present. We suspect, however, that selection effects would increase the likelihood of finding support for the correlational model, because persons with *consistent* belief and behavioral patterns should be more likely to complete and return the questionnaire. If this hypothesis is correct, then typological analysis of samples not subject to self-selection should find *fewer* cases fitting into the consistent patterns, and hence even less support for the correlational model.

A further caution stems from the presence of some numerically infrequent clusters. Most of the powerful quantitative causal modeling techniques (e.g., LISREL) preclude the use of nominal variables except as a series of dichotomous variables. In this example, the numerically infrequent types would undoubtedly lead to a violation of the multi-variate normal assumptions that characterize these techniques.

Conclusions

The preceding discussion emphasizes the description of the 13 types and the methodological implications of these findings. Clearly, however, theoretical implications are present as well. These findings closely suggest that families develop unique patterns of solidarity within the intergenerational system; unfortunately, the technique of clustering is primarily descriptive and as such does very little to explain *why* these patterns develop. The emergence of proximity as the dominant variable in the typological structure suggests, however, that this often ignored aspect of family structure is very important. Proximity especially influences the opportunities for association, which is a requisite for many but not all forms of service exchange. Association and assistance do not, however, necessarily translate into positive regard for one another.

One application of typological procedures that warrants examination employs in-depth, exploratory, qualitative interviews with a limited subsample of families closest to each type's centroids. By focusing on these "most typical" cases, and guided by an understanding of the existing patterns that characterize each family, qualitative interviews can explore the underlying rationales and family histories that lead to the development of each family cluster. While exploratory and non-representative, this approach provides one avenue to explore in developing theoretical linkages that explain the emergence of a particular family cluster. Qualitative analysis often provides suggestive data on the motivating factors that produce these patterns of intergenerational cohesion.

Qualitative suggestions must, however, be quantitatively verified. A second implication of this research addresses the empirical specification of the *causes and consequences* of these patterns of family cohesion. What are the determinants of type membership, and the dynamics of the factors leading to one pattern versus another? What consequences does type membership have for integration in alternative networks, or are the effects reciprocal? Are there consequences for mental health? We do not intend to try to enumerate all the possible causes or consequences, for that would require a book in itself. The point is that the role of the intergenerational family system in gerontological thinking has been simplistically viewed for too long, and that complexity must be addressed. To be sure, the demands of complexity are partially offset by the theoretical principle of parsimony, but parsimony at the expense of understanding is of little use either. A clear program of theory construction linked to empirical investigation of the role of the family throughout the life cycle is clearly needed to begin to address these deficiencies.

NOTES

1. An earlier version of this chapter by Mangen and McChesney appeared in *Research on Aging* (7[1]:121-136, 1985).

2. This would constitute a second-order factor in psychometric terminology.

3. For an excellent review of the range of clustering techniques, see Anderberg (1973) or Van Ryzin (1977).

4. Readers interested in the unstandardized distributions are referred to the appropriate chapter in this book.

5. Note, however, that we did not examine all six concepts in this study. Because of the complexity introduced by the different role relations in a three-generation study, we restricted this analysis to four dimensions and five measures.

6. The computer programs used are available in Anderberg (1973). The specific algorithm used is titled PROC7 in Anderberg's terminology.

7. Types 10 and 11 merge at the next stage of clustering.

11

Family Intergenerational Solidarity Revisited

Suggestions for Future Management

VERN L. BENGTSON
DAVID J. MANGEN

This volume presents one of the first systematic attempts to describe and measure family relations between generations across the life course. The individual chapters report the results of a program of research that examines intergenerational solidarity, based on an unusual three-generation study design. We have examined the theoretical, conceptual, and measurement issues pertaining to six dimensions of solidarity, using LISREL modeling as well as more traditional methods of assessing reliability and validity.

The central theme of this book is that the complex relationships reflected in intergenerational family interaction can be summarized by measurement of a common construct—solidarity—that is differentiated into six conceptual components. We argue that the theoretical development of this domain of relationships in family sociology and gerontology is dependent upon the precise definition and measurement of these central concepts. The volume presents a rationale for the six dimensions, and tests the adequacy of measurement in our unique sample. This is a necessary methodological step prior to addressing what has been described as "the pervasive contemporary myths concerning deterioration of family bonds in old age" within American society (Shanas, 1980).

Data for this research are based on the first wave (1972) of a panel study of 2044 individuals aged 16-91 who were members of some 500 three-generation families. These families had been randomly sampled from a population of 840,000 members of a prepaid medical health plan in Southern California. Each respondent completed a 1.5 hours, self-administered questionnaire focusing on attitudes, interactions, perceptions of family relationships, and psychological well-being. Most of the questions involved precoded, fixed-alternative items but some were open-ended, designed to elicit more idiosyncratic perspectives on individual goals and family relations.

A major difficulty encountered in the original data analysis involved assumptions of conceptual equivalence between constructs and measures. No clear conceptualizations were available reflecting family relations between adult children and their parents, and no reliable scales had been devised to measure such relationships (Bengtson, Olander, and Haddad, 1976). The use of these data, and other survey data involving family relations in old age, was limited to reporting item-by-item comparisons that often showed little variability and skewed distributions. Moreover, the theoretical rationale for such items had not been worked out, and their validity was open to question.

The initial analysis of these data, conducted in 1975-1979, revealed that the original conceptualization of family bondedness was incomplete, and that the issues of intergenerational cohesion were far more complex than envisioned in the original design. At the same time, contemporary theory and research methodology in sociology began to address some of the issues raised by the original analysis. Much more concern with conceptualization and measurement (Mangen and Peterson, 1982a, 1982b, 1984) as well as theory development (Burr, Hill et al., 1979a, 1979b) characterizes current social research, and statistical procedures enabling analysis of more complex theoretical models have been developed (Jöreskog and Sörbom, 1979).

The analyses that we report in this book have been guided by these contemporary developments in sociology. Our secondary analysis of the original data focuses on the theoretical underpinnings as well as the overall measurement properties of the instruments used to measure the dimensions of solidarity or cohesion. In this chapter, we review our success at accomplishing two major goals: (1) to explicate theoretically the concept of solidarity, and (2) to document the measurement properties of six dimensions of the solidarity construct.

The Measurement Strategy

One major aspect of conceptualizing solidarity involves the unit of analysis employed in substantive analyses. In Chapter 3, we suggest that several levels of analysis are possible. The *generational* level of analysis is the most straightforward, using individuals differentiated by ranked generational position as the basic unit of analysis. We suggest in Chapter 3 that the dominant goal of a generational analysis is comparison between the generations and the development of reliable and valid scales that are isomorphic across generations. For every dimension and every generation, we are able to develop scales that are congruent across generations, and in most cases these scales exhibit acceptable reliability and validity.

The lineage level of analysis may be approached from two perspectives: (1) a *family* level of analysis, where measures that reflect the cohesiveness of the complete intergenerational family are desired, and (2) the *role relationship* level of analysis, where the focus is on the cohesiveness in a specific dyadic relationship (e.g., mother and son). We suggest that the role relationship model is more appropriate because it recognizes that adults differentiate their feelings toward one another. We argue that an analysis of role relationship data requires attention to correlated errors of measurement that stem from multiple evaluations of the relationship by each party to the role relationship. The substantive analyses presented in Chapters 4-9 document the validity of this concern. With the exception of the family structure dimension, lineage-level analysis reveals systematic patterns of nonrandom measurement error both within and between generations. Clearly, attention to correlated measurement error is required.

Summary of Results

Chapter 2 addresses the theoretical basis for the family solidarity construct, reviewing literature ranging from the early founders of sociological thinking to the present. We review the historical development of the construct as seen from more clinically oriented scholars concerned with treating pathological or disturbed families. There is a remarkable degree of consistency in the theoretical treatments of solidarity by these diverse scholars. There is, however, a historical tendency toward defining solidarity in multidimensional terms. Also, at least with regard to intergenerational relations, there is a tendency to use "mechanical solidarity" (Durkheim, 1893/1933) conceptualizations and ignore issues of role differentiation.

The conceptualization of solidarity that we use in this research reflects these tendencies. We define six concepts (Bengtson and Schrader, 1982) that serve as the basis for our analysis. The results of our analyses of each of these dimensions is discussed below.

Family Intergenerational Structure

In Chapter 4, family structure is defined as the *pattern of role relationships (kinship networks) bonded by spatial constraints (proximity) that is enacted by family members over time*. Within the context of the intergenerational family system, structure is an opportunity function; both the number of relationships and their proximity are parameters limiting possible family interaction.

The operationalization of family structure concepts in this study presents few problems. The number of children and grandchildren, the marital status of members of each of the three generations in the sample, the gender composition of intergenerational dyads, and the age range and age variance of children in each of the generations describe the structural characteristics of the intergenerational family. In addition, two measures of residential proximity, actual distance in miles and functional categories reflecting how difficult a visit might be, are employed. Intergenerational reliability of reports is generally high.

Although the hypothesis that *number* of kin served as an opportunity function is not directly tested, the hypothesis that *proximity* of kin is a limiting factor is supported. In Chapter 10, we find that proximity is highly correlated with two major indices of family interaction—association and exchange—but is minimally correlated with affect. Moreover, proximity is the dominant variable in the intergenerational typology developed in Chapter 10.

Affectual Solidarity

Nominally defined as the *nature and extent of positive sentiment toward other members of the family*, affectual solidarity is measured by ten items reflecting five indicators of sentiment. Self-report and attributional measures are included for each indicator. Three global items are also employed.

Factor analyses indicate that one underlying construct explains most of the variance in the ten items. Alpha reliabilities for the ten-item scales are high. Construct validity is indicated by the single-factor structure for each dyadic relationship and by the congruence of structures across the various dyadic relations. Convergent validity is indicated by the moderately high correlations between the ten-item scale and global indicators. Discriminant validity is indicated by the absence of correlations across role relationships, and the low correlations of the scales with an eight-item measure of social desirability.

In the lineage-level LISREL analysis, however, the correlations between the paired affect scales are lower than anticipated. G1-G2 Affect correlates with G2-G1 Affect significantly (r = 0.349), as do G2-G3 Affect and G3-G2 Affect (r = 0.426; see Table 5.8). Clearly, each respondent evaluates the relationship uniquely. In general, the older generation evaluates the affect more positively than the younger generation.

Associational Solidarity

The association dimension of solidarity is defined as the *frequency and patterns of interaction in various types of activities.* In the original survey, nine items measure the type and frequency of such activities. These reflect formal and ritualistic contact, informal and regularized contact, and indirect contact. Seven of the nine indicate face-to-face interaction, while two measure indirect contact.

Factor analysis indicates a single dimension present in the data, with two items, both measuring the indirect contact dimension, loading poorly. The hypothesized three-factor structure does not emerge. Proximity influences the meaning of the two indirect contact indicators, invalidating their inclusion in the final scale.

The final seven-item scale exhibits a clear unidimensional structure. The first factor explains between 41% and 52% of the total variance of the seven items. Alpha coefficients for the scales range from .76 to .87, suggesting a reasonably reliable measure. Correlations of the single-item indicators with the appropriate scales are moderately high, as are the correlations between the paired scales, suggesting convergent validity (Table 6.5). Children tend to report more frequent, and parents less frequent, interaction. Discriminant validity is generally quite good, although a child's reports of interaction with mother and interaction with father are strongly correlated. We attribute this to substantive reality, however, and not to an absence of discriminant validity. In the LISREL analysis, method bias is revealed between the ten-item scales and the single-item indicators, even though the correlations between the paired dimensions are quite strong.

Consensual Solidarity

This dimension of intergeneration solidarity reflects the *degree of similarity in values, attitudes, and opinions* between parents and children. This is measured in two ways: (1) the absolute difference between a parent's opinion and that of his or her child; (b) the attributed difference, reflected in the difference between the respondent's opinion and that which he or she estimates his child (or parent) to hold. The differencing function requires, however, that equivalent attitudinal scales be developed for all responding generations and for all attributions.

In this analysis, three congruent dimensions of sociopolitical attitudes and two congruent scales reflecting religious orientations are used as the basis of the differencing procedure. The reliabilities of the two religious dimensions are quite good, but the three scales measuring sociopolitical attitudes, while adequate, are less internally consistent. In part, this is due to the fact that two of these three scales are doublets composed of only two items.

Eleven difference scores are derived from five scales for use in the lineage analysis of consensus. Five difference scores reflect the objective difference between the generations, three reflect the child's perception of that difference, and the final three reflect the parent's perception of that difference.

Results of this analysis are mixed. In general, examination of mean score for each of the 11 derived consensus measures indicates an overwhelming skew toward consensus between generation dyads. In comparing attributed with actual consensus, however, there is a general tendency to underestimate the differences as compared with objective measures of disagreement. Moreover, parents are more likely to see consensus than are children. Validity data are mixed. The LISREL models of consensus do not include all 11 derived measures, there are inconsistencies between the G1-G2 and G2-G3 dyads, and a substantial pattern of correlated errors is manifest.

We conclude that this dimension of family solidarity requires further conceptual as well as methodological work. If we assume that the methodological procedures used in this analysis to capture consensus are appropriate, then either the issues (i.e., political conservatism, religious practice and belief, marriage norms, and black demands) used as the basis for deriving the consensus measures are not the basis for consensus in intergenerational relations. If we assume that the underlying issues are the correct fundamental concepts upon which consensus is built, then methodological problems must be present. We suspect that both perspectives are in part correct.

From the conceptual perspective, the emergence of the black demands and marriage norms dimensions in the generational analysis was not expected; it may be that these factors are historically specific to the era of the early 1970s, and that the underlying consensus construct is distorted by this specificity. Alternatively, it may be the case that we have abstracted too far in conceptualizing consensus. Intergenerational consensus may focus upon family related issues, and not on the abstract issue of political conservatism. Measuring the amount of conflict within the family may well be more straightforward.

From the methodological perspective, several points are germane. First, use of the differencing procedure may be completely inappropriate, or perhaps the differencing should occur at the level of the *items* and not the *scales*. Second, the assumptions of the LISREL model may be inappropriate to this concept; perhaps multidimensional scaling algorithms are required. Finally, the dimensions used in assessing consensus may be insufficiently reliable to serve as the basis for the derived measures; perhaps a greater number of items reflecting each concept are required to enhance reliability.

Functional Solidarity or Exchange

The exchange dimension of solidarity, defined as the *degree to which family members exchange services or assistance*, is a key aspect of family solidarity. Conceptually, exchange may reflect what structuralists refer to as interdependence, and as such this dimension reflects the only remaining link in this conceptualization to Durkheim's (1893/1933) organic solidarity. Alternatively, exchanges may reflect issues of power, dependency, and justice, and it is from this perspective that our analysis proceeded.

Only five items in the survey reflect this dimension of solidarity, reflecting the exchange of services (two items), gifts (one item), and financial assistance (two items). Unfortunately, the financial items reveal little variation. The service items are very broad based, and it is impossible to distinguish clearly issues of interdependence, power, or justice. The service items are significantly correlated, however, and the LISREL analysis suggests that the simple frequency of exchanges may be determined adequately by applying these items. Even here, however, caution is recommended because of possible distortions by generation: either the G1 consistently underreports, or the G2 consistently overreports, the extent of service exchanges. More work is needed to elaborate this crucial dimension of solidarity. An extensive reconceptualization is presented in Chapter 8.

Normative Solidarity

As components of family solidarity, familial norms address both the degree of perceived filial responsibility (familism) as well as normative solidarity, or the degree of intergenerational consensus regarding filial responsibility. Theoretically, we define intergenerational familial norms as the *standards of behavior that govern and mediate intrafamilial interactions and expectations of the family as a social system, while "normative solidarity" is defined as the degree of intergenerational consensus regarding filial responsibility.* The measurement of familism is more straightforward than measuring consensus (see, for example, the preceding discussion of the consensus dimension), and the results of this analysis reflects this fact.

Assessment of measurement at the level of familism was moderately successful. While the original ten items lack internal consistency in each of the generations or a congruent factor structure across the generations, an abbreviated five-item version that reflects a familism component is congruent across generations but exhibits marginal reliability. Measurement of normative consensus is not, however, warranted with these measures.

We believe that the abbreviated five-item scale constitutes a starting point for further analysis of familism and normative solidarity. For researchers interested in a short measure of familism, our analysis suggests that our five-item scale indeed captures a familism component but that greater specificity in items and a greater number of items is required. We encourage others to build upon our results. For the researcher who is interested in a more detailed examination of familism and normative solidarity, in Chapter 9 we present a conceptual elaboration that we feel warrants examination. We encourage others to borrow this conceptualization, or to develop explicit alternatives.

An Intergenerational Family Typology

Chapter 10 uses typological procedures to examine the relationships among the dimensions of solidarity, in contrast to all of the other chapters, where the emphasis is on a single dimension of the solidarity construct. In one sense, this analysis allows us to determine whether or not solidarity is an *empirical construct* or if it is more appropriate to view it in *meta-construct* terms as a label that subsumes conceptually related but empirically distinct dimensions. In short, this chapter may be seen as a test of the utility of trying to develop a grand theory of solidarity as opposed to middle-range theories specific to each of the concepts or dimensions.

Typological procedures, when used in combination with correlational procedures, permit testing such a sweeping hypothesis. If solidarity is an empirical construct, then the linear model should hold. This model, implicitly assumed in much family research, suggests that families are more cohesive if they (1) live proximally, (2) associate frequently, (3) assist one another, and (4) care about one another. In empirical terms, a correlation matrix among the measures should reveal uniformly high correlations. The results presented in Chapter 10 suggest that two conceptual blocks are present, one composed of the behavioral indicators and the other composed of affectual measures. Correlations among variables within each block were moderately high, but the correlations between the blocks were quite low, suggesting that at least two higher order constructs characterized the data.

By using cluster analysis to create types, the analysis focuses on simplifying the number of objects (cases) to determine if a small number of family types adequately describes the data. If the linear and additive model is the more appropriate characterization of solidarity, then the clustering procedure yields a limited number of types characterized by parallel patterns of mean scores across the types. That is, families who give a highly cohesive response on one dimension would also report high cohesion on the others, and vice versa. If the linear model is inappropriate, intersecting patterns of mean scores plotted across types emerge. That is, families may be cohesive on one dimension but fragmented on others. The hierarchical cluster analysis supports, to some extent, the nonlinear hypothesis.

A total of 13 family types emerge from the cluster analysis; generally, these types reflect four major groups: (1) the "moderates" (53.1% of the sample), characterized by near average scores on the five variables that constitute the grouping procedure; (2) the "exchangers" (12.6%), who share the characteristic of being well above the average in the amount of service assistance provided to the G1 family member; (3) the "geographically distant" (15.7%), who are live a considerable distance from one another; and (4) the "socially distant" (18.5%), who are of average geographic proximity but have low levels of association and moderate to extremely low levels of affect.

Three of the types, constituting 34.6% of the sample, exhibit patterns consistent with the linear additive model. An additional three types, constituting 12.2% of the sample, are consistent on all dimensions except proximity. Thus, using the liberal definition of consistency, slightly less than one half the sample is characterized by solidarity as an empirical construct, while slightly more than 50% of the sample is characterized by inconsistent patterns. Interactions are clearly present in the data, and the relationships among the variables are better explained by a nonlinear typological structure.

These findings suggest that the relationships among our dimensions of family solidarity are not as simple as originally suggested. We will return to this concern when discussing our final recommendation for future work.

Recommendations

In this book we have attempted (1) to present the conceptualization of solidarity and its components; (2) to develop reliable, valid, and documented measures of each dimension; and (3) to describe data from the first wave of a longitudinal study on the dimensions of solidarity. Based upon this analysis, we have several recommendations for persons contemplating research on intergenerational relations. These recommendations fall into three classes: (1) recommendations for the *use* of the measures that we report here; (2) recommendations for the continued *development* of measures in this area; and (3) recommendations for continued *theoretical development* in assessing intergenerational relationships.

Use of Measures

The recommendations below for the use of measures are ba:
the assumption that the prospective user understands and ac
theoretical foundation upon which the measure is based. G
assumption, and based upon the analyses reported throug!
book, other researchers can use measures for three of the dime
solidarity with a high degree of confidence, while the other thre
greater caution.

The measures of intergenerational family structure, aff
association all demonstrate acceptable reliability and valid
structural measures are straightforward, and those measures re
the goals of the proposed research can be adopted easily. For a

TABLE 11.1   Summary of Item Content: Structure, Affect,
                and Association Dimensions

Family Structure:

1. Thinking now of your daughter _____ , did she ever have any *child-ren*
   1a. [If yes] What is the name of her oldest child?
   1b. [If not obvious] Is that a boy or a girl?

2. When was she born?

3. Was she adopted?

4. Is she still living?
   4a. [If deceased] When did she die?

5. [If still living] In what city and state does she live?

6. [If still living] Has she ever married?
   6a. [If ever married] Is she still married to this person, or is she se]
       widowed, or divorced?
   6b. [If widowed/divorced] Has she remarried?
   6c. [If never married or separated (6a)] Is she living with someone
       if they were married?

Affect:

Scale Items—

1. How well do you feel your father (mother/child) understands you?

2. How well do you feel your father (mother/child) trusts you?

3. How fair do you feel your father (mother/child) is toward you?

4. How much respect do you feel from your father (mother/child)?

5. How much affection do you feel your father (mother/child) has fo1

6. How well do you understand him (or her)?

7. How much do you trust your father (mother/child)?

---

association, use of the entire scale is recommended, although our analysis indicates that the single-item indicators will yield appropriate data should survey instrument length be an important consideration. Table 11.1 presents the item stems for these three dimensions.

For the other three dimensions (normative, exchange, and consensual solidarity), we suggest a more cautious perspective. We believe that the five-item reduced form measure of normative solidarity does reflect an underlying but abstract familism content, but is not appropriate for measuring normative consensus. Furthermore, our analyses suggest that this measure requires further development even as a familism measure. Thus we feel that this measure can be used, but we encourage users at least to examine the measurement properties of the measure in their data.

TABLE 11.1 Continued

8. How fair do you feel you are toward your father (mother/child)?
9. How much do you respect your father (mother/child)?
10. How much affection do you feel toward your father (mother/child)?

Single-Item Indicators—
11. Taking everything into consideration, how close do you feel is the relationship between you and your father (mother/child)?
12. How is communication between yourself and your father (mother/child)— how well can you exchange ideas or talk about things that really concern you?
13. Generally, how well do you and your father (mother/child) get along together?

Association:

Scale Items—
WITH YOUR (*INSERT REFERENT*): How often do you do the following?
1. Recreation outside the home (movies, picnics, swimming, trips, hunting, and so on)
2. Brief visits for conversation
3. Family gatherings like reunions or holiday dinners where a lot of family members get together
4. Small family gatherings for special occasions like birthdays or anniversaries
5. Talking over things that are important to you
6. Religious activities of any kind
7. Dinner together

Single-Item Indicator—
8. How often do you do things together with this (*insert referent*)?

The two-item measure of service exchange is appropriate for use in other research if service exchanges are an ancillary as opposed to central component of the proposed research. If exchanges are central, further development is required.

Recommendations with regard to consensual solidarity are perhaps the most difficult, in large part because the empirical evidence is conflicting. On the one hand, the generation-level measurement of religious belief, religious practice, and, on the whole, political conservatism, is reasonably good. As measures of these three concepts, we feel confident in recommending these measures for use. On the other hand, deriving a measure of consensus is more problematic. Use of the political conservatism scale to derive the three perspectives of consensus is warranted to a greater degree than any of the other dimensions, although even here the measurement structure in the LISREL models is less than ideal due to low explained variance of the parental view of consensus on political conservatism. In fact, a simple single-item indicator of agreement with parents or children on important social and political issues may be as valid.

Development of Measures

Even though we confidently recommend three of our measures for use in future research, further development of these measures is also encouraged. We do not consider this to be contradictory; rather, it comes from the recognition that both theory and research have progressed since the original survey, and improvement is always possible.

Because the measures of structure, affect, and association exhibit acceptable measurement properties, our recommendations for further development are few. The only problematic aspect of measuring structure pertained to proximity in the G2-G3 dyad, where G3 adolescents in college claimed the distance from college to home as appropriate, while their parents claimed residence at home. The only recommendation that we make for the affect scale is that researchers consider including some negative affect stimuli to tap that end of the affect continuum. While the affect scale does not correlate with a measure of social desirability, inclusion of negative affect stimuli may help control for response acquiescence. The seven-item association scale measures intergenerational contact sufficiently; our primary recommendation here comes from exchange theory and a concern for alternatives. We suggest that the degree of involvement or association with the alternatives to the intergenerational family system are important conditioners that modify how we interpret equivalent levels of intergenerational association. In short, we recommend that measures of *association with alternatives* be developed, not that the association scale we analyze here be modified.

A much greater amount of development is suggested for the other substantive domains. Major conceptual reworkings of normative solidarity and exchange are presented in their respective chapters. Both of these reconceptualizations are heavily based upon exchange theory principles, and assume that a major focus of the study is the referent concept. Indeed, we suspect that these reconceptualizations are so extensive that it may not be practical for any one study to include all of the dimensions or facets suggested. Recognizing this, we present the reconceptualizations because we believe that the specificity of the reworked concepts will assist researchers who wish to focus on one or more of the dimensions.

Our suggestions for the development of the final dimension—consensus—are both methodological and conceptual. Our analysis of this dimension convinces us that it is an important aspect of intergenerational relationships, and that the procedures we use address portions of the concept. There is, however, sufficient imprecision in the measurement models to cause concern. Methodologically, we suggest a number of alternative scoring schemes and statistical models that may capture the essence of consensus more precisely.

The lack of variance in the derived consensus measures suggests, however, that an alternative conceptual approach and simplified analytical scheme are required. Rather than deriving the degree of consensus from the actual or perceived differences between family members, we suggest that a conceptualization based on conflict theory focus on the stated disagreements between family members. This is a more direct approach to assessing consensus, and requires fewer levels of abstraction between data and concept.

Table 11.2 presents some sample items for these revised concepts that address the concerns raised by our analysis. These measures have not been field tested, so data are not available to assess the efficacy of the items.

Our recommendations for continued development of the consensus dimension focus on using the conflict theory approach to develop measures that focus on possible areas of disagreement in families. Two of the illustrative items we develop use issues similar to those analyzed in

TABLE 11.2   Illustrative Items Measuring Revised Concepts

Consensus	Exchange	Normative
1. In the past year, how often have you and your (referent) disagreed about religion and religious issues?	1. In the past month, how often have you helped your (referent) with grocery shopping? (Exchange Frequency: Service Dimension)	1. Children should be obligated to provide financial support to their aged parents. (Familism: Financial Aid Dimension)
2. In the past year, how often have you and your (referent) disagreed about how you raise your children?	2. In the past month, how many hours did you spend helping your (referent) with grocery shopping? (Exchange Value: Service Dimension)	2. Children who help parents with household chores have every right to expect favors in return. (Reciprocity: Instrumental Dimension)
3. In the past year, how often have you and your (referent) argued about politics and political candidates?	3. In the past month, how often has your (referent) turned to you for advice on child rearing? Exchange Frequency: Advice Dimension)	3. When I tell my mother about my deepest concerns, I expect her to share her deepest concerns with me. (Distributive Justice: Affective Dimension)

Chapter 7 (politics and religion), but focus on disagreements with a specific family member (referent), while the third item emphasizes family issues by assessing disagreements over child-rearing practices. For each of these items, a one-year time frame is explicitly structured into the measure. While, generally, a shorter time frame is desired in order to minimize recall and telescoping errors, potential disagreements are often episodic and tied to symbolic events such as holidays, and so on. Thus use of a short time frame (e.g., two weeks) would likely result in little variance in the responses.

The three sample items measuring exchange focus on the frequency and value dimensions presented in the Chapter 8 reconceptualization. Measures of distributive justice and reciprocity are not required, because these are derived from the frequency and value scales. Note here that a one-month time frame is structured into the items, and that specific forms of assistance are determined. The sample item assessing the value of the exchange assumes that value is equivalent to the rewards forgone by providing the service. Value then equals the *annual income* of the service provider divided by the number of yearly hours spent in remunerative labor, with this quotient multiplied by the number of hours spent providing service. In equation form, this equals:

$$\text{Value} = (\text{Service Hours}) \times (\text{Annual Income}/\text{Labor Force Hours})$$

Note, however, that this measure would yield an exchange value of zero for any service provider who is not in the labor force. Because a substantial amount of the service provided to older persons is provided by daughters or daughters-in-law, and because many of these women are not employed, computation of the economic value of the home-making services provided by a nonworking spouse is required.

The sample items measuring the normative dimension reflect two strategies of measurement. The first two items use "children" in the abstract, while the third item personalizes the stimuli to the relationship of the respondent and his or her mother or other referent family member as appropriate. If normative solidarity is theoretically viewed as an abstract phenomenon anchored in the broad social structure, then use of the more abstract approach is recommended. If, however, normative solidarity is anchored in the immediate *family* social structure, then use of the more specific and personalized approach is recommended.

Theoretical Development

Our work has theoretical implications for the study of inter-generational relationships. First, from the level of overarching conceptual frameworks, we suggest that Durkheim's (1893/1933) concept of organic solidarity be reintroduced into the study of intergenerational relationships. Many of our suggestions for modifying the exchange dimension derive fundamentally from this concern. It is curious that the study of intergenerational relationships has evolved away from the concept of organic solidarity, especially because role differentiation is often studied in husband-wife relations (Mangen, 1982).

On a more fundamental level, the analysis reported in Chapter 10 and throughout the remainder of this book leads us to believe that it is inappropriate to focus too much theoretical attention on solidarity as a higher order construct. While the concept of solidarity is extremely useful as a meta-construct designed to organize discussion and add parsimony, the typological results presented in Chapter 10 clearly indicate that each dimension of solidarity captures a fundamentally unique aspect of the relationship. This conclusion is supported by the analysis of Atkinson, Kivett, and Campbell (1986), who found unique determinants of each dimension of solidarity that they analyzed. What is required at this time is the development of middle-range theories of solidarity. Such theories should address the causes and consequences of each dimension of solidarity, as well as the relationships *among* two or three of the dimensions. This will contribute substantially to our understanding of intergenerational family dynamics.

In future analyses, we intend to focus our attention on substantive models suggested by middle-range theories. Fortunately, funding for a longitudinal follow-up to this study has been obtained. This will permit a more detailed and precise examination of changes over time in family dynamics. This is fundamental to the development of precise middle-range theories.

References

Acock, A. C. and V. L. Bengtson. 1975. "Intergenerational Transmission of Religious Behavior and Beliefs." Paper presented at the Pacific Sociological Association, Victoria, British Columbia.

————1978. "On the Relative Influence of Mothers and Fathers: A Covariance Analysis of Political and Religious Socialization." *Journal of Marriage and the Family* 40:519-530.

————1980. "Socialization and Attribution Processes: Actual Versus Perceived Similarity Among Parents and Youth." *Journal of Marriage and the Family* 42:501-515.

Adams, B. N. 1968. *Kinship in an Urban Setting.* Chicago: Markham.

————"Mate Selection in the United States: A Theoretical Summarization." Pp. 259-267 in *Contemporary Theories About the Family*, Vol. 1, edited by W. R. Burr et al. New York: Free Press.

Aldous, J. and R. Hill. 1965. "Social Cohesion, Lineage Type and Intergenerational Transmission." *Social Forces* 43:471-482.

Alwin, D. and D. Jackson. 1981. "Applications of Simultaneous Factor Analysis to Issues of Factorial Invariance." Pp. 249-279 in *Factor Analysis and Measurement in Sociological Research*, edited by D. Jackson and E. Borgatta. Newbury Park, CA: Sage.

Anderberg, M. 1973. *Cluster Analysis for Applications.* New York: John Wiley.

Angell, Robert Cooley. 1965. *The Family Encounters the Depression.* Gloucester, MA: Peter Smith. (Original work published 1936)

Aristotle. 1961. "Politics." Pp. 276-339 in *The Pocket Aristotle*, edited by J. D. Kaplan, translated by Benjamin Jowett. New York: Washington Square Press.

Atkinson, M. P., V. R. Kivett, and R. T. Campbell. 1986. "Intergenerational Solidarity: An Examination of a Theoretical Model." *Journal of Gerontology* 41(5):408-416.

Back, K. W. 1951. "Influence Through Social Communication." *Journal of Abnormal and Social Psychology* 46:9-23.

Bales, Robert F. and Philip E. Slater. 1955. "Role Differentiation in Small Decision-Making Groups." Pp. 259-306 in *Family, Socialization and Interaction Process*, edited by T. Parsons and R. F. Bales. New York: Free Press.

Bengtson, Vern L. 1970. "The Generation Gap: A Review and Typology of Social-Psychological Perspectives." *Youth and Society* 2:7-31.

————1975. "Generation and Family Effects in Value Socialization." *American Sociological Review* 40:358-371.

————and K. D. Black. 1973a. "Intergenerational Relations and Continuities in Socialization." Pp. 207-234 in *Personality and Socialization,* edited by P. Baltes and W. Schaie. New York: Academic Press.

————1973b. "Solidarity Between Parents and Children: Four Perspectives on Theory Development." Paper presented at the Theory Development Workshop, National Council on Family Relations, October.

Bengtson, Vern L., L. Burton, and D. J. Mangen. 1981. "Family Support Systems and Attribution of Responsibility: Contrasts Among Elderly Blacks, Mexican-Americans and Whites." Paper presented at the annual meetings of the Gerontological Society of America and the Canadian Association of Gerontology, Toronto, Canada, November 10.

Bengtson, Vern L., N. Cutler, D. Mangen, and V. Marshall. 1985. "Generations, Cohorts, and Relations Between Age Groups." Pp. 304-338 in *Handbook of Aging and the Social Sciences,* edited by R. Binstock and E. Shanas. New York: Van Nostrand Reinhold.

Bengtson, Vern L., M. J. Furlong, and R. S. Lauffer. 1974. "Time, Aging, and the Continuity of the Social Structure: Themes and Issues in Generational Analysis." *Journal of Social Issues* 30:1-30.

Bengtson, Vern L. and J. A. Kuypers. 1971. "Generational Differences and the Developmental Stake." *Aging and Human Development* 2:249-260.

Bengtson, Vern L., Edward B. Olander, and Anees A. Haddad. 1976. "The 'Generation Gap' and Aging Family Members: Toward a Conceptual Model." Pp. 237-263 in *Time, Roles, and Self in Old Age,* edited by J. F. Gubrium. New York: Human Sciences Press.

Bengtson, Vern L. and Sandi S. Schrader. 1982. "Parent-Child Relations." Pp. 115-128 in *Research Instruments in Social Gerontology.* Vol. 2, edited by D. J. Mangen and W. A. Peterson. Minneapolis: University of Minnesota Press.

Berger, J., M. Zelditch, B. Anderson, and B. Cohen. 1972. "Structural Aspects of Distributive Justice." Pp. 119-146 in *Sociological Theories in Progress.* Vol. 2, edited by J. Berger and M. Zelditch. Boston: Houghton Mifflin.

Berkowitz, L. 1954. "Group Standards, Cohesiveness, and Productivity." *Human Relations* 7:509-519.

Bettelheim, B. 1965. "The Problem of Generations." Pp. 76-109 in *The Challenge of Youth,* edited by E. Erickson. New York: Anchor.

Black, K. D. and V. L. Bengtson. 1973. "The Measurement of Family Solidarity: An Inter-Generational Analysis." Paper presented at the annual meeting of the American Psychological Association, Montreal, Canada, August 27.

Blalock, H. M., Jr. 1975. "Indirect Measurement in Social Science: Some Nonadditive Models." Pp. 359-379 in *Quantitative Sociology,* edited by H. Blalock et al. New York: Academic Press.

————1979. "The Presidential Address: Measurement and Conceptualization Problems: The Major Obstacle to Integrating Theory and Research." *American Sociological Review* 44(6):881-894.

————1982. *Conceptualization and Measurement in the Social Sciences.* Newbury Park, CA: Sage.

Blau, P. and O. D. Duncan 1967. *The American Occupational Structure.* New York: John Wiley.

Blenkner, M. 1965. "Social Work and Family Relationship in Later Life." In *Social Theories and the Family*, edited by E. Shanas and G. F. Streib. Englewood Cliffs, NJ: Prentice-Hall.

Blood, R. and D. Wolfe. 1960. *Husbands and Wives*. New York: Free Press.

Borg, I., ed. 1981 *Multidimensional Data Representations: When and Why*. Ann Arbor, MI: Mathesis Press.

Boulding, K. E. 1958. *The Skills of the Economist*. Cleveland, OH: Howard Allen.

Bovard, E. W., Jr. 1956. "Interaction and Attraction to the Group." *Human Relations* 9:481-489.

Bowen, Murray. 1960. "The Family as the Unit of Study and Treatment." *American Journal of Orthopsychiatry* 31:40-60.

Bowerman, Charles E. and John W. Kinch. 1959. "Changes in Family and Peer Orientation of Children Between the Fourth and Tenth Grades." *Social Forces* 37:206-211.

Bradburn, N. M. and S. Sudman. 1979. *Improving Interview Method and Questionnaire Design*. San Francisco: Jossey-Bass.

Braun, P. and V. L. Bengtson. 1972. "Religious Behavior in Three Generations: Cohort and Lineage Effects." Paper presented at the 25th annual meeting of the Gerontological Society, San Juan, Puerto Rico.

Braungart, R. 1974. "The Sociology of Generations and Student Politics: A Comparison of the Functionalist and Generational Unit Models." *Journal of Social Issues* 30(2):31-54.

Broderick, C. 1984. "Review of Families: What Makes Them Work [book review]." *Journal of Marriage and the Family* 46(2):501-502.

Brody, E. M. 1978. "The Aging of the Family." *Annals of the American Academy of Political and Social Science* 438(July):13-27.

————1981. "'Women in the Middle' and Family Help to Older People." *Gerontologist* 21(5):471-480.

Brown, Roger. 1965. *Social Psychology*. New York: Free Press.

Burchinal, L. G. 1964. "The Premarital Dyad and Love Involvement." Pp. 623-674 in *Handbook of Marriage and the Family*, edited by H. T. Christensen. Chicago: Rand McNally.

Burgess, E. W. and L. S. Cottrell. 1939. *Predicting Success or Failure in Marriage*. New York: Prentice-Hall.

Burgess, E. W. and P. Wallin. 1953. *Engagement and Marriage*. Philadelphia: Lippencott.

Burr, Wesley R. 1970. "Satisfaction with Various Aspects of Marriage over the Life Cycle: A Random Middle Class Sample." *Journal of Marriage and the Family* 32:29-37.

————R. Hill, I. Nye, and I. Reiss, eds. 1979a *Contemporary Theories About the Family*. Vol. 1. New York: Free Press.

————eds. 1979b *Contemporary Theories About the Family*. Vol. 2. New York: Free Press.

Burr, Wesley R., Geoffrey K. Leigh, Randall D. Day, and John Constantine. 1979. "Symbolic Interaction and the Family." Pp. 42-111 in Contemporary Theories About the Family. Vol. 2, edited by Burr et al. New York: Free Press.

Burt, Ronald, ed. 1978. *Applied Network Analysis. Sociological Methods & Research* [special issue] 7(2):123-256.

Bytheway, B. 1977 "Problems of Representation in the Three Generation Family Study." *Journal of Marriage and the Family* 39:243-250.

Campbell, Angus, Philip E. Converse, and Willard Rogers. 1976. *The Quality of American Life*. New York: Russell Sage.

Campbell, R. T. and E. Mutran. 1982. "Analyzing Panel Data in Studies of Aging: Application of the LISREL Model." *Research on Aging* 4(1):3-41.

Cantor, M. H. 1975. "Life Space and the Social Support System of the Inner City Elderly of New York." *Gerontologist* 15:23-27.

————1976. "The Configuration and Interests of the Informal Support System in a New York City Elderly Population." Paper presented at the 29th Annual Meeting of the Gerontological Society, New York, October 13-17.

Cartwright, Dorwin and Alvin Zander. 1960. *Group Dynamics: Research and Theory*. Evanston, IL: Row, Peterson.

Cattel, R. 1966. "The Scree Test for the Number of Factors." *Multivariate Behavioral Research* 1:245-276.

Cavan, Ruth and Katherine Ranck. 1938. *The Family and the Depression*. Chicago: University of Chicago Press.

Cicirelli, V. G. 1980. "A Comparison of College Women's Feelings Toward Their Siblings and Parents." *Journal of Marriage and the Family* (February):111-118.

————1981. *Helping Elderly Parents: The Role of Adult Children*. Boston: Auburn House.

Collins, Barry E. and H. Guetzkow. 1964. *A Social Psychology of Group Processes for Decision-Making*. New York: John Wiley.

Collins, Barry E. and Bertram H. Raven. 1969. "Group Structure: Attraction, Coalitions, Communication, and Power." Pp. 102-204 in *The Handbook of Social Psychology*, Vol 4, edited by G. Lindzey and E. Aronson. Reading, MA: Addison-Wesley.

Connell, R. W. 1972. "Political Socialization in the American Family: The Evidence Re-Examined." *Public Opinion Quarterly* 36:321-333.

Cook, K. S. 1975. "Explorations, Evaluations and Equity." *American Sociological Review* 40(3):372-388.

Cook, K. S. and R. E. Emerson. 1978. "Power, Equity and Commitment in Exchange Networks." *American Sociological Review* 43(5):721-739.

Coxon, A.P.M. 1982. *The User's Guide to Multidimensional Scaling*. Exeter, NH: Heinemann.

Cromwell, R. and D. Olson. 1975. "Multidisciplinary Perspectives of Power." Pp. 15-37 in *Power in Families*, edited by R. Cromwell and D. Olson. New York: Halstead Press.

Crowne, D. and D. Marlowe. 1964. *The Approval Motive*. New York: John Wiley.

Davies, P. M. and A.P.M. Coxon, eds. 1982. *Key Texts in Multidimensional Scaling*. Exeter, NH: Heinemann.

Deutsch, M. 1968. "Field Theory in Social Psychology." Pp. 412-487 in *The Handbook of Social Psychology*. Vol. 1, edited by G. Lindzey and E. Aronson. Reading, MA: Addison-Wesley.

Douvan, E, and J. Adelson. 1966. *The Adolescent Experience*. New York: John Wiley.

Durkheim, E. 1933. *The Division of Labor in a Society*, translated by G. Simpson. New York: Free Press. (Original work published 1893).

Elder, G. 1980. *Family Structure and Socialization*. New York: Arno Press.

Elder, G. H., Jr. 1984. "Family and Kinship in Sociological Perspectives." In *The Family*, edited by R. Parke. Chicago: University of Chicago Press.

Emerson, R. M. 1972a. "Exchange Theory, Part I: A Psychological Basis for Social

Exchange," Pp. 38-57 in *Sociological Theories in Progress*, vol. 2, edited by J. Berger, M. Zeldich, Jr., and B. Anderson. Boston: Houghton Mifflin.

————1972b. "Exchange Theory, Part II: Exchange Relations and network Structures." Pp. 58-87 in *Sociological Theories in Progress*, vol. 2, edited by J. Berger, M. Zeldich, Jr., and B. Anderson. Boston: Houghton Mifflin.

Falding, H. 1965. "A Proposal for the Empirical Study of Values." *American Sociological Review* 30:223-233.

Farber, B. 1957. "An Index of Marital Integration." *Sociometry* 20:117-34.

Festinger, L. 1950. "Informal Social Communication." *Psychological Review* 57:271-272.

————ed. 1980. *Retrospectives on Social Psychology*. New York: Oxford University Press.

————S. H. Gerard, B. Hymovitch, H. Kelly, and B. H. Raven. 1952. "The Influence Process in the Presence of Extreme Deviates." *Human Relations* 5:327-346.

Festinger, L., S. Schachter, and K. Back. 1960. Pp. 241-259 in *Group Dynamics: Research and Theory*, edited by D. Cartwright and A. Zander. Evanston, IL: Row, Peterson.

Feuer, L. 1969. *The Conflict of Generations*. New York: Basic Books.

Firth, R. 1936. *We, the Tikopia*. London: George Allen & Unwin..

Flacks, R. 1967. "The Liberated Generation: An Exploration of Roots of Student Protest." *Journal of Social Issues* 23(July):52-72.

Friedenberg, E. 1969. "Current Patterns of Generational Conflict." *Journal of Social Issues* 25(2):21-38.

Fuguitt, G. V. and S. Lieberson. 1974. "Correlation of Ratios or Difference Scores Having Common Terms." Pp. 128-144 in *Sociological Methodology 1973-1974*, edited by H. L. Costner. San Francisco: Jossey-Bass.

Gallagher, B. J. 1974. "An Empirical Analysis of Attitude Differences Between Three Kin-Related Generations." *Youth and Society* 4:327-349.

Gelfand, D. E. 1982. *Aging: The Ethnic Factor*. Boston: Little, Brown.

George, L. K. 1980. *Role Transitions in Later Life*. Monterey, CA: Brooks/Cole.

Gilford, R. and V. Bengtson. 1979. "Measuring Marital Satisfaction in Three Generations: Positive and Negative Dimension." *Journal of Marriage and the Family* 41:387-398.

Glenn, N. D. 1980. "Values, Attitudes and Beliefs." In *Constancy and Change in Human Development*, edited by O. G. Brim, Jr., and J. Kogan Cambridge, MA: Harvard University Press.

Goffman, E. 1959. *The Presentation of Self in Everyday Life*. Garden City, NY: Doubleday.

Goldfarb, A. I. 1975. "Psychodynamics and the Three-Generation Family." In *Social Structure and the Family*, edited by E. Shanas and G. Streib. Englewood Cliffs, NJ: Prentice-Hall.

Goode, W. J. 1959. "On the Theoretical Importance of Love." *American Sociological Review* 24(February):38-47.

Goulder, A. 1960. "The Norm of Reciprocity: A Preliminary Statement." *American Sociological Review* 25:161-178.

Greenberg, J. 1984. "Evaluating the Cost of Services." Pp. 317-347 in *Research Instruments in Social Gerontology*. Vol. 3, edited by D. J. Mangen and W. A. Peterson. Minneapolis: University of Minnesota Press.

Hadden, J. K. and R. R. Evans. 1965. "Some Correlations of Religious Participation Among College Freshmen." *Religious Education* 60:277-285.

Hagestad, G. O. 1981. "Problems and Promises in the Social Psychology of Inter-generational Relations." Pp. 11-46 in *Stability and Change in the Family,* edited by R. Fogel et al. New York: Academic Press.

————1982. "Life-Phase Analysis." Pp. 463-532 in *Research Instruments in Social Gerontology,* edited by R. Fogel et al. New York: Academic Press.

Hamblin, R. L. 1974. "Social Attitudes: Magnitude Measurement and Theory." Pp. 61-120 in *Measurement in the Social Sciences,* edited by H. M. Blalock. Chicago: Aldine.

Hare, A. P. 1962. *Handbook of Small Group Research.* New York: Free Press.

Harman, H. 1976. *Modern Factor Analysis.* Chicago: University of Chicago Press.

Harris, D. K. and W. E. Cole. 1980. *Sociology of Aging.* Boston: Houghton Mifflin.

Heider, F. 1958. *The Psychology of Interpersonal Relations.* New York: John Wiley.

Heise, D.1969. "Separating Reliability and Stability in Test-Retest Correlation." *American Sociological Review* 34:93-101 .

Heller, P. L. 1970. "Familism Scale: A Measure of Family Solidarity." *Journal of Marriage and the Family* 32:73-80.

Hess, R. and G. Handel. 1959. *Family Worlds: A Psychological Approach to Family Life.* Chicago: University of Chicago Press.

Hill, R. 1949. *Families Under Stress.* New York: King's Crown.

————1977. "Response to Bytheway." *Journal of Marriage and the Family* 39:251-252.

————N. Foote, J. Aldous, R. Carlson, and R. MacDonald. 1970. *Family Development in Three Generations.* Cambridge: Schenkman.

Hill, Reuben and Paul Mattesich. 1979. "Family Development Theory and Life-Span Development." Pp. 161-204 in *Life-Span Development and Behavior.* Vol. 2, edited by Paul B. Baltes and Orville G. Brim. New York: Academic Press.

Hobbes, T. 1950. *Leviathan.* New York: Dutton. (Original work published 1651)

Hochchild, A. R. 1975. "The Sociology of Feeling and Emotion." Pp. 280-307 in *Another Voice,* edited by M. Millman and R. Moss Kantor. Garden City, NY: Double Day Anchor.

Hoffman, M. L. and L. W. Hoffman, eds. 1964. *Review of Child Development Research.* Vol. 1. New York: Russell Sage.

Homans, G. C. 1950. *The Human Group.* New York: Harcourt, Brace and World.

————1974. *Social Behavior: Its Elementary Forms.* New York: Harcourt, Brace, Jovanovich.

Houser, B. B., S. L. Berkman, and A. Long. 1981. "Filial Expectations and Outcomes for Older Women." Paper presented at the 11th Annual Brigham Young University Family Research Conference, February.

Hyman, H. 1969. *Political Socialization.* New York: Free Press.

Itkin, W. 1952. "Some Relationship Between Intra-Family Attitudes and Pre-Parental Attitudes Toward Children." *Journal of Genetic Psychology* 80:221-252.

————1955. "Relationship Between Attitudes Toward Parents and Parents' Attitudes Toward Children." *Journal of Genetic Psychology* (86):329-352.

Jackson, Jacquelyne J. 1980. *Minorities and Aging.* Belmont, CA: Wadsworth.

Jansen, L. T. 1952. "Measuring Family Solidarity." *American Sociological Review* 17:727-733.

Jasso, G. 1978. "On the Justice of Earnings." *American Journal of Sociology* 83(6):1398-1419.

Jennings, M. K. and R. G. Niemi. 1968. "The Transmission of Political Values from Parent to Child." *American Political Science Review* 42:169-184.

Jessup, D. J. 1981. "Family Relationship as Viewed by Parents and Adolescents: A Specification." *Journal of Marriage and the Family* (February):95-107.

Jones, E. E. and E. Davis. 1965. "From Acts to Dispositions: The Attribution Process in Person Perception." Pp. 219-265 in *Advances in Experimental Social Psychology.* Vol. 2, edited by L. Berkowitz. New York: Academic Press.

Jones, E. E. and H. B. Gerard. 1967. *Foundations of Social Psychology.* New York. John Wiley.

Jones, E. E. and V. A. Harris. 1967. "The Attribution of Attitudes." *Journal of Experimental Social Psychology* 3:1-24.

Jöreskog, K. G. and D. Sörbom. 1978. *LISREL User's Guide IV.* Chicago: International Education Services.

————1979. *Advances in Factor Analysis and Structural Equation Models.* Cambridge, MA: Abt Associates.

————1981. *LISREL User's Guide.* Chicago: International Educational Services.

————*LISREL VI User's Guide.* Mooresville, IN: Scientific Software.

Kaldoun, I. 1958. *The Muqaddinah: An Introduction to History,* translated by F. Rosenthal. New York: Pantheon. (Original work published 1348)

Kandel, D. and G. Lesser. 1972. *Youth in Two Worlds.* San Francisco: Jossey-Bass.

Kelly, H. H. 1967. "Attribution Theory in Social Psychology." Pp. 192-240 in *Nebraska Symposium on Motivation, 15,* edited by D. Levine. Lincoln: University of Nebraska Press.

————1971. *Attribution in Social Interaction.* Morristown, NJ: General Learning Press.

————1973. "The Process of Causal Attribution." *American Psychologist* 28:107-128.

Kemper, T. D. 1978. "Toward a Sociology of Emotions." *American Sociologist* 13(February):30-41.

Kerckhoff, A. C. 1965. "Nuclear and Extended Family Relationships: A Normative and Behavioral Analysis." Pp. 93-112 in *Social Structure and the Family,* edited by E. Shanas and G. Streib. Englewood Cliffs, NJ: Prentice-Hall.

————1966a. "Family Patterns and Morale in Retirement." Pp. 173-192 in *Social Aspects of Aging,* edited by I. H. Simpson and J. C. McKinney. Durham, NC: Duke University Press.

————1966b. "Norm Value Clusters and the 'Strain Toward Consistency' Among Older Married Couples." Pp. 138-159 in *Social Aspects of Aging,* edited by I. H. Simpson and J. C. McKinney. Durham, NC: Duke University Press.

Kinch, J. W. 1963. "A Formalized Theory of the Self-Concept." *American Journal of Sociology* 68:481-486.

Kipnis, Dorothy M. 1957. "Interaction Between Members of Bomber Crews as a Determinant of Sociometric Choice." *Human Relations* 10:263-270.

Koos, E. L. 1973. *Families in Trouble.* New York: Russell and Russell. (Original work published 1946)

Kuhn, Alfred. 1974. *The Logic of Social Systems.* San Francisco: Jossey-Bass.

Landecker, W. S. 1951. "Types of Integration and Their Measurement." *American Journal of Sociology* 56:332-340.

Larson, C. 1953. "Participation in Adult Groups." Unpublished doctoral dissertation, University of Michigan.

Latowski, E. and M. Kelner. 1970. "Youth: The New Tribal Group." Paper presented at the meeting of the American Anthropological Association.

Laumann, Edward O. and Franz U. Pappi. 1976. *Networks of Collective Action*. New York: Academic Press.

Lee, G. R. 1979. "Effects of Social Networks on the Family," Pp. 27-56 in *Contemporary Theories About the Family*. Vol. 1, edited by W. R. Burr et al. New York: Free Press.

Leigh, G. K. 1982. "Kinship Interaction over the Family Life Span." *Journal of Marriage and the Family* (February):197-208.

Lerner, R. M. and J. R. Knapp. 1975. "Actual and Perceived Intra-Familial Attitudes of Late Adolescents and Their Parents." *Journal of Youth and Adolescence* 4:17-36.

Lewin, K. 1948. *Resolving Social Conflicts*. New York: Harper.

Lewis, R. A. and G. B. Spanier. 1979. "Theorizing About the Quality and Stability of Marriage." In *Contemporary Theories About the Family*. Vol. I, edited by W. R. Burr et al. New York: Free Press.

Lidz, T., A. R. Cornelison, S. Fleck, and D. Terry. 1957. "The Interfamilial Environment of Schizophrenic Patients." *American Journal of Psychiatry* 114:241-248.

Locke, H. J. 1951. *Predicting Adjustment in Marriage: A Comparison of a Divorced and a Happily Married Group*. New York: Henry Holt.

————and K. M. Wallace. 1959. "Short Marital Adjustment and Prediction Tests: Their Reliability and Validity." *Marriage and Family Living* 21:251.

Locke, J. 1962. "An Essay Concerning the True Original, Extent and End of Civil Government." Pp. 3-143 in *Social Contract*, edited by E. Barker. New York: Oxford University Press. (Original work published 1690)

Lodge, M. 1981. *Magnitude Scaling*. Sage University Papers: Quantitative Applications in the Social Sciences (No. 25). Newbury Park, CA: Sage.

Lopata, H. Z. 1973. *Widowhood in an American City*. Cambridge, MA: Schenkman.

————1979. *Women as Widows: Support Systems*. New York: Elsevier North Holland.

Lott, A. J. and B. E. Lott. 1961. "Group Cohesiveness, Communication Level, and Conformity." *Journal of Abnormal and Social Psychology* 62:408-412.

Macfarlane, J. W. 1941. "Inter-Personal Relationships Within the Family." *Marriage and Family Living* 3:30-31.

Mangen, D. J. 1982. "Dyadic Relations." In *Research Instruments in Social Gerontology*. Vol. 2, edited by D. J. Mangen and W. A. Peterson. Minneapolis: University of Minnesota Press.

————and W. A. Peterson, eds. 1982a. *Research Instruments in Social Gerontology, Vol. 1, Clinical and Social Psychology*. Minneapolis: University of Minnesota Press.

————eds. 1982b. *Research Instruments in Social Gerontology, Vol. 2, Social Roles and Social Participation*. Minneapolis: University of Minnesota Press.

————eds. 1984. *Research Instruments in Social Gerontology, Vol. 3, Health, Program Evaluation and Demography*. Minneapolis: University of Minnesota Press.

————and R. Sanders. 1982. "Introduction." Pp. 3-23 in *Research Instruments in Social Gerontology*. Vol. 1, edited by D. J. Mangen and W. A. Peterson. Minneapolis: University of Minnesota Press.

Markides, K. S. and S. W. Vernon. 1984. "Aging, Sex-Role Orientation, and Adjustment: A Three-Generation Study of Mexican Americans." *Journal of Gerontology* 39(5):586-591.

Marshall, V. W. and C. Rosenthal. 1985. "The Relevance of Geographic Proximity in Intergenerational Relations." Paper presented at the annual meeting of the Gerontological Society of America New Orleans, November.

————and J. Synge. 1983. "Concerns About Parental Health." Pp. 253-273 in *Older Women*, edited by E. Markson. Toronto: D. C. Heath.

Mayer, M. 1976. "Kin and Neighbors: Differential Roles in Differing Cultures." Paper presented to the 29th Annual Meeting of the Gerontological Society of America, New York, October.

McDougall, W. 1908. *An Introduction to Social Psychology*. London: Methuen.

McGrath, J. E. and I. Altman. 1966. *Small Group Research*. New York: Holt, Rinehart & Winston.

Mead, G. H. 1934. *Mind, Self, and Society*, edited by Charles W. Morris. Chicago: University of Chicago Press.

Mead, M. 1970. *Culture and Commitment*. New York: Basic Books.

Miller, B. C. 1976. "A Multivariable Developmental Model of Marital Satisfaction." *Journal of Marriage and the Family* 38:643-657.

Minuchin, S. 1974. *Families and Family Therapy*. Cambridge, MA: Harvard University Press.

Mitteness, L. S. and C. N. Nydegger. 1982. "Dimensions of Parent-Child Relations in Adulthood." Paper presented at the annual meeting of the Gerontological Society of America, Boston, November.

National Council on the Aging. 1975. *The Myth and Reality of Aging in America*. Washington, DC: Author.

Nisbet, R. 1970. *The Social Bond*. New York: Alfred Knopf.

Nye, F. 1979. "Choice, Exchange, and the Family." Pp. 1-41 in *Contemporary Theories About the Family*. Vol. 2, edited by W. Burr et al. New York: Free Press.

————and W. Rushing. 1966. "Toward Family Measurement Research." Pp. 31-34 in *Proceedings of the Family Measurement Conference*. Washington, DC: Department of Health, Education and Welfare.

————1969. "Toward Family Measurement Research." In *Marriage and Family*, edited by J. Hadden and E. Borgatta. Itasca, IL: F. E. Peacock.

Offer, D. 1969. *The Psychological World of the Teenager*. New York: Basic Books.

Olson, D., H. McCubbin, H. Barnes, A. Larsen, M. Muxen, and M. Wilson. 1983. *Families: What Makes Them Work*. Newbury Park, CA: Sage.

Olson, D., C. S. Russell, and D. H. Sprenkle. 1983. "Circumplex Model of Marital and Family Systems. VI: Theoretical Update." *Family Process* 22:69-83.

Orden, S. R. and N. M. Bradburn. 1968. "Dimensions of Marriage Happiness." *American Journal of Sociology* 73:715-731.

Pareto, V. 1935. *The Mind and Society*. 4 Vols, edited by A. Livingston. New York: Harcourt, Brace.

Parsons, Talcott. 1951. *The Social System*. New York: Free Press.

————1955a. "The American Family: Its Relations to Personality and to the Social Structure." Pp. 3-33 in *Family, Socialization and Interaction Process*, edited by T. Parsons and R. F. Bales. New York: Free Press.

————1955b. "Family Structure and the Socialization of the Child." Pp. 35-131 in *Family, Socialization and Interaction Process*, edited by T. Parsons and R. F. Bales. New York: Free Press.

Payne, S., D. A. Summers, and T. Stewart. 1973. "Value Differences Across Three Generations." *Sociometry* 36:20-30.

Plato. 1962. *The Republic of Plato*, translated by Francis MacDonald Cornford. New York: Oxford University Press.

Reiss, I. L. 1960. "Toward a Sociology of the Heterosexual Love Relationship." *Marriage and Family Living* 22:139-145.

Roethlisberger, F. and W. Dickson. 1939. *Management and the Worker*. Cambridge, MA: Harvard University Press.

Rosow, I. 1965. "Intergenerational Relationships: Problems and Proposals." Pp. 341-378 in *Social Structure and the Family*, edited by E. Shanas and G. Streib. Englewood Cliffs, NJ: Prentice-Hall.

————1967. *Social Integration of the Aged*. New York: Free Press.

————1974. *Socialization to Old Age*. Berkeley: University of California Press.

Rossi, P. H. and S. L. Nock, eds. 1982. *Measuring Social Judgments*. Newbury Park, CA: Sage.

Roszak, R. 1969. *The Making of a Counter Culture*. Garden, City, NY: Doubleday.

Rousseau, Jean-Jacques. 1962. "The Social Contract." Pp. 169-307 in *The Social Contract*, edited by E. Barker, translated by G. Hopkins. New York: Oxford University Press. (Original work published 1762)

Rubin, Z. 1970. "Measurement of Romantic Love." *Journal of Personality Social Psychology* 16:265-273.

————1973. *Liking and Loving: An Invitation to Social Psychology*. New York: Holt, Rinehart & Winston.

Safilios-Rothschild, C. 1969. "Family Sociology or Wives' Family Sociology? A Cross-Cultural Examination of Decision-Making." *Journal of Marriage and the Family* 31:290-301.

Sagi, P. C., D. W. Olmsted, and F. Atelsek. 1955. "Predicting Maintenance of Membership in Small Groups." *Journal of Abnormal and Social Psychology* 51:308-311.

Scanzoni, J. 1979. "Social Processes and Power in Families." Pp. 295-316 in *Contemporary Theories About the Family*. Vol. 1, edited by W. Burr et al. New York: Free Press.

Schachter, S., N. Ellertson, D. McBride, and D. Gregory. 1951. "An Experimental Study of Cohesiveness and Productivity." *Human Relations* 4:229-238.

Schiffman, S. S., M. L. Reynolds, and F. W. Young. 1981. *Introduction to Multidimensional Scaling*. New York: Academic Press.

Schuessler, K. F. 1982. *Measuring Social Life Feelings*. San Francisco: Jossey-Bass.

Schuman, H. and S. Presser. 1981. *Questions and Answers in Attitude Surveys*. New York: Academic Press.

Seelbach, W. C. 1977. "Gender Differences in Expectations for Filial Responsibility." *Gerontologist* 17(5):421-425.

————and W. J. Sauer. 1977. "Filial Responsibility Expectations and Morale Among Aged Parents." *Gerontologist* 17(6):492-499.

Shanas, E. 1962. *The Health of Older People*. Cambridge, MA: Harvard University Press.

————1978. *National Survey of the Aged* (Final report, HEW OHD 90-A-369). Washington, DC: U.S. Department of Health, Education and Welfare.

————1980. "Older People and their Families: The New Pioneers." *Journal of Marriage and the Family* 42(1):9-15.

————P. Townsend, D. Wedderburn, H. Friis, P. Milhoj, and J. Stehouwer. 1968. *Old People in Three Industrial Societies*. New York: Atherton Press.

Shand, A. F. 1914. *The Foundations of Character*. London: Macmillan.

Shaver, K. G. 1975. *An Introduction to Attribution Process.* Englewood Cliffs, NJ: Prentice-Hall.

Shaw, M. 1976. *Group Dynamics.* New York: McGraw-Hill.

Shepherd, C. 1964. *Small Groups.* Scranton, PA: Chandler.

Sherif, M., M. Sherif, and R. E. Nebergall. 1965. *Attitude Change.* Philadelphia: W. B. Saunders.

Shyrock, Henry S., Jacob S. Siegal et al. 1976. *The Methods and Materials of Demography.* New York: Academic Press.

Singleman, P. 1972. "Exchange as Symbolic Interactionism." *American Sociological Review* 37(4):414-424.

Slater, P. E. 1970. *The Pursuit of Loneliness.* Boston: Beacon.

Spanier, G. B. 1976. "Measuring Dyadic Adjustment: New Scales for Assessing the Quality of Marriage and Similar Dyads." *Journal of Marriage and Family* 38:15-28.

Sprey, J. 1979. "Conflict Theory and the Study of Marriage and the Family." Pp. 130-159 in *Contemporary Theories About the Family.* Vol. 2, edited by W. R. Burr et al. New York: Free Press.

Stark, R. and C. Y. Glock. 1968. *American Piety.* Berkeley: University of California Press.

Strauss, M. 1964. "Measuring Families." Pp. 335-400 in *Handbook of Marriage and the Family,* edited by H. T. Christiansen. Chicago: Rand McNally.

Streib, G. F. 1965. "Intergenerational Relations: Perspectives of the Two Generations on the Older Parent." *Journal of Marriage and the Family* 35:469-476.

————and C. J. Schneider. 1971. *Retirement in American Society.* Ithaca, NY: Cornell University Press.

Streib, G. F. and W. E. Thompson. 1960. "The Older Person in a Family Context." In *Handbook of Social Gerontology,* edited by C. Tibbitts. Chicago: University of Chicago Press.

Stryker, S. 1955. "The Adjustment of Married Offspring to Their Parents." *American Sociological Review* 20:149-154.

————1965. "Relationships of Married Offspring and Parents: A Test of Mead's Theory." *American Journal of Sociology* 62:308-319.

Suchman, E. 1956. "Social Sensitivity in the Small Task-Oriented Group." *Journal of Abnormal and Social Psychology* 52:75-83.

Sudman, S. and N. Bradburn. 1974. *Response Effects in Surveys.* Chicago: Aldine.

————1982. *Asking Questions.* San Francisco: Jossey-Bass.

Sussman, M. B. 1965. "Relationships of Adult Children with Their Parents in the United States." In *Social Structure and the Family,* edited by E. Shanas and G. F. Streib. Englewood Cliffs, NJ: Prentice-Hall.

————and Burchinal. 1962. "Kin Family Network." *Marriage and Family Living* 24:231-240.

Tedin, K. L. 1974. "The Influence of Parents on the Political Attitudes of Adolescents." *American Political Science Review* 68:1579-1592.

Terman, L. M. 1938. *Psychological Factors in Married Happiness.* New York: McGraw-Hill.

Theodorson, G. A. and A. G. Theodorson 1969. *Modern Dictionary of Sociology.* New York: Thomas Y. Cromwell.

Thomas, L. E. 1974. "Generational Discontinuity in Beliefs: An Exploration of the Generation Gap." *Journal of Social Issues* 30(3):1-22.

Thomas, W. I. 1972. "The Definition of the Situation." In *Symbolic Interaction,* edited by

Jerome G. Mannis and B. M. Meltzer. Boston: Allyn & Bacon (Original work published 1931).

Townsend, P. 1968. "Welfare Services and the Family." Pp. 102-131 in *Old People in Three Industrial Societies*, edited by E. Shanas et al. New York: Atharton.

Treas, J. 1977. "Family Support Systems for the Aged: Some Social and Demographic Considerations." *Gerontologist* 17(6):468-491.

Troll, L. E. and V. Bengtson. 1979. "Generations in the Family," Pp. 127-161 in *Contemporary Theories About the Family*. Vol. 1, edited by W. R. Burr et al. New York: Free Press.

Troll, L. E., S. J. Miller, and R. C. Atchley. 1979. *Families in Later Life*. Belmont, CA: Wadsworth.

Troll, L., B. L. Neugarten, and R. J. Kraines. 1969. "Similarity in Values and Other Personality Characteristics in College Students and Their Parents." *Merrill-Palmer Quarterly* 15:323-336.

Tryon, R. C. and D. E. Bailey. 1970. *Cluster Analysis*. New York: McGraw-Hill.

Turner, A. N. 1957. "Foreman, Job and Company." *Human Relations* 10:99-112.

Turner, R. H. 1970. *Family Interaction*. New York: John Wiley.

U.S. Bureau of the Census. 1981. *Statistical Abstract of the United States*. Washington, DC: Government Printing Office.

Van Ryzin, J., ed. 1977. *Classification and Clustering*. New York: Academic Press.

Veroff, Joseph, Elizabeth Douvan, and Richard A. Kulka. 1981. *The Inner American*. New York: Basic Books.

Vogel, E. F. and N. W. Bell. 1960."The Emotionally Disturbed Child as a Family Scapegoat." Pp. 412-427 in *The Family*, edited by N. W. Bell and E. F. Vogel. New York: Free Press.

Ward, J. H. 1963."Hierarchical Grouping to Optimise an Objective Function." *Journal of the American Statistical Association* 58(301):236-244.

Wheaton, B., B. Muthen, D. F. Alwin, and G. F. Summers. 1977. "Assessing Reliability and Stability in Panel Models." Pp. 84-136 in *Sociological Methodology 1977*, edited by D. R. Heise. San Francisco: Jossey-Bass.

Wynne, L. et al. 1958. "Pseudo-Mutuality in the Family Relations of Schizophrenics." *Psychiatry* 21:205-222.

Yankelovich, D. 1970. "The Generation Gap: A Misleading Halftruth." Paper presented at the meeting of the Eastern Sociological Society.

Yarrow, L. J. and M. R. Yarrow. 1964. "Personality Continuity and Change in the Family Context." Pp. 489-523 in *Personality Change*, edited by P. Worchel and D. Byrne. New York: John Wiley.

About the Contributors

Vern L. Bengtson is Director of the Gerontology Research Institute and Professor of Sociology at the University of Southern California. He has contributed to the research literature on family intergenerational relations and the social psychology of aging. He is editor (with Joan Robertson) of *Grandparenthood* (Sage) and (with Robert Lauffer) of *Youth, Generations, and Social Change* (Society for the Psychological Study of Social Issues). His training is from the University of Chicago. He has been involved in two editions of the *Handbooks on Aging* (Van Nostrand Reinhold) and the Brooks-Cole series in social gerontology, as well as numerous other publications including *The Social Psychology of Aging* (Bobbs-Merrill).

Rebecca L. Gronvold is a doctoral student in sociology at the University of Southern California, and an instructor in sociology at California Lutheran College. Her interests combine demography, gerontology, and family sociology. She is currently completing a dissertation chaired by Kingsley Davis, which examines nonmarital cohabitation among older adults in the United States. Most recently she has completed a needs assessment of Ventura County while affiliated with the Center for Economic Research at California Lutheran College for the United Way of Ventura County.

Paula Hancock completed her doctorate in sociology at the University of Southern California in 1985. Her training is in demography and social organization. She has spent a year in the State of Bahrain as a researcher involved in the development of a health monograph based on the decennial census. Her dissertation involved demographic implications of womens' labor force participation, welfare, and undocumented workers. Currently she works on forecast membership for the Kaiser Permanente Health Plan.

Pierre H. Landry, Jr., is a Research Analyst working in strategic planning for a private utility company. His training at the University of Southern California has been in evaluation research, methodology, and the sociology of deviance. His current interests lie in the design, development, and evaluation of large-scale indicator systems used in monitoring and forecasting demands on social and technological resources.

David J. Mangen is the founder and President of Mangen Research Associates, a Minneapolis-based research and consulting firm specializing in gerontological issues. Already well-known for his contributions to research measurement in the social sciences, he is the editor (with Warren A. Peterson) of the three-volume *Research Instruments in Social Gerontology* handbooks (University of Minnesota Press). He serves on the editorial board of *Research on Aging* and *Journal of Geronotology*. His training is from the University of Minnesota (in family studies and gerontology) as well as the Midwest Council of Social Research on Aging. His current research involves an in-depth examination using Monte Carlo probability methods of the effect of correlated measurement error on structural models of change. Previously, he was on the faculty of the Leonard Davis School of Gerontology at the University of Southern California.

Mary E. Martin, C.S.C., is a doctoral candidate in sociology at the University of Southern California. She is specializing in gerontology, medical sociology, and family sociology. Her dissertation chaired by Vern Bengtson concerns filial responsibility and caregiving in three-generation families.

Kay Young McChesney is a family sociologist and a family therapist. Her major research interest is the feminization of poverty. Her research on homeless mothers and their children has received national media attention. She is currently Director of the USC Homeless Families Project and received her Ph.D. in sociology from the University of Southern California in 1987.

Richard B. Miller is a doctoral student in sociology at the University of Southern California. He is specializing in family sociology, aging, and family therapy. His current research interests include family change, grandparenthood, and intergenerational relationships in aging families.

Gerald Jay Westbrook has worked as Research Consultant at the University of Southern California's Andrus Gerontology Center, and served as Director of Professional Services for a home health care agency, and also as Assistant Director of Product Development for ElderMed. Currently, he is Gerontologist with ARA Living Centers, an instructor in the deparment of sciences at UCLA extension, a member of the L.A. City/County Area Agency on Aging's Long Term Care Task Force and Elder Abuse Task Force, and a Center Fellow at the UCLA/USC Long Term Care Gerontology Center. He is also a nationally recognized expert on the design and implementation of animal-assisted therapy programs, and a private consultant on mass media and aging. Finally, he serves as Media Coordinator for the American Society on Aging.